S

th   F

w

Published by the National Institute of Adult Continuing Education
(England and Wales)
21 De Montfort Street, Leicester, LE1 7GE
Company registration no. 2603322
Charity registration no. 1002775

First published 2000

CATALOGUING IN PUBLICATION DATA
A CIP record for this title is available from the British Library
ISBN 1 86201 091 9

Typeset by The Midlands Book Typesetting Company, Loughborough
Cover design by Boldface, London EC1
Printed in Great Britain by Redwood Books

Contents

Introduction

Jane Thompson

Some things about the politics involved in widening participation in higher education are well known. They are reflected in David Blunkett's landmark speech at the University of Greenwich about the challenges to be faced in Higher Education in the twenty-first century (Blunkett 2000a). Underlining the government's starting point, the minister made it very clear that 'it is with the challenge of globalisation that the education policy now starts' (*ibid*). By globalisation he means, of course, the economic, social and cultural characteristics of late capitalism:

> the increased internationalisation of production and trade; the real time integration and volatility of global financial markets, and enhanced mobility of capital; intensified environmental and political inter-dependency; and socio-cultural transformations consequent upon new information and communication flows. (*ibid*)

He might also have added, the increasing de-regulation, casualisation, racialisation and feminisation of labour markets. The desperate migration of refugees, economic migrants and asylum seekers across borders originally opened up to exploit cheap labour and to facilitate trade. The intensified environmental degradation and political instability created in poorer countries as a consequence of richer countries measuring their economic and political (non-) interventions in direct relation to the interests of Western capitalism. Or the increased opportunities to exert socio-cultural domination – including the appropriation of 'virtual learning markets' – through ICT developments established and controlled by the West. But he chose not to. Instead Blunkett concentrated his attention on the extent to which 'the powerhouses of the new global economy are innovation and ideas, skills and knowledge' (*ibid*). All of them considerations which place

> higher education at the centre of these developments. World class higher education ensures that countries can grow and sustain high skill businesses, and attract and retain the most highly skilled people…(higher education) is at the heart of the productive capacity of the new economy (including the knowledge economy) and the prosperity of our democracy'. (*ibid*)

In a world in which e-commerce transcends national boundaries, education has become a marketable commodity that can be traded globally (Chapters 3 and 12). In his Greenwich speech, Blunkett announced plans for an e-university and urged his audience 'to pursue entrepreneurial activity' within 'a global market for higher education' (*ibid*). This is a climate in which the inability of nation states to provide educational services is perceived as a commercial opportunity, 'an immediate by-product of which is the demise of local universities, particularly in Africa ... and the loss of diversity in approaches to problem solving, artististic expression, and ways of engaging with information.' (Chapter 3).

Meanwhile, on the home front, because of 'the knowledge economy' and the 'skills deficit', Higher Education is required to become 'a powerful instrument of social justice, since it serves not only as a driver of wealth creation, but as a critical determinent of life chances' (*ibid*). For Blunkett this means that

> a modern higher education sector must be open and inclusive. It must pursue wider social inclusion as an institutional objective. Success must be understood and measured by how far institutions serve the population as a whole – and that means people from all social class backgrounds and ethnic groups, and those with disabilities, at whatever stage of their lives. This will mean better access courses and similar initiatives which root higher education in the local community and open up provision to previously excluded groups ... Social justice requires the democratisation of participation in higher education, which, in turn requires reform and modernisation of the sector itself (*ibid*).

According to this view, then, widening participation in higher education is a way of 'stretching a system' that was once designed for an elite to accommodate a much wider social mix of students – particularly those from previously excluded groups – largely as a response to the economic implications of globalisation, but also in the interests of social inclusion.

But is this the whole picture? And what does it actually mean? Despite New Labour's obvious commitment to servicing the interests of private enterprise and the labour market as well as widening the social mix of students in higher education, we would do well to remember that major structural inequalities, and the problems they create, are not caused by education, and cannot be resolved by educational initiatives operating in isolation or – as is more frequently the case – in preference to taking structural inequalities seriously. Increasing the numbers of students in Higher Education from non-traditional backgrounds could just as easily produce 'new forms of legitimation' which obscure the fact that material inequalities are systematically reproduced in other ways – in particular through the wealth and poverty that are the hall mark of market economies and globalisation (Chapter 12).

Acting to minimise the conflicts that occur when inequalities of wealth, material resources, knowledge, information and influence are allowed to escalate in relation to the development of free market economies has also become a priority. Whether the political inclination is to champion social justice and social inclusion, as a way of promoting social cohesion or to 'blame the victims' of powerful structural inequalities for causing their own problems, neither political tendency wants a society that is at war with itself. Thatcherism once maintained that increasing unemployment was 'a price worth paying' for enterprise and the freedom of the market. Now governments of both the right and the centre-right in the UK know the consequences – and the costs, if only to the tax payer – of disaffection and 'unproductive' lives. Leading – not surprisingly – to a renewed interest in the possibilities of neighbourhood renewal and urban regeneration through the rediscovery of community.

So far as New Labour is concerned, academia is expected to help deliver Tony Blair's conviction that 'education is the best economic policy we have' (Ecclestone 1999). It must also contribute to New Labour's related vision that people in 'the most disadvantaged and economically deprived communities' can be part of 'the solution to rebuilding those communities', by way of a 'civic revival' in 'participative democracy…confidence in citizenship' and in 'the survival of democracy itself' (Blunkett 2000b).

This is an agenda which provides higher education with an enormous challenge. Not least because there are many in academia who have a different – older, more intellectual – understanding about the purposes of education, and who see no reason to revise their opinion. The Chief Inspector of Schools Chris Woodhead, for example, recently voiced a fairly 'off-message' response to government thinking in this respect, in a lecture he gave to the Royal Society of Arts about lifelong learning. Echoing Michael Oakeshott, writing 50 years earlier (Oakeshott, 1950), he described the particular virtue of a university as being 'a place apart' in which 'the young (*sic*) can be involved in conversation with men and women who are engaged in the pursuit of learning', without there being any requirement for 'the conversation' to be vocational or useful or ethical. He spoke in favour of diversification so that 'some universities at least' might be allowed to get on with what they do best – conversation and scholarship – which is 'essential to our civilsation', leaving those that are 'more into globalisation than others' with the task of getting 'new students…working on qualifications that will lead to employment and to contributing to our national economic good' (Woodhead 2000).

Of course Woodhead was speaking for many in Higher Education when he put the onus on schools to improve the A level results of their 'disadvantaged' pupils in order to meet the standards necessary to widen participation. And in defending tradition against the clamour for modernisation and change, he spoke with the authority of considerable institutional support. 'Life and work in the academy today – at least in the rich world – is dominated by two overwhelming priorities, both of which are driven by the same underlying imperative; first to publish in high status, international journals (and so to make money through the competitive assessment of institutional 'outputs'); second, to acquire lucrative, externally funded research (and so to make money in the competitive contract culture).' (Chapter 12).

This is not a world in which the leading players automatically welcome collegiality and mutuality when it comes to their potential rivals. No sooner were the former polytechnics given new university status in 1992 than some older foundations, those with specific reputations and vested interests to defend, began to organise themselves as the Russell Group, and to disassociate themselves as the top 19 research and 'selecting universities' from those whose market position would increasingly come to rely on 'recruiting' new and different kinds of students.

It was this same momentum which encouraged the Greenaway Report (2000) commissioned by the Russell Group to recommend that Higher Education be properly regarded as a free market, one in which the cost to students of different degree programmes should be calculated in line with the status of different universities, the market value of different degrees and the competitive capacity of some universities to recruit students prepared to pay more for their education than others. There are no prizes for guessing where all of this could lead us. As Peter Scott points out, despite all the evidence to the contrary – implying growth and increased pluralism in higher education – the predominant impression in many universities, especially those which pre-date 1992, is of a 'crowded elite system' in which academics are struggling to preserve a culture and a tradition that is reluctant to take on board the need for change and which frequently equates expansion and diversity with declining standards and dumbing down (Scott 1995).

And while government rhetoric – based on neo-liberal assumptions about globalisation and the knowledge economy – has increased the pressure on higher education to demonstrate more commitment to recruiting older, poorer, part-time and non-traditional students, and HEFCE has directed relatively generous funding towards widening participation (HEFCE 99/33; 99/56), both initiatives can be treated fairly pragmatically by those who want the minimum amount of change.

Universities on the whole – especially older universities – do not regard themselves as popular resources whose credibility lies in their obligations and responsiveness to local communities and disadvantaged constituencies. As we have seen, they are concerned principally with the defence of their own academic and intellectual freedoms and with research. In these circumstances it has been relatively easy to consign discussion and responsibility for widening participation to a discrete department, to a relatively small number of senior managers, or to those (newer) universities which either choose or are obliged to concern themselves with access and widening participation in order to survive; leaving the more elite institutions to concentrate on publications, research and postgraduate provision.

Pragmatism also means, of course, that experimental initiatives concerned with widening participation can be allowed to flourish for as long as they are 'viable' and 'appropriate' – according to a powerful institutional consensus about what constitutes viability and appropriate provision (Preece 1999). But they can just as easily be jettisoned when funding incentives are changed, when institutional cultures are asked 'to accommodate a difference too many' (Chapter 9) or when more traditional preoccupations with research ratings and postgraduate provision stake their more powerful claims to resources and precedence. In this context, social class is not an out-of-date or 'an abstract concept, but is real and operative in the daily lives of non-traditional students. For working class and other previously excluded groups, Higher Education remains difficult to access and is exceedingly difficult to survive.' (Chapter 11)

But this is also an agenda – articulated in terms of economic *and* civic revival – which presents a challenge to those in adult education who welcome institutional change. Those who have already used the language of participation, access, citizenship, social justice, democracy, community and class to argue that education is a critical component in the pursuit of emancipation and in the struggle for progressive social change. (Allman 1999; Crowther, Shaw and Martin 1999; Mayo 1997; Mayo and Thompson 1995; Thompson 1980, 1997; Youngman 2000)

Even the somewhat beleaguered extra-mural tradition which, in common with its more radical counterpart, draws inspiration from the teachings of Tawney and Raymond Williams – about a critical and questioning approach to what counts as knowledge – understands about 'cultivating humanity' (Nussbaum 1997) and promotes its defence of liberal education in some of the poorest communities. Although it might be seen as out of step with the vocational priorities of globalisation and funding bodies, and with the kinds of accredited provision that universities tend to favour these days, in Glasgow at least working class students, based in communities of multi-deprivation, are studying Aristotle and Plato in terms that connect to the priorities of 'their class' and 'their kind' (Chapter 8).

Similarly, in Ireland women's community-based education is thriving and has been considerably shaped by feminist ideas and practice, by its connection to grass-roots organisations *and* the academy, and by the contribution of theories dealing with complexity, contradiction and ambiguity (Chapter 7).

In south-east London a partnership approach between the Learning From Experience Trust, Lewisham College, the Community Education Department of Lewisham Borough Council and Goldsmiths College is looking at ways in which 'action learning in the community' can be used to connect widening participation initiatives to the authority of lived experience *as well as* 'make the case for the institutional changes necessary to make the goals of wider access and social inclusion effectively realised in practice' (Chapter 10).

In East and West Sussex, development models drawn from the third world – involving participatory rural appraisal (PRA) and participatory action research (PAR) – are being developed through long-term partnerships with community and voluntary-sector organisations and the communities in which they work and which are rooted in the belief that universities should engage with communities using their privileged position to gain access to resources for the purposes that communities themselves identify (Chapter 2).

In attempting to recognise different knowledge bases, this work continues the fight for individuals and communities who are not considered to have the right to define their own knowledge.' It enlists the allegiance of academics to help 're-locate resources to communities to enable them to investigate and explore their knowledge and then demand other forms of knowledge'. In turn, academics working in solidarity with local people also learn from them 'about their experience and find ways to articulate this understanding within the changing knowledge base of the academy' (Chapter 2).

This is the kind of education which draws on what Keith Jackson has called 'the adult education of engagement':

> The view that adults bring something which derives both from their experience of adult life and from their status as citizens to the educational process; that adult education is based on a dialogue rather than a mere transmission of knowledge and skill; that education is not only for personal development but also for social movement; that adult education constructs knowledge and does not merely pass it on; that adult education has a dialectical and organic relationship with social movements (Jackson, 1995).

What he is talking about is a socially and politically committed form of education 'which is partisan in the broadest sense that it reflects particular interests – particularly those of exploited, oppressed and marginalised groups – and takes their side...this kind of educational work is about adopting a political position as distinct from assuming a professional identity' (Chapter 12).

In *Stretching the Academy* we support the view that the current, general interest in widening participation (and also combating social exclusion, promoting community regeneration, creating a culture of lifelong learning and encouraging active citizenship) may provide opportunities to radicalise these policies and to intervene strategically in institutional practices in ways that help to influence them (Thompson, Shaw and Bane 2000). But we also know that the roots of such concerns in *both* economism *and* radicalism require careful and constant interrogation – not only of the ideas involved but also how they are deployed. 'When concepts such as widening participation rattle off the tongues of politicians, educationalists and journalists alike,' we should be clear that it 'is used in different contexts and for different purposes and its meaning should not be taken for granted' (Chapter 2). The examples we discuss pose critical questions about the extent to which we can not only 'stretch' but also 'turn' the academy, create the space, re-theorise the discourse, influence the practice, operate dialectically and strategically within and against the systems in which we work – to make the most of present circumstances that have placed participation and democratic renewal back on the political agenda.

A related concern lies in 'the terms and conditions' within which participation occurs. In other words, what is to be participated in? And how is the power balance which mediates such participation to be addressed? Current trends in higher education policy, theory and practice – so far as non-traditional students are concerned – frequently leads to narrowly conceived and economistic forms of vocationalism and competence. 'The dominance of the government's rhetoric of the workplace – upgrading skills, new and improved competencies, expanded portfolios and so on – positions the learner in a very restricted way, namely as a potential worker, so that he or she is encouraged to choose a course of study that will lead to some sort of vocational qualification' (Chapter 4). In addition, the legacy of Thatcherism – now embraced by New Labour – means that to a greater or lesser extent Higher Education has become part of the (global) marketplace in which knowledge has become widely commodified, tied to consumerism and offered as credentialism – in competition, rather than collaboration, with rival institutions. 'Within this pervasive market context, the (global) learner is seen as a customer, a consumer of learning (Robertson 2000). Self-directed learning is seen as a process in which the learner should be able to 'shop around to find the best buy' to meet his or her requirements. Learning is thus commodified. 'Buying learning is no different from buying a car or a packet of cornflakes' (Chapter 5).

In this kind of economy, managerialism multiplies – contributing enormously to an audit culture which places profit before purpose and which turns discussion about values and significance in Higher Education into discussions about costs and balance sheets. Implicit in these assumptions – for both 'producers' and 'consumers' alike – is the view that education is instrumental, involving a judgement about 'the most cost effective level of investment in learning which will yield the greatest returns' in terms of a flexible and multi-tasking workforce on the one hand, and individual earning potential on the other (Chapter 5).

This concentration on the learning market, credentialism and the 'racheting up of the work ethic' – whether or not there is worthwhile work to be had – encourages the belief, in learners as well as providers, that there is no other way of thinking about the purposes of education. As a result, 'two of the three tendencies of education – personal and cultural development, and social understanding and engagement – are in danger of being subordinated to vocational training with the consequent diminishing of the larger sense of self and social relations' (Chapter 4).

In addition, the focus on 'self-directed learning', with its construction of the student as a consumer, also shifts the emphasis from education to learning; and from teaching as a purposeful intervention intended to engage student's critical intelligence, to the non-directive facilitation of individual and individualised learning. In the process, the proper preoccupation with high standards of achievement, and with improving the general excellence of teaching that students should expect to receive as part of their educational experience, quickly gets reduced to what can be measured most easily in quality assurance excercises and what can be audited most efficiently (Chapter 9). 'What the new pedagogy of mass Higher Education demands of teachers is not that they teach well, but that they enable students to learn. While this is an attractive notion … what is missing, in most cases, from the contemporary version of "learner focus" is precisely the recognition of identity and socio-cultural situatedness of the student which characterised (and still characterises) the best of critical pedagogy in adult education' (Chapter 1).

At the same time, the growing literature relating to teaching and learning in higher education is dominated by psychodiagnostic versions of pedagogy which focus on the diagnosis of different learning needs, styles and approaches, and on the various techniques for dealing with them (Zukas and Malcolm 1999). There is very little evidence in any of this literature 'of any clear understanding of the interaction between the classroom and the rest of the world, or of the shaping and production of knowledge in educational contexts' (Chapter 1). Or that pedagogy is a matter of principle and purpose rather than mere technique (Chapter 12). So long as teaching and learning within higher education continues to 'indicate a marked preference for maintaining conventional educational delivery systems and shows little evidence of a willingness to critque the knowledge base that informs these systems … participation in education (will remain) largely conditional on conformity to pre-determined truths about what constitutes knowledge and how learning should take place' (Chapter 3). In these circumstances it is hard to see how 'this new higher education, with its "neutral" focus on the anonymous learner, [will be] any more inclusive or democratic than its earlier manifestation, which assumed that all of its students would be young, white, middle-class men destined for elite jobs' (Chapter 1). And under these conditions, 'engaging with learners who have experienced peripherality is tantamount to intellectual colonisation' (Chapter 3).

Current trends in adult education policy, theory and practice also require interrogation and caution. Stirred by the progressive tone of some New Labour language, there is a danger that rhetorical assertions about the importance of widening participation, combating social exclusion and recognising social capital, for example, take too little account of the material, gendered, racialised and ideological context in which all of these initiatives are located.

For example, developing community leaders who will lead the way from exclusion to inclusion is one of the big ideas in new government policies on neighbourhood renewal (SEU 2000). But 'a policy which is based on individuals in this way remains a conservative approach to what claims to be a radical solution to participate in learning and society' (Chapter 2). Similarly, the inclusion/exclusion debate still defines the problem of poverty and lack of access to social and economic resources as being primarily about 'the dysfunction of particular groups in deprived communities. The solution offered ... is for the people concerned to adjust to a taken-for-granted middle class norm of behaviour, such as re-training, to enable integration. Widening participation strategies [become] the methods that providers of re-training and education use to include (excluded) individuals in social activity'(Chapter 2). These are strategies which – in the case of New Deal, for example – rely on more than a little coercion. Community regeneration initiatives, framed within an intention of 'normalising the unemployed or disaffected' (Preece 1999) and adjusting them to dominant values, could be explained as yet another example of the State using community education to 'gentle the masses'. In an effort to 'stretch' the academy, therefore, adult educators 'should be careful that [they] are not falling into the trap of state/capitalist coercion' (Chapter 2).

Also gaining influence in the debates about widening participation and combating social exclusion is a growing enthusiasm for the idea of social capital, especially in relation to supporting and integrating communities and promoting active citizenship. At first glance the concept seems to have much to recommend it, especially from a feminist perspective, because it moves from the defence of individualism to a recognition of social connections between people. But the absence in the literature of any attention to power, and to the micro-relations of power that exist between and within social relationships is a serious omission. 'In shifting our gaze away from dominant, and more obvious, power relations (onto the social interaction of least powerful groups) we are encouraged to shift our gaze away from power relations altogether ... the horizontal ties that exist between and within communities are not comprised of equal relations, however they are conceptualised. Nor are they necessarily mutually beneficial. They are, rather, embedded within matrices of power, struggle and resistance through which people come to know their place and their possibilities' (Chapter 6).

Because the main purpose of the literature is to distinguish between the kinds of social capital that promote the possibility of learning, social cohesion and capacity building, compared to the kinds which impede integration and social development in communities, the silence concerning ideology is also problematic. It becomes critical – for reasons that are well known – to ask who judges the social behaviour of others? for what purposes? and on whose terms?

Not least because 'there is a gender blindness in accounts of social capital. For example, when we read of parents who do not spend enough time with their children, whom do we really mean? ... Similarly when we discuss the poor, we should note that the majority of the world's poor are women ... When we argue for the bonds of collectivities to be strengthened who do we think is already doing the bulk of this unpaid emotional and physical work?'(Chapter 6). And all of this in circumstances where women have very little control and not much power over the men they are supposed to take care of and seek to civilise (Thompson 2000). 'To fail to mother, (or to do it badly) or to fail to care for others, is to fail to be a moral woman ... When we read, as in Coleman's

(1988) work, that parents are not investing enough time and energy with their children, we are reading a disciplinary discourse directed at perceptions of women's moral failures' (Chapter 6).

In addition to what counts as theory and knowledge, this understanding needs to be negotiated actively in relation to a more democratic dialogue between academics and students, in different settings and in various sites of struggle. Active knowledge making – in solidarity between teachers and students – is not about rejecting the knowledge of the academy or defending uncritically the authority of personal experience. Rather it is concerned 'to test knowledge against the template of lived experience', to produce knowledge and theory from critical reflection on experience and 'to harness the ways of understanding and acting that emerge from this process to a common and collective purpose' (Chapter 12).

So far as teaching is concerned, pedagogy should be regarded as 'a matter of principle and purpose rather than mere technique'. Methods of teaching and learning must allow the teacher to learn and the student to teach – as well as the other way round. 'The idea of pedagogy that generates 'knowledge from below' is liberating in two senses; first because it claims that knowledge itself can be emancipatory and that what counts as knowledge can be contested; second because it suggests that alternative and sometimes subversive ways of knowing and acting can be liberated through teaching and other kinds of educational work' (Chapter 12).

The challenge presented by widening participation in higher education, therefore, is not in our view about 'helping' the socially excluded; or squeezing more non-traditional students into increasingly overcrowded lecture theatres, or sitting them in front of on-line learning packages in order that technical facilitators can enable them to function as self-directed learners. Neither is it simply a question of providing vocational qualifications that will hold out the promise of a better stake in the global labour market. It is not even about 'stretching' a system that was designed for an elite to accommodate a wider cross-section of the population in the interests of meritocracy.

Rather, it is about developing a sustained critique of current rhetoric, developing a distinctive *social* theory of knowledge derived from a politically committed analysis and theory of power which leads to a form of pedagogy that is concerned to democratise knowledge making and learning, in ways that redefine the very parameters of what counts as higher education – a challenge that goes beyond rhetoric and pragmatism, which reclaims social purpose and which stands for a newly democratic settlement in Higher Education.

References

Allman P (1999) *Revolutionary Social transformation: democratic hopes, political possibilities and critical education*, London and Connecticut: Bergin and Garvey

Blunkett D (2000a) '*Higher education in the twenty-first century*', speech, 15 February, University of Greenwich

Blunkett D (2000b) Urban Renaissance Conference, 9 May, Balsall Heath, Birmingham

Coleman J (1987) *Social Capital in the Creation of Human Capital*, in G. Radnitzky and P. Bernholz (eds), *Economic Imperialism: the economic method applied outside the field of economics*, New York: Paragon

Crowther J, Shaw M and Martin I (1999) *Popular Education and Social Movements in Scotland Today*, Leicester: NIACE

DfEE (1998) *The Learning Age: a renaissance for a New Britain*, CM 3790

Ecclestone K (1999) 'Care or Control? Defining learner's needs for lifelong learning', in *British Journal of Educational Studies* Vol 47, No 4, December 1999

Greenaway D (2000) *Funding Universities to Meet National and International Challenges*, London: The Russell Group

HEFCE Circular 99/33

HEFCE Circular 99/56

Jackson K (1995) 'Popular Education and the State: a new look at the community debate', in Mayo M and Thompson J (eds), *Adult Learning, Critical Intelligence and Social Change*, Leicester: NIACE

Mayo M (1997) *Imagining Tomorrow: adult education for transformation*, Leicester: NIACE

Mayo M and Thompson J (1995) *Adult Learning, Critical Intelligence and Social Change*, Leicester: NIACE

Nussbaum M (1997) *Cultivating Humanity: a classical defense of reform in liberal education*, Cambridge: Harvard University Press

Oakeshott M (1950) 'The Idea of a University', in *The Listener*, 43, 424–6

Preece J (1999) *Combating Social Exclusion in University Adult Education*, Aldershot: Ashgate

Robertson D (2000) 'Students as consumers', in Scott, P. (ed), (2000) *Higher Education Reformed*, Brighton: Falmer Press

Scott P (1995) *The Meanings of Mass Higher Education*, SHRE and Open University Press

Social Exclusion Unit (SEU) (2000) *National Strategy for Neighbourhood Renewal: a framework for consultation*, http://www.cabinet-office.gov.uk/seu

Thompson J (ed) (1980) *Adult Education for a Change*, London: Hutchinson

Thompson J (1997) *Words in Edgeways*, Leicester: NIACE

Thompson J (2000) *Women, Class and Education*, London: Routledge

Thompson J, Shaw M and Bane L (eds) (2000) *Reclaiming Common Purpose*, Leicester: NIACE

Woodhead C (29 February 2000) *Lifelong Learning: a utopian dream?*, Royal Society of Arts

Youngman F (2000) *The Political Economy of Adult Education and Development*, London: Zed/NIACE

Zukas M and Malcolm J (1999) 'Models of the Educator in HE', paper presented to BERA Annual Conference, University of Sussex

1 Joining, invading, reconstructing: participation for a change?

Janice Malcolm

> higher education has social obligations which start with the proper
> performance of the academic tasks of teaching, promoting learning and the
> creation and testing of knowledge – and without them higher education
> is preaching or journalism or consultancy – and then go to work with
> values and groups outside its walls. (Kogan 1999)

Much of this chapter relates to my own experience, both inside and outside the
community of teachers in higher education, but there is a purpose to my self-
absorption. First, the opportunity to include myself in an academic 'story' is
irresistible; it is something we all do privately but the conventions of academic
life mean that we rarely write about it. Second, I hope that including something
of my own experience will help to clarify what it is that concerns me about the
contemporary practice – as opposed to the feelgood rhetoric – of 'widening
participation'. My biographical contributions are intended to illustrate both the
positive and the negative aspects of the world we have lost in higher education,
using the 'double frame' of my individual experience within the contextual
reality of higher education (HE) (Alheit and Dausien 1999:2), and to consider
how adult educators could help to shape the world still to be found through
widening participation.

Joining: the petitioner at the gate

I am a product of 'widening participation' in one of its earlier incarnations. I
was a girl from a sink estate who went to a girls' grammar school and did well.
The grammar school seemed the height of social and intellectual sophistication
to me, reflecting as it did the aspiring middle-class conventionality of the
majority of its pupils and teachers. I did my best to absorb this apparent
sophistication despite the highly unpropitious social and economic
circumstances to which I returned each evening, and the inevitable personal
conflicts which this caused. I thought I had managed reasonably well, until I
went to university in 1974. There I suddenly found myself surrounded by first,
men, and second, true sophisticates of both sexes, many of whom had been to
public school, who had always expected to go to university and who apparently
understood exactly what was required of them. My feeling of being an outsider
at school was as nothing to this new experience. School, despite being strange
in many respects, did feel in the end like a place where I could legitimately claim
membership: it was intended for bright girls, and that's what I was. It took only

a short time at university to realise that this place was definitely *not intended for me.*

> *Our linguistics tutor does not talk to women, which makes tutorials difficult. Work by women students is regularly returned to us covered in red ink and sarcastic comments; on one occasion the tutor has crossed out whole pages of my essay.*
>
> *I am sitting in a group in the students union; we are discussing the resignation of the Labour Prime Minister, speculating about a general election. 'The working class will vote however the Sun tells them to, of course, they believe everything the tabloids say,' announces a world-weary ex-public schoolboy. I ask him where he has gleaned his extensive knowledge of working-class behaviour. 'I spent three days working in a factory once,' he assures me. 'I know what they're like.'*
>
> *The philosophy lecturer stands at the front of the lecture theatre, diminutive in his academic gown. He waves at us a slim paperback on Cartesian dualism. He is recommending that we read it, since we are obviously failing to grasp the subject as he would wish. He assures us, to knowing sniggers from most of his audience, that the book is so simple even a woman could understand it.*
>
> *The professor in charge of the German department gives a series of (compulsory) lectures on early German romanticism. He carries in a folder of yellowing notes; they are rumoured to be the notes that he took himself as an undergraduate 30 years previously. He reads them out in a monotone. We struggle to remain awake, write derivative poetry on cigarette packets, look hopefully out of the window for distractions. By the fourth week of the course, three students remain out of the 40 for whom this is a compulsory course. Eventually even they cannot drag themselves along, despite their strong work ethic. The course just 'disappears', although we still sit an examination on it. We wonder (later, when the degree results appear) if perhaps this is the reason why no one has got a first for the last 20 years.*
>
> *Another elderly man teaches us – what was it supposed to be? I don't remember the subject. I remember principally listening to his stories of the boys he seduced in Heidelberg in the thirties, and his renditions of the pious sayings which hung on the samplers over his bed. We come across the word 'kitsch' and, innocents that we are, admit that we do not know what it means. He teaches us so that we never forget: he walks around the classroom homing in on items of our clothing or personal adornment to illustrate what it means. His classes are renowned for their vicious wit; we all pray that he will not notice us but pick on someone else.*

It is interesting to speculate how these lecturers would have characterised the expected learning outcomes from their classes, or demonstrated their commitment to reflective practice. But perhaps it is unfair to select these rather dismal incidents; I actually learned a great deal at university and *some* of my teachers were excellent. They cared with passion about the knowledge which they produced, and shared the productive experience with us imaginatively and creatively. But what I want to show here is how and why I failed to be a true member of the university community. In four years I was taught by only two women, who were exceptional academics but whose rarity and brilliance made them seem even more strange to me. They and some of their male colleagues modelled for us what it was to care about and create a subject, but there was little they could do to help me overcome my feeling of being in the wrong place. I met almost no one who came from a background similar to my own, and certainly not among the staff. The relations between myself and my teachers were shaped for me by the structures and content of undergraduate teaching and the cultural assumptions on which it was based – as well as by the dislocating personal experiences I have just described. Without the confidence that comes from being in the right place and knowing it – from being situated, at home, *joining in* a scholarly community – it was impossible for me to conceive of becoming like them, of being an apprentice to them, of taking responsibility myself for the co-production of knowledge. This is easily explained, of course, since I was clearly not a junior version of a male, competitive, middle-class academic with a public school education – and that's what academics generally were.

I wanted access to something and I got it, if only partially and with an emotional struggle. I did all that was required of me in terms of academic performance, but the distance between me and the university (and thus all that it represented) was such that I would never really feel a member of it, nor would I ever be treated as one. 'Habitus' was something I understood long before I came across Bourdieu. Not surprisingly, I fled the university after graduation and took a short if circuitous route to the refuge of adult education.

Invading: barbarians on the move

Other adult educators have trodden a path similar to my own. I worked in community education, trying to promote access to education, including HE, for people who lived on estates like the one I had grown up on, or were excluded in other ways. I was aware, however, that the distance between these people and the universities could never be closed solely by the efforts of those seeking access. The culture of universities themselves would need to change if they were to be 'habitable' for all, but it was not at all clear to me how this was to come about.

My understanding of adult education, when I started teaching and organising (language and literacy) classes in the early 1980s, was that despite being a marginalised educational activity it had a central, rather undefined political purpose. I had not yet read much on the politics of education, other than Freire and some stirring German texts on anti-authoritarian approaches to schooling (eg Kohl 1971). Desperately trying to square my embryonic educational politics with the apparent contradictions of the sugarcraft and beauty classes that some of my colleagues promoted, I decided that what I was doing was essentially different and radically purposive. If education was the citadel, where knowledge was preserved 'uncontaminated by the deluge of barbarism outside' (Eliot 1980/1932) then I was helping my barbarian students to dig tunnels and find other clandestine routes into it. They were not to conceive of themselves as unwelcome petitioners at the gate, as I had felt myself to be, but as spies, *agents provocateurs* and even warriors in the battle against the unequal distribution of knowledge–wealth and the deprivation which it caused. Our joint purpose was to understand and break down (or simply climb over, if possible) the fortifications surrounding knowledge. This was doubtless arrogant and naive but it was extremely well intentioned. I was a feminist and a socialist; I felt I had a duty to make the fruits of human endeavour available to all who wanted them, and to enable its hidden (for example female, working class, black) and unrecognised fruits to be recognised for what they were. At the time, adult education was a natural and fairly congenial home for would-be radicals in need of the means to make a living.

The important thing about adult education in relation to my purpose here was its focus on pedagogy, on the centrality of the *student*, rather than the syllabus, to the educational process. Our understanding of the situatedness of our students, in terms of their class, race or gender, and of the relationship between knowledge and power, meant that we had to question not only processes within the classroom but, crucially, what constituted educational knowledge within and across disciplines. What our students knew in abundance, we realised, often did not count as knowledge. Universities, as bastions of power, decided what 'real' knowledge was and admitted to it only those who met their criteria. The HE access movement within adult education responded to this by fighting to have 'our' students admitted and thus 'empowered'. Those of us outside universities could not directly change what happened within them, but the new 'interdisciplines' such as women's studies encouraged us to hope that someone on the inside could and would. From outside, we could prepare our students to be well armed, critical and confident participants in higher education whose presence, whose difference, would eventually force the culture of universities to change. This is of course a retrospective rationalisation. In reality I'm not sure that I ever devoted sufficient thought at the time to how the admission of 'our' students would change the robust culture of higher education, or indeed how they could realistically cope with it once they were 'in'. From here it seems that I should have considered more carefully what, exactly, they were gaining access to.

Accommodating: when AE met HE

Until a point not so long ago, the distinct identities of adult education and higher education were easily discernible. Higher education was the domain of universities which offered an academic form of education for its own sake (albeit with a high social economic and value) to a small and select stratum of the population; alternatively it was the rather more vocational, not quite so select but still aspirational offerings of the polytechnics. Adult education was self-consciously extramural and different, whether it appeared under the university imprint or emanated from the more diverse LEA-funded and voluntary sectors. Higher education guarded and fed the flame of truth – or at least universities did. What polytechnics did was less clearly defined, but seemed to involve meeting the State's economic and technological needs while showing due deference to the flame of truth – a trick which was always difficult to perform with dignity. Adult education, on the other hand, had emerged from the confluence of a number of traditions which sought to achieve *social* change – in some cases democratic and radical to varying degrees, in others cases religious, and seeking the moral improvement or salvation of the population. Even the much-maligned 'keep-fit and flower arranging' category of adult education provision could lay disputed claim to a civilising mission or a desire to improve the nation's physical and mental well-being. Whatever the social aim – and some were obviously more laudable than others – the fact that the aims *were* social meant that students were the focus. Getting students in and, more problematically, giving them what they 'needed' were the major preoccupations of many engaged in adult education. This was in contrast to the situation prevailing in the universities, where knowledge was the focus, and students were admitted to partake of it, strictly on the institution's terms and only when they had overcome the many obstacles which defended the university from the outside world.

This is a simplistic summary of a rather complex situation but it serves, I hope, to illustrate some essential differences in the traditional ethos of the two sectors. The citadel of higher education is a well-worn metaphor not least because of its unpleasant accuracy; it is not difficult to conceive of traditional higher education as a well-fortified castle or sacred space, full of treasures and heavily guarded, admittance to which is almost impossible for ordinary people. A stroll around Oxford serves to remind us of this reality: beautiful, rich and ancient buildings dominate their surroundings but are accessible only through a small, guarded gateway, with permission. Adult education always seemed to me to be more akin to the country market or fair proceeding noisily outside the walls, where all could trade their labour, skills, services and culture, and where new, perhaps subversive, ideas and folk tales could be preached and exchanged. This is a romantic metaphor that has lost much of its allure as the fortifications separating the citadel and the street market have been chipped away, arguably to the detriment of both.

Initially, expansion in higher education could be seen as yet another way of mopping up unemployment. Just as the school leaving age had been raised not-so-surreptitiously to 18 by requiring school-leavers to undergo training and denying them benefits, so expanding HE would effectively keep another cohort of people busy while apparently pursuing laudable educational aims. At the same time, longer-term economic pressures and some rather intuitive popular theorising suggested that getting a higher proportion of the population into HE would help to improve the 'competitiveness' of the national economy against that of other countries. Without going into either the ideological or economic arguments for and against this position, we can see that there were ways in which this essentially economic agenda could appear to be an opportunity for the access movement. The softening impact of the new European discourse of 'social exclusion' made it all the more likely that adult educators would be able to accommodate themselves to an education policy which promoted egalitarianism through widening participation in higher education – especially since other sources of funding for adult education had been cut off one after another.

Unfortunately, widening participation is inevitably a costly business; moreover, given the mandatory nature of student grants it was becoming increasingly difficult to justify HE students getting financial support when other students, such as those in further education, did not. In policy terms this inequity was a sitting target; instead of providing proper student funding for all, the new 'inclusive' Government railed against the historical privilege of higher education, and nobly insisted that from now on *no* student should be entitled to a grant. The widening participation initiative has thus coincided with the abolition of student grants, their replacement by student loans, and the extension of tuition fees to universities, all of which are likely to discourage underrepresented social groups from even considering higher education.

The Secretary of State for Education has come to give a lecture on lifelong learning and human capital – or some such topical combination – at the university where I now work. The lecture is a riotous event, with schoolchildren demonstrating noisily outside and students from the SWP heckling mercilessly inside. The scripted lecture remains undelivered because of the disruption; instead the visitor engages in combative arguments with the students and other hecklers, deriding their 'whining' about loss of unearned privilege (student grants, reasonable funding levels) and defending the egalitarianism of his wish to give a 'useful' education to all instead of a useless one to a middle-class few. I am sure he believes what he is saying; it resonates with a rhetoric of class struggle which would once have appealed to many adult educators. Later, I look at the official press release for the lecture that he was supposed to give. I learn that 'he called on the accountancy profession and investment analysts to take the lead in devising new ways of measuring knowledge and creativity, not just plant and equipment', and that a learning culture must be about 'partnership – Government, business and individuals pooling resources together – to underline the importance of learning, which today is the key to employability, job security and higher earnings' (DfEE 1999). This seems, somehow, a more honest account of the realities of 'widening participation' than the quasi-radical demagoguery I witnessed in the lecture hall.

So what does this new wave of widening participation mean in terms of the experience of those students who gain entry to what was once the HE citadel? Who gets in and, a question that is much less frequently asked, what do they get out of it? It is clear that the student population, the experiencers of HE, is now different from that which I joined in 1974. The diversity and inclusiveness for which adult educators campaigned has been won in some respects, albeit through a series of Faustian bargains. Half of all students are women; most of them are not school-leavers; they are much more ethnically diverse. Expansion has ensured that there are many, many more students altogether, both at undergraduate and postgraduate levels. So participation has widened in some respects, but in terms of class there has been very little movement. Applicants from an unskilled (social class V) background, like my own, still constitute less than 2 per cent of home applicants to HE (UCAS 1998); while this is a slight improvement, it hardly constitutes a storming of the citadel. This percentage is unlikely to improve given the contemporary financial pressures on HE students, so social and cultural alienation will in all probability continue to characterise the experience of those few who do gain entry. However they may have to learn to call it by another name, since class is being gradually replaced by geodemographic classifications which enable our postcodes to say more about our social and economic identity than any other indicator (Tonks 2000). By abandoning the unhelpful and complicated ideas of class, gender or race in favour of 'widening participation', HE is enabled to sidestep many of the problems accompanying the influx of new communities of students; another linguistic innovation makes the problems vanish by characterising all students simply as 'learners'.

Selling: reproduction citadels at bargain prices!

> In the contemporary scene, we have to counteract a prevailing discourse which seeks to reduce the work of academics to that of a technical enterprise based on the needs of the market rather than scholarly practices informed by ethical frameworks (Smyth and Hattam 2000:159)

It is a discourse which has obviously not been confined to higher education, and resistance to it has not been very strong, although this may change as the process of benchmarking and codification in academic subjects begins to encroach more obviously on the content of disciplinary teaching. Funding constraints, standardisation and layers of scrutiny have all contributed to fragmentation of the academic community and a focus on the individual performance of teachers and students.

I have been teaching in Higher Education for 10 years and am now looking at the situation from within. Those students who secure entry to the contemporary citadel will find a different world from that which I sketched in the first part of this chapter. It is most unlikely that any of their teachers will have time to wander the classroom pouncing on unfortunate manifestations of their taste, or indeed on anything else about them. Students are less likely to have to face overtly bigoted remarks from lecturers, and if they do, some official procedure for redress will doubtless be available to them. They will find themselves in large teaching groups, with sometimes several hundred in one lecture. Even in 'small groups' their teachers may have difficulty remembering all of their names; personal contact between tutors and students will be limited. On modularised courses they cannot help but experience a degree of anonymity and isolation as they rub shoulders fleetingly in teaching sessions with new groups of fellow-students, drawn from different courses all over the university. They will be encouraged to 'take responsibility for their own learning', and this will be most evident when they find that much of the teaching available to them is in the form of downloadable notes, materials and assessment tasks which they can access without entering the university at all or having contact with a human teacher. Essentially, the relationship between students, their peers and their teachers has been transformed.

The daily student experience may be very different, but in many ways the lack of attention to the student as a person and as a community member is not that dissimilar to the regime which I experienced – and that I wanted to change. Students do matter now, but principally in their capacity as funding units or disembodied learning mechanisms rather than as whole beings with community identities; in that sense it is still the case, and possibly to a greater extent than before, that students will inevitably feel that HE is a place 'definitely not intended for me'. The secure, leisured aimlessness and pedagogic inertia of the useless lecturers of yesteryear will have been replaced by something else, but it will not necessarily be any better. All of us are under much more pressure than ever before to describe and justify what we do in our teaching. It is almost impossible to imagine any teacher getting away for long with the 'disappearing class' on German romanticism; either the quality assurance process or the angry students would mean that it rapidly became a public issue. We are increasingly aware that our teaching has to be seen to be satisfactory, even if it does not yet have the same significance as our research, and entire new edifices of control and support have been constructed to ensure that it is. Given this welcome new concern about the teaching role, why should we be worried about the pedagogic experiences to which the newly-widened student constituency is exposed?

Higher Education pedagogy in the 'old' HE was not codified or scrutinised, and perhaps not even thought about very much. Students were expected to learn largely by osmosis, through exposure to the informally constituted community of scholars, academics and their books – clearly difficult if one arrived as a smuggled-in minority alien from a different world and speaking a different language. But osmosis is not expected to suffice any more. What the new pedagogy of mass Higher Education demands of teachers is not that they teach well, but that they 'enable students to learn'. This is an attractive notion and seems to suggest that adult education's ideals of student-centred pedagogy, starting from where the students are, ownership, etc, have become common currency in what was once a notoriously elitist system. However what is missing in most cases from the contemporary version of 'learner-focus' is precisely that recognition of the identity and socio-cultural situatedness of the student which characterised (and still characterises, I hope) the best of critical pedagogy in adult education.

The burgeoning literature of teaching and learning in HE is dominated by 'psychodiagnostic' versions of pedagogy which focus on the diagnosis of learning needs, styles and approaches and the appropriate techniques or tools for dealing with them (Zukas and Malcolm 1999). There is little evidence in much of this pedagogic literature of any clear understanding of the interaction between the classroom and the rest of the world, or of the shaping and production of knowledge in educational contexts. Knowledge is, indeed, more or less absent from the teaching and learning discourse, which rarely trespasses on disciplinary territory (Malcolm and Zukas 2000). For the adult educator, the ideological and other implications of treating students as disembodied, decontextualised learners of predetermined curricula must be a matter of concern. How is this new higher education, with its 'neutral' focus on the anonymous learner, any more inclusive or democratic than its earlier manifestation, which assumed that all of its students would be young, white, middle-class men destined for elite jobs?

On the face of it there has been an obvious improvement on the previous situation, where the only pedagogic demand on teachers was that they turn up more or less punctually on a reasonably regular basis; teachers clearly should be expected to take their teaching seriously. However we should not confuse the drive for measurable and codified teaching practices and learning outcomes, which slot so neatly into cost-driven quality assurance and funding regimes, with the critical, emancipatory and egalitarian traditions in adult education. The realities of contemporary student life are different from those in either the ancient citadel or the anarchic street market. The citadel has *become* the market; not a romantic medieval souk, but more the sordid modern version, where fake designer labels, second-rate food and tacky imitations of beautiful things compete for the customer's attention and money. This market is not a community meeting place where big ideas are discussed and knowledge is democratised, but a gathering of individuals out to get the best bargain for themselves – students as individualised, self-directed consumers of learning, teachers as … hustlers, perhaps? 'The notion of hustler seems to us to be appropriate as academics within universities are increasingly defined (and define themselves) in terms of doing the economic dirty work of government' (Smyth and Hattam 2000:171).

Reconstructing: no reproductions

This is not what we some of us had in mind when we promoted access to higher education, any more than we wanted our students to share the alienation which I and others like me experienced at university. We wanted higher education to change, but not like this. Obviously adult educators are not personally responsible for the degeneration of some aspects of Higher Education that has accompanied expansion. Teachers and students inside and outside HE have all adopted various strategies in response to imposed, economically – and ideologically – driven change which, with hindsight, they might consider foolish and short-sighted. The lure of expansion and inclusion was irresistible, even as we experienced and railed against the commodification of education and of our own work. How could we not be in favour of widening participation? But now that the results are becoming increasingly clear, when we can see what students actually get from being included in HE, it is surely time to consider how 'knowledge-work'[1] can be retrieved from the bargain basement and turned into something which we and our students can negotiate with dignity and purpose.

Adult educators working in universities have a particular responsibility to participate in this process. Higher Education as a whole, to the extent that it is still a community, has not distinguished itself in the defence or reconstruction of knowledge-work to date. The growth of quality assurance procedures, which demand evidence of quality while, in some cases, actively damaging it, has been allowed to continue with little meaningful resistance. It is, after all, very easy (and increasingly common) to accuse those who criticise 'the new', of elitism, nostalgia and self-interest – in short, of representing the 'forces of conservatism'. We are understandably reluctant to face such accusations, however obtuse they may be. The 'teaching and learning' saga discussed above is only the latest manifestation of the tendency for academics, sensitive to any hint of such criticism, to accede to the banal 'modernisation' of their work and the contracting-out of their responsibilities. Adult educators within higher education have much to offer in terms of experience and understanding of working with their disciplines and their students, to the benefit and transformation of both. While some have taken their expertise into the depths of the university or to the heights of policy making, many of us have taken the line of least resistance, along with our other academic colleagues, by remaining in our trenches and doing whatever is achievable within them, coming out from time to time to do a bit of hustling when it seems necessary.

My own priority would be the reclaiming and reconstruction of teaching as a form of knowledge production by teachers, for reasons which have been explained elsewhere (Malcolm and Zukas 2000; Zukas and Malcolm 1999). Others might wish to look at related aspects of academic and disciplinary work, where what we offer our students has often become a shoddy imitation of what we, as adult educators, once fought hard for them to have. Whatever our focus, if we are to retain intellectual and ethical integrity, some actual rather than vicarious citadel storming – or more constructively, citadel building – seems to be called for. Participation in higher education might then become something worth opening up to more, and different, students for reasons other than (their and our) personal economic benefit and market survival.

Note

1   Thanks to Dave O'Reilly for this term – wherever it came from.

References

Alheit P and Dausien B (1999) '"Biographicity" as basic resource of lifelong learning', paper presented at European conference 'Lifelong Learning – Inside and Outside Schools', University of Bremen

DfEE (1999) 'Human capital the key to business future – Blunkett', press release 115/99, Department for Education and Employment

Eliot T S (1980) 'Modern education and the classics', *Selected Essays* London, Faber & Faber, first published 1932

Kogan M (1999) 'Higher education communities and academic identities', keynote address to SRHE annual conference, UMIST

Kohl H R (1971) *Anti-autoritärer Unterricht in der Schule von heute: Erfahrungsbericht und praktische Anleitung*, Hamburg, Rororo

Malcolm J and Zukas M (1999) 'Models of the educator in HE: problems and perspectives', paper presented to STLHE, 'Collaborative Learning for the 21st Century' University of Calgary

Malcolm J and Zukas M (2000) 'Becoming an educator: communities of practice in HE', in McNay I (ed) *Higher Education and its Communities* Buckingham: SRHE/Open University Press

Smyth J and Hattam R (2000) 'Intellectual as hustler: researching against the grain of the market', *British Educational Research Journal*, Vol 26 No 2, pp 157–75

Tonks D (2000) 'Access to UK Higher Education, 1991–98: using geodemographics', *Widening Participation and Lifelong Learning*, 1, 2

UCAS (1998) *Annual Statistical Tables: 1998 Entry*, Cheltenham: Universities and Colleges Admissions Service

Zukas M and Malcolm J (1999) 'Models of the educator in HE', paper presented to BERA Annual Conference, University of Sussex

2 Beyond rhetoric: reclaiming a radical agenda for active participation in Higher Education

Mary Stuart

> We will be judged on our success in creating a culture of self-improvement for the many and not for the few. (DfEE 1998)

The current rhetoric used in education does worry me. It is not that I wish to be mealy mouthed and critical of attempts to engage larger sections of the population in learning, nor that I am dissatisfied with some of the policy statements and funding arrangements for a more equitable distribution of resource, but I worry because the language of education does have the power to create action and when concepts such as widening participation rattle off the tongues of politicians, educationalists and journalists alike, their meaning should be clear. However, this is far from the reality. 'Widening participation' is used in different contexts and for different purposes and its meaning should not be taken for granted. The notion of widening participation outlined in *The Learning Age* (1998) of 'self-improvement for the many' could also have several meanings. It would be foolish, therefore, to assume that there is a necessary connection between older notions of a social purpose, popular or radical education and the widening participation agenda.

There are, in any case, few agreed definitions in post-compulsory education. Within institutions, the different political perspectives of different practitioners contest similar terminology. Resources are allocated within the criteria of current policy but the definitions of those policies continue to be debated by funders, managers and practitioners. Consequently, projects to engage a broader section of our communities in learning are often based on competing philosophical beliefs that have different implications and effects for those 'participating'. In this climate, when widening participation can be defined as bringing in new groups of students, individually or collectively, to the academy or, as different modes of delivery, part-time or sub-degree, to attract a broader base of learners, or even, as a mechanism for the transformation of higher education; it is important to be specific about the claims made of the activity. Otherwise widening participation in education is in danger of being all things to all people and pleasing none of them.

In this chapter I explore some of the rhetoric and definitions of 'participation', examining the relationship between definition and action. The chapter argues that there are at least three different interpretations of the term 'widening participation' with each definition building on a particular perspective of the role of Higher Education and the nature of society. Some definitions relate specifically to the economic interests of a changing workforce and some are more concerned with preventing marginalisation within communities. Each of these perspectives can be more or less radical and I highlight one methodology for participation in Higher Education grown out of approaches used in third world development that is philosophically linked to the ideal of a popular education. I begin by examining the connection between widening participation in higher education and a move towards a mass Higher Education system.

Widening participation and massification

The work of adult education within universities to offer equality of learning opportunities for all classes has a long history. Williams (1959) is one of most celebrated examples of that tradition. He argued that it was through his workers' education classes that many of his theories of culture, still current in the academy today, developed. He suggests a two way process of engaging with the 'working class'. His learning from such groups is not patronising but academically challenging, creating a new set of academic methodologies including the beginnings of a study of popular culture and media which has transformed the map of the academy. However, in Raymond Williams' time the work between the WEA and universities was a marginal activity within an elitist system. Less than 20 per cent of the population had the opportunity to study at university in the early 1960s and continuing full-time study beyond 16 in any form was unusual. From the 1960s there was the beginnings of a move towards lifetime learning but although adult education across Britain grew enormously between 1961 and 1975, as Stock (1996) notes, students tended to come from middle class backgrounds and were usually recurrent learners. To encourage new adult learners, a barrage of interventionist style policies and programmes were introduced including high-profile adult literacy campaigns in the 1970s and equal opportunities directed funds from local authorities such as the ILEA (Inner London Education Authority) in the early 1980s. Targeting funds at non-participants came to be seen as a more appropriate use of more limited resources. Universities during this period continued to provide the more traditional extension programmes with an increasingly middle-class student group. The approach of the university/WEA partnerships in decline by the 1960s may have achieved something for individuals, the elite of the working class perhaps, but the mass of the working class were not liberated through education, nor I suggest could they be. To sound a little like an old-fashioned dialectician, the capitalist imperative creates the material conditions through which 'education' as a system developed and was sustained. As Preece (1999) points out:

they (the WEA) were granted state funding on condition they only accepted university lecturers as a teaching resource. This was in order to provide a 'stable' curriculum in competition with the more grass roots funded National Labour Colleges which developed around the same period. ... The development of university LAE must therefore be understood from the perspective of its originators – a philanthropic minority of the ruling class – which necessarily had a vested interest in maintaining the status quo. (p 7)

Despite belief to the contrary, much of the engagement by universities with working-class realities in the first half of the twentieth century was philosophically based in social change through self-improvement, individually radical but not enormously socially challenging, and it is significant that the current rhetoric of government policy, as noted above, is still individualistic even if mass individualism. The development of the polytechnics from the recommendations of the Robbins report (1963) into higher education heralded the beginning of a mass Higher Education system. It challenged the 'classical' curriculum of higher education and increased the numbers of individual participants in the higher education system.

Access programmes also developed during the 1980s and validating bodies sprung up all over the country. It was largely women who had been denied education earlier in their lives who took up the opportunities offered by Access. The gender balance in higher education has shifted significantly with more than half of undergraduates now being women (Thompson 1995).

In the early 1990s the funding council for universities took on a similar approach to that employed in local authorities during the 1980s. Specific funding was allocated for work with 'educationally disadvantaged groups' (UFC 1990). In other words, a shift in thinking had occurred about the role for Higher Education to work with 'socially alienated' groups. Like local authority provision which had assumed, during the 1960s, that increasing provision would increase the participation rates of 'alienated' groups, the growth in numbers in universities had increased the number of middle-class students rather than gaining new students from the working class. Like local authorities, intervention and targeting specific groups became the strategy and policy of funders and government. The language of educationally disadvantaged students used in the early 1990s was based on a deficit model and focused on the dis-abilities of non-participants. In attempts to secure funds, universities increasingly defined their communities as deficient. Targeting specific groups therefore who are not participating (McGivney 1992) seldom implied that the system had to change; rather the implication was that the targeted groups had to change to fit in with the standards of Higher Education.

In 1995 new funds for 'widening provision' became available to all universities, old and new, through competitive bidding. Widening provision could be a challenging term. It was not about participation, but examining and changing provision within the academy. Implicit in this funding was a belief that 'targeted groups', the non-participants in HE, required guidance. It was based on ideas espoused in numerous reports and articles that access required information, and retention required guidance (McNair 1993; Houghton 1998; Johnston and Croft 1998; Fraser 1999). The applications for funds that were successful used guidance as a major plank of their strategic plans. However, while guidance about routes into and through higher education was less patronising than the language of 'educationally disadvantaged', it was still focused on a taken-for-granted structure of higher education learning, highlighting student retention, successful completion and credits and qualifications.

Numbers of participants in Higher Education had risen from less than one in five of the population in the 1960s to one in three in the 1990s but the numbers of people from poorer backgrounds participating in Higher Education had decreased (Wicks 2000). The Dearing report (1997) on Higher Education did not see widening participation as higher education's problem setting the difficulties within further education and schooling. In other words the history of participation in Higher Education is largely a history of elitism which ordinary people, women, Black and minority ethnic groups, disabled people and the working class have battled to gain access and contribute to knowledge development. A range of policy strategies and legislation from the second half of the twentieth century (Robbins 1963; F and HE Act 1991) attempted to widen access but despite claims that massification and a Higher Education system based on continuing learning was being established (Duke 1992) it is clear that we have not, as yet, fully secured this. My 'worry' is not about 'widening', or massification, but rather about the terms of participation, in other words what is there to participate in and how is the power balance of participation addressed.

Widening participation and exclusion

The current government definition of widening participation is summed up by Malcolm Wicks, the current lifelong learning minister, when he argued that widening participation was about access to, and flexible study of, higher education (Wicks 2000). The overall thrust of the Government's argument focuses on an education for the workplace. In highlighting barriers to learning, the minister pointed to methods of study as the main barriers. His solutions were centred on flexible study that enabled learning in the workplace through part-time and internet-based learning. Lifelong learning here takes on the agenda of the needs of global capitalism where 'upskilling' is the main focus of learning 'taken up over the lifespan' (Wicks 2000). In this debate standards are equated with benchmarking providing 'what students and employers can expect from a course' (Wicks 2000). In other words, a major part of the current government's rationale for challenging the elitism of Higher Education is about competitiveness in the marketplace. As Jackson (1995) points out, it is important to examine rhetoric and practice in the context of global changes to capitalism and the attempts by communities and workers to redefine some sense of their value in this climate. Where connections between widening participation and communities are made by government the language relates to the work of the social exclusion unit. Here the idea of 'ambassadors' who could return to communities to celebrate their achievements and provide encouragement for others is central to strategy. Developing 'community leaders' who will lead the way from exclusion to inclusion is part of the big idea of the new policies on neighbourhood renewal (SEU 2000). A policy that is based on individuals in this way remains a conservative approach to what claims to be a radical solution to participate in learning and society. The link between exclusion and widening participation therefore also worries me.

Exclusion is directly related to ideas of inclusion and strategies to develop social inclusion focus on, as Preece (1999) notes, 'normalising the unemployed or disaffected. As such, it legitimates the status quo of those systems which might otherwise be regarded as contributing to the very problem being addressed' (p 10). In other words, the inclusion/exclusion debate defines the problem of poverty and lack of access to social and economic resources as being about the dysfunction of particular groups in those communities. The solution offered in this model is for these people to adjust to a taken-for-granted middle-class norm of behaviour, such as retraining, to enable integration. Widening participation strategies are the methods that providers of retraining and education will use to include these individuals in social activity. Field (1999) notes that practitioners and researchers in the field of widening participation have not as yet realised the extent of coercion in the field of participation. He cites the example of the New Deal training programmes but also says:

> Without anyone much noticing, a great deal of professional development and skills updating is carried out not because anyone wants to learn or is ready to learn, but because they are required to learn ... changing expectations of customers from customers and citizens more generally: for a range of problems ... the answer is to provide training, whether its subjects want it or not. (p 11)

The relationship between the social exclusion debate, coercion, work and training and participation in learning does create concern. In our attempt to challenge the elitism of the academy we should be careful that we are not falling into the trap of state/capitalist coercion. Yet there is another trap, which as community educationalists, we can fall into and that is our so-called missionary zeal (Johnston 1999).

Owning up – widening participation and individual experience – a perspective from my life history

From 1981 until 1984 I 'scrounged' off the State. When I was 23 I fell pregnant with twins, developed high blood pressure and had to give up work. Soon after that I was made homeless and spent the first six weeks after my twins were born in a hostel for homeless people before being offered a council house on an estate in south London. I even experienced the classic line from a social worker who asked me if I had got pregnant so I could get a council house. While living on the estate I signed up for an Open University degree and became what would be today a useful statistic for the postcode analysis. I suppose I was also the type of student that could be discussed at conferences and in articles as a 'widening participation success'. In thinking about my work in education since then I have to admit that this life history has shaped my beliefs and actions. It is why I worry at some of the rhetoric used in education over the years. Was I a remedial learner, a woman returner, a socially excluded non-participant who had been encouraged into the world of education or simply a woman who wanted to find a language for all that she had experienced since being born into a challenging social milieu? It was not that I wanted to understand the world better, as many educationalists, and I at times, have been guilty of thinking learners want. Rather I wanted to articulate my understanding, to argue my case better and to challenge oppression more. Shaw and Crowther (1995) set out more or less exactly what I was looking for:

> If we are to engage with students on issues arising from purpose and experience, we need to provide opportunities for them to develop arguments, defend positions and come to a view which can be articulated and reviewed or renewed in light of new experience. (p 215)

I did not think I was socially excluded, although I suppose I demonstrated many of the signs of social exclusion, having been homeless, poor, with no say in the allocation of resources and yes, living with a particular economy that people who live outside of this sort of environment regard as suspect. Getting a car through an MOT required riveting bashed-out catfood cans to the floor so that the rust was not detected. Furnishing the house required taking perfectly good sofas and chairs out of skips from the richer part of the neighbourhood (at night so no one would see you) and not asking where cheap goods came from when 'the man' came to the door. That was how I, and many other people on the estate, lived and while, of course, I did not want to be poor – no one does – I did not feel helpless or isolated and I did not see education as a golden chalice. It did, however, get me out of poverty on my own terms. Like many people who have 'got an education', I left the estate, got a job in the profession, increased my earnings enormously and became what I guess would be called 'socially included'. Looking back on these changes now, I do not feel that any of the inclusion/exclusion or widening participation language applies to me, and if it does not apply to me I suspect most of the so-called socially excluded groups who are being encouraged to participate in education do not think it applies to them either. There are a number of worries for me from my own case study. One of them relates to the elements of 'outreach' work which smack of 'do-gooding' and a remedial approach to learners which, ultimately, maintains the status quo of higher education. I did not want someone to offer me a chance, provide me with a ladder up or design a package of support and guidance for me 'since individuals from non-participating groups are often unaware of their learning needs' (Fraser 1999:15). It is a dilemma for practitioners who work with people who do not know the culture and language of Higher Education but it is imperative to work towards an honest and adult relationship with community members who take on learning. As Field has pointed out, we have a huge normative assumption 'that participation is a Good Thing' (Field 1999:11). Perhaps before we can claim that participation itself is valuable we need to be clear what the terms of participation are in our higher education system.

Another worry that springs from my own experience is the role of education in supporting individuals to move out of their communities. Successful participation does require the learning of a different culture and language which does not sit easily with previously learnt knowledge. I am, if I am owning up, constantly aware that there are many parts of myself that I hide from the academy and the middle-class English world that I inhabit. My experience is not that unusual – there are many examples of such stories – but the dilemma for community educationalists remains in how we can best enable individuals to deal with shifting cultures and equally to move beyond an individualistic approach to learning which our Higher Education system, based in assessment and accreditation, advocates.

Widening participation and active citizenship

Much of the debate about widening participation as a method of challenging exclusion has echoes of discussions about citizenship and education for a social purpose. Growing out of a more radical tradition of community based university education, a number of continuing education departments through the twentieth century have argued for the development of learning programmes with industrial working-class communities (Ward and Taylor 1986). During the 1980s this work took on a particular political feel with the decline in the British manufacturing base (Francis 1989; Trotman and Lewis 1990) including work with mining communities during and beyond the miners' strike (Reynolds 1995), trade unions (Forrester 1995) and with the demand from second-wave feminism and the peace movement which led to the growth in women's education programmes and 'peace studies' that redefined many academic disciplines by re-examining the contribution of women to knowledge development (Delmar 1986; Thompson 1983, 1995).

Citizenship is a contested and shifting concept. It is not a fixed state. It was Thatcher who talked about 'the enemy within', redefining who had citizenship rights. Currently, again, the debate about asylum seekers re-opens the debate about citizenship and the nature of British society. Like the notion of education, citizenship can be exclusive and inclusion within society can be used as a threat to limit citizenship rights and create boundaries around communities. Participating and being included in what is, encourages people to fit in and to take for granted a set of unspoken rules of what education and citizenship are. Rather, citizens rights need to be won by critiquing taken-for-granted notions of entitlement (Martin 1999). Johnston (1999) reflects on different models of citizenship suggesting that there is a need to recognise learning for different aspects of citizenship; inclusive citizenship, pluralistic citizenship, reflexive citizenship and active citizenship. He argues that citizenship encompasses both rights and inclusion and that learning across the lifespan would be a vital part of active citizenship. This typology of citizenship is useful in identifying what is problematic about current rhetoric on widening participation for it seems that while politicians, funders and managers of higher education embrace 'widening participation', what they are embracing is only focused on one form of participation, akin to inclusive citizenship as Johnston describes or as Martin (1999) puts it:

> in a democratic learning society education for active citizenship has to be about not simply how to be a citizen (i.e. fitting in) but rather about deciding what being a citizen should mean. (p 92) (my brackets)

Perhaps the concept of active participation or a participation that allows critique is more useful for a radical approach to higher education. Implicit in the idea of changing notions of citizenship is a belief in difference and different knowledges within a society. This is not to say that there is no truth but simply that truth is contextual and that sophisticated understandings and interpretations of knowledge do not always reside in the established institutions of society such as the academy but may be found in different communities. This is perhaps the most significant challenge to higher education but it does not automatically come from the participation debate. It is through the connection of debates on citizenship and social advocacy for citizenship rights that questions of knowledge, not about what is but rather about what might be, refocuses a radical vision for participation in Higher Education.

University knowledge is not universal knowledge, the whole edifice of universities is based on fashions of discourse, threads of conversations that excite groups of researchers. This is not to fully concede to some of the postmodernists such as Derrida (1976) who see no possibility for constructive action; rather it is to question who makes knowledge and suggest that our truth making in the academy is only one way of talking about material conditions. Taking these ideas into the arena of different communities' involvement in higher education I would like to suggest one possible way of widening participation that is not dictated by the academy but is rather about a democratic partnership between researchers/practitioners and communities.

Working our way forward – one radical approach to participation

Rogers (1992) highlighted that there was a different approach to adult education in the third world, particularly that it focused on development needs for communities rather than individualised needs as in the West, but as Jackson (1995) rightly points out, Rogers does not deal with the issue of capital in driving state policies in the third world. However, there are other development models that we in the West can learn from the third world. Participatory Rural Appraisal (PRA), or participatory action research (PAR) as it is sometimes called, is a community development methodology used in a number of third world countries to identify development needs in rural areas (Burkey 1996). It is not part of the many education or literacy programmes in the third world, it is about development more generally. It is not about teaching, it is about learning; learning not for rural communities as such, although this is a substantially important unintended consequence, but rather about a community's advocacy for development, by teaching the officials who need to articulate locally relevant policy. The methodology of PRA works in partnership with members of communities to facilitate their advocacy for their needs. Traditional knowledge gathering in these circumstances has been rightly criticised for being disempowering (Gluck and Patai 1991). For example, who (and how) do you interview?; how can you be sure that your 'city' eyes see what is important and ethically do you have a right to 'watch others'? and so on. The methodology recognises that communities 'are not homogeneous entities' (Burkey 1996:40) and works to ensure that issues of power are addressed not only between researchers and communities are addressed but also between different interest groups within communities. Hence PRA works with a range of tools that involve the whole community to investigate a particular issue that requires a solution. The issue could be about a clean water scheme, siting a chemical waste plant in the area or developing an appropriate literacy scheme for adults in the area. As such it could be seen as an example of 'really useful knowledge' (Johnson 1979) because the work is directed at real-life experience and the solutions can be seen to have a direct impact on conditions.

Drawing on the principles of this methodology and through long-term partnerships with a number of voluntary and community-sector organisations in East and West Sussex, plans developed during 1998 to establish a learning exchange network (LEN) as a resource for voluntary and community organisations, their workers, paid and unpaid, and the communities in which they worked. Rooted in a belief that universities should engage with communities using their privileged position to gain access to resources for the purposes that communities identify, the university continuing education centre applied for funding from the European Social Fund to build the capacity of the voluntary sector. The main purpose of the fund was to provide training for the voluntary and community sectors and the network does this but it does this through a participatory appraisal system. Working with organisations who join the network, funding is allocated on set criteria agreed by a democratically elected steering group to organisations who wish to understand the skills and knowledge which their volunteers and paid employees possess and highlight where they wish to undertake further training. The funding can be used by the organisations in different ways and a number of participatory appraisal techniques are discussed with them. Sometimes organisations will use researchers from the university to research with the staff and volunteers what their future needs will be, sometimes they will use members of their own staff to undertake the analysis and sometimes they will draw in the expertise of other network members who can assist their organisation or group. PRA argues for the 'return of knowledge to the people and encourages the people themselves to preserve this knowledge in forms available to other poor people' (Burkey 1996:63) and LEN works on this principle.

The network is facilitated by two part-time community development researchers, one for East Sussex and one for West Sussex. They maintain a database of organisations in LEN with information on offers and requests from members for support to find solutions to identified problems in their community. LEN also organises events at the request of members and produces a monthly newsletter with details of training opportunities around the counties. The network has over 100 member organisations from larger voluntary sector groups such as Age Concern and umbrella organisations such as Councils for Voluntary Services, and smaller organisations such as 'Sofas and Stuff', a furniture recycling organisation in rural West Sussex, or 'Speak Out' a citizen advocacy project in Brighton and Hove.

So is this radical?

Allman and Wallis (1995) argue that as well as 'vision' and 'commitment' 'the radical educator must also be realistic'(p 19). Realism is not, I think, an excuse for giving in to the current audit culture of Higher Education or giving up on different approaches to addressing a problem. It is rather about ensuring that you are fulfilling criteria as stipulated in whatever audit is required but equally ensuring that the project with community members takes on a life of its own beyond the imagination of the university. The network is fulfilling the criteria of ESF: it is building the capacity of the voluntary and community sectors by providing training, but it is doing it by letting the agenda be controlled not by the university but by the network members. Drawing on the PRA philosophy the network believes that knowledge creation and development should be a partnership between those with first hand experience of problems and those with training in developing frameworks and languages of understanding. This is the radical aspect of the project. It is attempting to recognise different knowledge bases and, as O'Rourke (1995) points out, this is an area of participation in higher education that has received little attention and is noticeably underdeveloped:

> If wider access involves renouncing the very processes and practices which could be interrogated and re-articulate those absences with the people who experience them, thereby transforming the nature and culture of the academy, then we have achieved very little. (p 122)

In other words, we need to continue to fight for individuals and communities who are not considered to have the right to define their own knowledge. We can use our privileged position to relocate resources to communities to enable them to investigate and explore their knowledge and to then demand other forms of knowledge. We need to learn from such communities about their experience and find ways to articulate this understanding within the changing knowledge base of the academy. For me that is an exciting and difficult project. It is not about widening participation in higher education simply for the self-improvement or greater inclusion of the masses, it is more radical than that. It is about challenging the academy to allow active participation from a wide range of communities and individuals who will help to redefine the parameters of higher education itself. This seems to me to be the challenge for a radical agenda for widening participation in higher education, one that goes beyond rhetoric and stands for a new form of democratic learning.

References

Allman P and Wallis J (1995) 'Challenging the post-modern condition: radical adult education for critical intelligence', in Mayo M and Thompson J (eds), *Adult Learning, Critical Intelligence and Social Change*, Leicester: NIACE

Burkey S (1996) *People First. A guide to self-reliant, participatory rural development*, Zed Books: London

Dearing R (1997) *Higher Education in the Learning Society*, London: National Committee of Enquiry into Higher Education

Delmar R (1986) 'What is feminism?', in Mitchell J and Oakley A (eds), *What is Feminism?*, Blackwell: London

Derrida J (1976) *Of Grammatology*, Baltimore: Johns Hopkins University Press

DfEE (1998) *The Learning Age: a renaissance for a new Britain*, Cm 3790

Duke C (1992) *The Learning University. Towards a new paradigm?*, Buckingham: Open University Press

Gluck S B and Patai D (1991) *Womens Words: the feminist practice of oral history*, New York: Routledge

Field J (1999) 'Participation under the magnifying glass', in *Adults Learning 10–14* Vol 11 No 3, November 1999

Forrester K (1995) 'Learning in working life: the contribution of the trade unions', in Mayo M and Thompson J (eds), *Adult Learning, Critical Intelligence and Social Change*, Leicester: NIACE

Francis D H (1989) 'Socio-economic and cultural problems of declining industrial regions: the case of South Wales valleys', in Alheit P and Francis H (eds), *Adult Education in Changing Industrial Regions*, Verlag Arbeiter-Bewegung und Gesellschaftswissenschaft

Fraser L (1999) 'Widening participation through pre-entry guidance for adults', in *Update on Inclusion Widening Participation in higher education* 15–17 Iss 1, spring 1999

Houghton A (1998) 'Extending the guidance boundaries: an exploration of educative and empowering guidance strategies for learners who have been long-term unemployed', in Preece J, Weatherald C and Woodrow M (eds), *Beyond the Boundaries: exploring the potential of widening provision in higher education*, Leicester: NIACE

Jackson K (1995) 'Popular Education and the State: a new look at the community debate', in Mayo M and Thompson J (eds), *Adult Learning, Critical Intelligence and Social Change*, Leicester: NIACE

Johnson R (1979) 'Really useful knowledge: radical education and working class culture', in Clarke J, Critcher C and Johnson R (eds), *Working Class Culture: studies in history and theory*, London: Hutchinson

Johnston R (1999) 'Adult learning for citizenship: towards a reconstruction of the social purpose tradition', in *International Journal of Lifelong Learning*, Vol 18 No 3, 175–90, (May–June 1999)

Johnston R and Croft F (1998) 'Mind the Gap: widening provision, guidance and cultural change in higher education', in Preece J, Weatherald C and Woodrow M (eds), *Beyond the Boundaries: exploring the potential of widening provision in higher education*, Leicester: NIACE

McGivney V (1992) *Motivating Unemployed Adults to Undertake Education and Training*, Leicester: NIACE

Martin I (1999) 'Lifelong learning for democracy: stretching the discourse of citizenship', in *Scottish Journal of Adult and Continuing Education*, Vol 5 No 2, 89–105

McNair S (1993) *An Adult Higher Education: a vision*, policy discussion paper, Leicester: NIACE

O'Rourke R (1995) 'All equal now?', in Mayo M and Thompson J (eds), *Adult Learning, Critical Intelligence and Social Change*, Leicester: NIACE

Preece J (1999) *Combating Social Exclusion in University Adult Education*, Aldershot: Ashgate

Reynolds S (1995) 'Amman Valley enterprise: a case study of adult education and community renewal', in Mayo M and Thompson J (eds), *Adult Learning, Critical Intelligence and Social Change*, Leicester: NIACE

Robbins Lord L C (1963) *Higher Education Report to the Advisory Council for Education*, London: HMSO

Rogers A (1992) *Adults Learning for Development*, London: Cassell

Social Exclusion Unit (SEU) (2000) National Strategy for Neighbourhood Renewal: a framework for consultation, http//www.cabinet-office.gov.uk/seu

Shaw M and Crowther J (1995) 'Beyond subversion', in Mayo M and Thompson J (eds), *Adult Learning, Critical Intelligence and Social Change*, Leicester: NIACE

Stock A (1996) 'Lifelong learning. Thirty years of educational change', in Raggatt P, Edwards R and Small N, *The Learning Society*, London: Routledge

Thompson J (1983) *Learning Liberation: women's response to men's education*, London: Croom Helm

Thompson J (1995) 'Feminism and women's education', in Mayo M and Thompson J (eds), *Adult Learning, Critical Intelligence and Social Change*, Leicester: NIACE

Trotman C and Lewis A (1990) 'Education and Training: the experience and needs of miners redundant from Cynheidre and Betws Collieries in South Wales', Valleys Initiative for Adult Education

UFC (1990) *Universities Funding Council Prospectus for Funding to Counter Educational Disadvantage in Higher Education*

Ward K and Taylor R (1986) *Adult Education and the Working Class: education for the missing millions*, London: Croom Helm

Wicks M (2000) Keynote Address to Universities Association of Continuing Education Conference, April

Williams R (1959) 'Going on learning', in *New Statesman*, 30 May

3 Peripherality, solidarity and mutual learning in the global/local development business

Anne Ryan

The periphery is a place apart; a place where remoteness is determined less by geographic location than by a powerlessness to exercise influence or control. To experience peripherality is to be on the outside rather than the inside, to be disengaged from the complex range of decision-making processes that shape everyday realities. Education is a priority item on local and global development agendas and is universally acclaimed as a fundamental prerequisite to combat the manifestations of peripherality.

This chapter claims that educational interventions which celebrate rather than problematise the experiences of those at the periphery are characterised by solidarity and mutual learning. Interventions of this nature have the potential to produce purposeful knowledge; knowledge that can address the urgent development needs of this era. The chapter further claims that educational initiatives which value conformity over difference, effectively ascribe a hegemonic position to existing elitist processes of knowledge creation and deplete the available range of diversity in perception, thought and creativity.

This chapter critiques the growing involvement of tertiary institutions in local and global development activities, both in their capacity as providers of educational services and as consultants to NGOs, bilateral and multilateral development agencies. The increasing international profile of higher education institutions means that their sphere of influence is widening, as are the factors that influence their responses. The chapter argues that the appropriateness of these responses is largely dependent on whether these initiatives democratise the processes of knowledge creation or enforce conformity within the narrow confines of the current formal system.

The development consultancy work being carried out by tertiary institutions is reviewed to determine the extent to which their contribution is enabling or constraining experimentation in environments where the delivery of conventional educational services is wholly inadequate.

The chapter also considers the responses of higher education institutions to sectors of the local and global population who were previously excluded from higher education, but are now viewed as potential constituents. While emphasising the distinction between the democratisation of learning opportunities and the democratisation of the processes of knowledge creation, the chapter determines the extent to which these new constituents are positioned as consumers of a pre-packaged educational product, or as co-creators of a new knowledge base. It considers how the dominant liberal approach to broadening access may not lead to greater participation in the processes of knowledge creation but may in effect consolidate existing elitist and exclusionary practices.

Throughout the chapter Higher Education is positioned as a sub-system within a broader formal educational system in which schooling is an integral part. This makes it possible to consider differences in responses to exclusion among providers of formal and non-formal education and to highlight the preference of the formal system for conformity. To counter the colonising role of Western academia the chapter argues in favour of a commitment to an educational approach that can facilitate the kinds of partnership and inclusiveness necessary to enable collaborative learning opportunities. It looks to a learner-driven community education approach to provide a model of educational provision that can effectively challenge the dominant system-driven formal educational provision.

Creating purposeful knowledge

A 1998 European Commission report proposes strategies to create purposeful knowledge that are dependent on a shift away from conventional methods of research towards a dynamic networking among a broad range of interested parties. The main obstacle to collaboration is identified as the tight boundary that separates disciplines, keeps theorist and practitioners apart and isolates the academy from those actively engaged in economic, social and cultural development (Caracostas and Muder 1998). The report (pp 145–48) emphasises that:

- knowledge should be produced with a view to its application
- defining the problem and setting the priorities for research requires consultation with different interest groups
- the search for a solution to an application problem requires a variety of skills, some technical, some social
- the sites at which knowledge is produced are no longer limited to universities or research centres
- a crucial part of the research task is to enable collaboration among the different participants
- quality control should be based on criteria that reflect the needs of the network of interests involved and should begin when the problems are begin defined and the priorities for research are being set.

This document could not be seen as emanating from a concern with the widespread exclusion of sectors of the world's population from the processes of knowledge creation, nevertheless its significance lies in the fact that it highlights a growing awareness that established conventional approaches to knowledge production are no longer appropriate. It promotes a basis for dialogue across interest groups and regards the different knowledge within each group as essential to the success of the overall endeavour. Accountability is not determined by the strictures of a particular discipline. Instead it is contingent on solving a real problem.

The success of this kind of collaborative venture depends on the quality of the relationship between the players. The stress on enabling collaboration implies a need for dialogue where the less powerful stakeholders are not forced to subsume their distinctive perspectives by adopting the language and frames of reference of the powerful. The task is rather to establish a relationship where mutual understanding is possible. Crucial to the success of such a process is the willingness of those whose expertise is highly regarded to risk respecting the knowledge of those who are not so positioned. The motivation to do so is based on a practical rather than moral imperative in that purposeful knowledge necessitates collaboration and its value is totally dependent on its applicability.

Support for a more inclusive base for knowledge creation is a step towards acknowledging the degree of collaboration and partnership needed to create purposeful knowledge. It is also likely to foster a wider debate on the nature of knowledge. The philosophical positionings of those taking part in this debate will influence the strategies adopted to promote inclusiveness.

Creating knowledge through solidarity

Santos (1999) provides useful theoretical insights into the challenge of defining, creating and applying purposeful knowledge. He calls for a postmodernist critical theory that is characterised by a responsiveness to the multiplicity of oppressions that exist thereby making the 'different struggles mutually intelligible' (p 34) and making resistance to what he calls 'the hybrid concept of globalisation' (p 35) possible and realisable; a critical theory that allows for the creation of a vision that is unashamedly aspirational in transcending the limitations of what currently exists and is sustainable only in so far as it continues to be the product of dynamic networking among the many agents of resistance and change.

Santos positions himself within an oppositional postmodernism in order to go beyond mere deconstruction and to distinguish between behaviours that are essentially either conformist or rebellious. He further distinguishes between two forms of knowledge creation, one that promotes conformism and another that promotes rebelliousness. These he terms 'knowledge-as-regulation, whose point of ignorance is called chaos and whose point of knowledge is called order, and knowledge-as-emancipation, whose point of ignorance is called colonialism and whose point of knowledge is called solidarity' (Santos, 1999:36). Santos uses the term 'colonialism' to encapsulate the narrow base whereby knowledge is controlled by an elite, all outside that base are relegated to a not-knowing position, and the differences or otherness of those who are outside are seen as problems to be overcome. Solidarity, on the other hand, refers to the end point of a dynamic process that perceives difference not as a problem, but as the prime site for creating new and purposeful knowledge.

Knowledge-as-emancipation, therefore, not only calls for a recognition of 'others' as knowing subjects but also calls for processes that enable meaningful engagement with those who have been silenced and objectified. Silence, Santos (1999:39) claims, is 'a construction that asserts itself as the symptom of a blockade', a blockade which, he says, results from the imposition of what were presented as 'universal values authorised by reason' but were in fact, reason as defined by the dominant race, sex and social class. For those outside these elite groupings the resulting 'destruction provoked silences that rendered unprounceable the needs and aspirations of the peoples and social groups whose forms of knowledge were subjected to destruction' (Santos 1999:39).

The need for meaningful engagement with those who have been excluded from creating knowledge is echoed in the epistemological concerns of radical adult education. A major concern of adult education is to create opportunities for those who have been silenced to acknowledge themselves as 'knowing', to value this 'knowingness' and to draw on it as a base for further learning. However, unless formal educational providers acknowledge the knowingness of new learners, those entering mainstream education from groups who were formerly excluded will be afforded opportunities to do no more than 'consume' knowledge created within the old paradigm of knowledge-as-regulation. The focus will be on enabling them to conform to the needs of the system and in so doing these new learners will be required to abandon their 'otherness' and resume their silence.

Education as a force for exclusion

Any discussion of higher education is difficult in isolation from the global realities that are shaping current approaches to provision. There is, for example, ample evidence that the current provision of formal educational services serves to consolidate the exclusion of the least advantaged of the world's population, either by denying them access or by reinforcing class and gender based differences among those who gain access. Consequently the potential of large sectors of the world's population to contribute to the creation of knowledge is severely curtailed.

The 1990 UN Education For All Summit declared education to be a fundamental human right and set a target of basic primary education for all by 2000. The summit went on to state that education can help ensure a safer, healthier, more prosperous and environmentally sound world. Ten years on it is estimated that worldwide at least 130 million children, two-thirds of whom are girls, receive no formal education whatsoever. In addition 150 million children who start school drop out before grade 5. This exodus is largely due to the high costs involved in keeping a child in school and the poor quality of the education provided in inadequately resourced schools. In Zambia, for example, it is estimated that three out every four grade 6 pupils are illiterate. Thus the target of education for all, set in 1990, remains far from realised in either quantitative or qualitative terms. It appears that the description of education made by the Zambian Minister of Education in 1976 still applies:

> The education system is like a train which travels on a single track bound for one destination, but which ejects most of its passengers, without stopping, at several points along the route. In other words, the system favours a small minority who are believed to be the most able academically, at the expense of the vast majority of others. By doing so, it promotes a spirit of selfish competition, rather than cooperation. It breeds individualism, elitism and class consciousness, since material wealth and the comfortable life seem to be the goal at the end of the academic ordeal.

Although the statistics are far less bleak within better-off countries, similar patterns of educational exclusion are evident. Across the world it is those from the most disadvantaged areas, or those who belong to the most disadvantaged sectors of the population, who are most likely to drop out, or be pushed out, of formal education. In a review of education policy in Ireland, Clancy (1999:91) makes the point that the social class background of parents is directly related to early school leaving and that among those who complete second level schooling 'the levels of attainment are strongly related to social background, with higher levels of attainment for those from higher socio-economic groups'. The link between socio-economic status and retention and performance rates are apparent across all OECD countries. Even where there is an increase in the number of participants from lower socio-economic groups at all levels of education, the gap in relative retention rates is not closing. A recent OECD study indicates that 'increased overall rates of participation of young adults does not necessarily mean that students from previously under-represented groups have increased their share' (Wagner 1999:4).

One has to conclude that while academic ability may appear to be the decisive factor that determines one's likelihood of gaining and retaining a seat on the 'educational train', this ability is decidedly class specific. It is also gender specific in the case of poorer countries, or in the case of certain subject areas in better-off countries. In any consideration of education from a global perspective it is clear that large numbers of people have been relegated to the status of outsider or bystander. Therefore, one has to further conclude that the educational opportunities provided are incapable of meeting the learning needs and life circumstances of those who are so poorly served. The exclusion or nominal involvement of such large numbers has a negative impact not only on those who are excluded but also on the educational system that lacks exposure to diversity in approaches to problem solving and ways of thinking.

Responses to exclusion

Attempts to broaden the learner base are evident in the world's poorer countries where the implementation of universal primary education (UPE) has dominated educational agendas for the past 10 years, while in the better-off countries a growing number of third-level institutions are engaging in outreach activities among local communities and undertaking development related consultancy work in Africa, Asia and South America. In addition there is a growing trend among universities in North America and Europe to market courses overseas and to broaden their on-campus student base by enabling access to a more diverse range of students than heretofore.

This expansion of education worldwide is undoubtedly driven by a complex range of forces including financial considerations, demands for greater equity, changing demographics, a desire to respond to new demands from pressure groups including industry, the availability of funding supports for initiatives that promote greater access and a commitment to a vision of education that is participatory and democratic. Whether these initiatives respond to the diversity of perspective and ways of thinking resulting from broadening the learner base or merely offer opportunities for larger numbers of learners to participate in a fundamentally unchanged and essentially elitist system is largely dependent on the extent to which these moves are driven by a liberal or radical vision of education and knowledge.

Figure 3.1 depicts the distinguishing characteristics of liberal and radical responses to the challenge of exclusion.

As outlined above, the liberal response to exclusion aims to expand and modify the existing systems to accommodate greater numbers from different sectors of the population. It assumes that exclusion results from a set of unfortunate circumstances occurring haphazardly – circumstances that can be compensated for by directing additional resources to support individuals who are judged on a case-by-case basis to be deserving and most likely to benefit from participation.

Such a response, according to Lynch (1999:309), will at best 'bring limited gain for the relatively advantaged among the disadvantaged'. She points out that:

> the internal logic of liberal policies … treats education as an autonomous site with an ability to promote equality internally irrespective of external forces. By ignoring economic and power inequalities outside of education in particular, it endorses social and economic systems which perpetuate inequality within education. In a global context of structured inequality, the

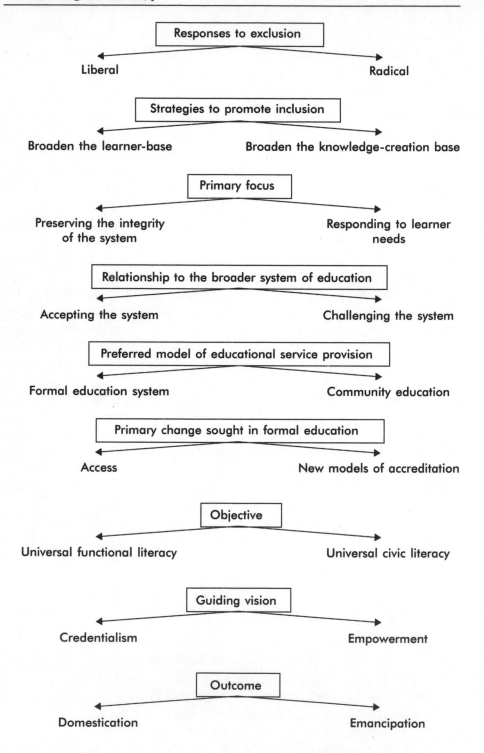

Figure 3.1 Liberal and radical responses to the challenge of exclusion

promise of liberal equal opportunities policies is realisable therefore for only a small minority of relatively advantaged people within a given disadvantaged group. (Lynch 1999:309)

A further distinguishing characteristic of the liberal approach is an unquestioning adherence to conventional delivery systems. The rigidity of this position reflects a belief that these systems are underpinned by what Santos termed 'universal values authorised by reason'. Such an unquestioning stance obscures the origins of these values and reasoning, thereby deflection attention from the systems propensity to perpetuate exclusion. This stance also attributes undue regard to delivery modalities so that how and where one acquires learning becomes as significant as what one has learned. As far back as the 1970s Illich (1971) questioned the capacity of conventional schooling to provide worthwhile education and more recently this issue has again been raised by Webster (1996). He claims that although circumstances have changed dramatically, the system of schooling has remained largely unchanged and is now outmoded. He describes the school as 'a modern institution in a postmodern world...a symbol of what has passed' (Webster 1996:72–73).

The radical response to exclusion is distinguished by its concern to tackle the causes of exclusion and in doing so it has no commitment to maintaining the integrity of the current educational system. On the contrary, it perceives the problem as endemic to the system in which it occurs and assumes that unless the system is fundamentally reformed, it will continue to exclude in ways that are eminently predictable. It further assumes that the factors that exclude specific groupings from participation in education also serve to exclude those same groupings from other services. As such, exclusion is a deep rooted, systemic and self-perpetuating problem.

Much of what informs community education is reflected in the radical position. In particular, community education provides a model of the kind of educational provision that is decidedly learner-driven and characterised as:

being firmly community-based, with local groups taking responsibility for playing a key role in organising courses, deciding on programme content and recruiting tutors;

an empowering process, working as an equal partner with the knowledge, skills and experience a learner can offer, and taking account of the cultural and other needs of participants;

an agent of social change and community advancement, which helps communities and individuals to develop strategies to take a more active role in decision-making on issues which affect their lives and those of their families and communities;

a process built on models of active participation, and inclusive decision-making. (Department of Education and Science, 1998:89)

While the community education described above generally targets adult learners, the age of the learner is of less significance than the shift in emphasis away from the needs of the system and towards the needs of the learner. Despite the possibilites for innovation and diversification afforded by this model, current provision indicates a strong preference for a system-driven approach, irrespective of its demonstrable short-comings.

Universal primary education versus schooling the universe

The dominance of a system-driven rather than a learner-driven vision of education is particularly evident in the drive to attain universal primary education (UPE). The influence of educational consultants, including those from higher education institutions, is a significant factor in promoting this kind of response. The focus is almost exclusively on expanding the current provision to reach greater numbers and to invest the bulk of available resources in revamping and rejuvenating existing delivery mechanisms. As mentioned earlier, even in countries where a commitment to UPE has raised levels of enrolment for both boys and girls, serious deficiencies remain. Very high levels of dropout and poor performance in examinations among children from economically disadvantaged families, uneven standards of provision and unresponsive and inert service delivery systems remain major, and to date largely intractable problems. An analyses of the situation from the perspective of the system rather than the learner tends to locate the problem within the reality of the lives of those excluded. The system's failure to serve the educational needs of girls, orphans, homeless children, those from the poorest families, especially those from female or child headed households, and children in the workforce, are explained in terms of the problems these children pose for the system. Inappropriate cultural practices, lack of appreciation of the value of education or an inability to pay for uniforms, books, lunches and the like are posited as reasons. Based on this analysis the main thrust of educational investment is to compensate for deficiencies in the learners life, effectively to 'change' those who are 'outside' so that they can 'fit' the image of those who are 'inside'.

Similarly, the poor quality of the education provided to those who do attend school is probematised as a reluctance on the part of trained teachers to work in remote areas, a tendency for teachers to move to other jobs in the private sector, lack of resources to provide ongoing in-service training for school staff, scarcity of teaching aids and irregular salary payments to teachers. While these are valid interpretations, focusing on the conditions as the source of the problems deflects from any fundamental questioning of the suitability of this model of educational service delivery to provide a useful service in what is likely to remain a resource-scarce environment.

In the face of dwindling resources and rising demand few consultants question the appropriateness of a model of schooling involving costly infrastructure, lengthy pre-service teacher training and centrally based administrative, distribution and quality control mechanisms. These consultants rarely conclude that low rates of enrolment and high rates of drop-out arise because the schooling provided is poorly adapted to the needs of the target population. Furthermore, accountability is rarely premised on a universal right to education but rather on an obligation to maintain the integrity of a system of schooling.

The widespread evidence of ingenuity, imagination and entrepreneurial initiative among impoverished individuals, families and communities implies a network of non-formal learning that supports this activity. The challenge of identifying this network and devising a system of formal education provision to augment rather than subvert this learning has been tried by development agencies in a number of countries. However, a lack of investment has curtailed the widespread application of these innovative approaches and the ongoing development of similar provision at secondary and tertiary levels.[1]

Given the broader development context in which the current educational expansion is taking place national governments are unlikely to opt for new models of educational provision unless such a shift is supported by donor agencies. As long as donor agencies are informed by Western educationalists is unlikely that substantial investment will be forthcoming or that the liberal response to UPE will be set aside.

Trading in the global learning market

The concern to democratise knowledge is taking place against a backdrop of globalisation. Korsgaard (1997) claims that over the past 20 years the economic competitiveness induced by globalisation has been felt in both formal and adult education where there is evidence of a move away from a learner-centred focus towards an 'economy-centred' purpose. The philosophy informing this emphasis 'is based on a neo-liberal way of thinking, regarding education as an investment in human capital and human resource development' (Korsgaard 1997:18).

The dominance of this way of thinking is evident in the marketing of tertiary level courses worldwide. In a world where e-commerce transcends national boundaries, education is increasingly being presented as a commodity to be traded globally. A recent speech by the Secretary of State for Education and Employment in Britain spoke of the need for an 'e-university' to capture a share of the 'global learning market' (Blunkett 2000:4–5). Within such a context the inability of nation states to provide educational services is perceived as an opportunity for 'universities to pursue entrepreneurial activity' within a 'global market for higher education (which) is already estimated to stand at 300 billion pounds sterling per year' (pp 14 and 3).

It is not uncommon to find the same courses on offer in many different countries. The main selling point is that the course, as well as the qualification, is identical to the one offered at the home campus. Embedded in this practice is a liberal assumption that knowledge is a value-neutral commodity that can be packaged for sale on the world market, that education results from the 'consumption of a course' produced in isolation from the context in which it is applied, and that learning is essentially a one way activity. A commonly posited rationale for educational activities of this nature is capacity building. This assumes that current capacity deficits are due solely to the size of the pool of qualified personnel within a country. It takes little account of the infrastructure needed to produce and replenish the pool of personnel and, perhaps more importantly it does not appreciate the value inherent in fostering indigenous centres of learning where cultural differences can be reflected in the curriculum and learning styles. An immediate by product of the current liberal market approach is the demise of local universities, particularly in Africa. As Western credentials become the standard and 'order' is imposed on 'otherness', a more long-term impact will undoubtedly be felt in the loss of diversity in approaches to problem solving, artistic expression and ways of engaging with information, thereby further contributing to the situation in which 'The mental space in which people dream and act is largely occupied by Western imagery … dangerously (crippling) humankind's capacity to meet an increasingly different future with creative responses' (Sachs 1992:4).

The liberal propensity for conformity in education leaves little room for these kind of creative responses to flourish. On the contrary, Blunkett's (2000:13) statement that 'in the knowledge economy, entrepreneurial universities will be as important as entrepreneurial businesses, the one fostering the other' implies a sought-after synchronicity between learning and business that indicates little concern for creating anything other than an educated, monocultural global workforce.

Access for outsiders

In Western universities the dominance of liberal approaches are also highlighted in on-campus access initiatives for those described variously as 'mature' students, students with 'special needs', 'older' learners, and 'non-traditional' students. The liberal response tends to emphasise the 'otherness' and 'outsider' status of these students. Their 'otherness' is defined in terms of how they process information or respond to established teaching and examining procedures and the specific supports they need such as childcare or wheelchair ramps. The focus in on the learner's ability to fit into the system rather than the capacity of the education offered by the institution to be inclusive. The outsider status of these learners is attributed to factors such as a lack of motivation to participate on their part, little encouragement from peer group and family, financial constraints, and fear of failure. An exclusive focus on supporting the individual student to overcome these constraints and to cope with the demands of the institution implies benign neutrality on the part of the wider educational system in creating this situation and a benevolence on the part of the tertiary institutions that are willing to accommodate these learners as exceptional cases.

Rather than locate the problem among those who are underrepresented, a radical approach recognises the institution as exercising preferences that are clearly reflected in selection procedures and progression routes and that effectively serve to exclude sectors of the population. A radical approach is concerned to reveal whose 'reason' is being presented under the guise of 'universal values' in determining what constitutes the typical learner, what knowledge is deemed worthwhile, how it is created, the purposes of learning and how it is measured and how these values are replicated throughout the entire educational system from pre-school onwards.

Critiques of the broader educational system that raise all of these questions have informed the provision of appropriate pre-entry courses and support services to learners and staff to make access for a broader range of learners possible. While these are important interventions and ones that need to be attended to, the tendency to remain aloof from critiquing the knowledge base of the entire formal educational system, has allowed piecemeal adjustments to be made to parts of the system, enabling it to flourish as a whole without fundamental change.

Radical adult education theorists and practitioners concerned with these realities are faced with the challenge of defining the principles that inform their analysis of the social, economic and educational context in which access initiatives are taking place, and in so doing to challenge institutions to acknowledge that the values imbedded in previous practices that excluded these learners, and in current liberal practices that seek to include them, constitute an unchanged elitist stance. Radical changes across the system require forums where all of the stakeholders, particularly those who are not well served at present, can voice their dissatisfaction and play an active part in refashioning the provision of educational services and the allocation of resources within the services, so that diversity can be nurtured as a source of strength. Forums of this nature are needed at the levels of policy making and co-ordination of provision as well as at the level of implementation.

Voices from the periphery

Individuals and communities which are at the periphery whether due to geographic, social, economic, religious or cultural circumstances experience particular constraints not least of which is self-consciousness with regard to their isolation and exclusion. What distinguishes these individuals and communities is their experience of exclusion as a dynamic process that marginalises them from a range of decisions that impact on their lives. There is a growing demand among those addressing the complex problems associated with peripherality for formal education to provide a forum to explore and disseminate the lessons they have learned.

The opportunities and constraints that impact on the establishment of relationships between peripheral communities and formal educational systems have much to do with the fundamental differences in philosophical positionings of both and in the 'kinds of knowledge' valued by both parties. The tendency for formal educational providers to direct their efforts towards succeeding and prospering in the global economy is inadequate to address the endemic complexities of exclusion experienced by peripheral communities.

Dissatisfaction with available courses has led large indigenous development agencies, such as ORAP[2] in Zimbabwe and BRAC[3] in Bangladesh, to come together to design and deliver a third level course for development practitioners incorporating content they know to be important. Demands for inclusion are also coming from groups who are concerned to influence more than just the content of courses. This is particularly true for women's community groups in Ireland. For many years these groups have engaged in educational activities that have experimented with collaborative and mutually supportive ways of learning. They have also heightened their awareness of how educational policies and practices perpetuate exclusion. These groups are searching for progression routes within the broader education system that will validate their learning to date and allow them to continue to learn in participative, collaborative ways. They particularly want access to universities because they recognise that university qualifications are valuable currency in the labour market. The implementation of APEL (Accreditation of Prior Experiential Learning) goes some way to enable access and afford recognition of the learning these groups have undertaken. However, these groups want more than access to the existing system. They want opportunities to participate in radically reshaping that system so that it can respond to their preferred way of learning and in so doing acknowledge these as valid and worthwhile. Furthermore they are concerned that progression through the formal system should not entail renouncing one's identity or alienation from core values.

Groups such as these are poised to engage with the 'gatekeepers' of knowledge. They merely need a platform where this engagement can be activated.

Colonising otherness: a final frontier

The success of radical responses to the challenge of democratising learning opportunities is particularly evident in learning environments outside the formal education system. In a range of geographic settings women's groups, community arts educators and others have developed innovative pedagogical processes that facilitate learners to overcome their silence and unleash their knowledge. In the main these processes have blurred the distinction between educator and learner and have enabled hitherto excluded groups to gain confidence in their status as knowing subjects. As their confidence grows, so too does their capacity and desire to determine the pace and direction of their ongoing learning and their engagement with society as a whole. These shifts from object to subject, from learner to self-educator are at the core of radical adult and community education within a knowledge-as-emancipation framework.

Achievements of this nature, however, have been largely confined to the domain of learning. The powerful position of the written word as a repository and carrier of knowledge has received little if any attention. Its supremacy has not been challenged either in terms of the appropriateness of its status in mainstream educational practices or the fact that it is the domain of an elite and relatively small cohort of experts and academics.

As highlighted in Figure 3.2 the area of learning has been afforded attention to make it relevant to a broad range of participants whose 'knowingness' is

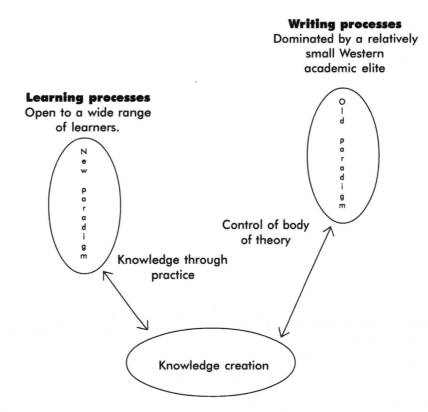

Figure 3.2 Emphasises how a focus on democratising learning rather than knowledge does not encompass the full knowledge-creation process

acknowledged and valued. However the codification of this knowledge into a widely accessible and influential medium of information dissemination remains largely undisturbed.

Research methodologies that acknowledge the 'knowingness' of those outside the system and that attempt to respect that knowing, have gone some way to create channels to allow a greater range of voices be heard. Nevertheless the pen or keyboard remains firmly in the hands of those who can speak the language and comply with the accepted 'norms' of the system. Furthermore 'ownership' of what is written rests with the writer not with those who are written about. The ownership conferred on the author of the written words serves to emphasise the power differentials between those who can contribute to the body of theory and those who cannot. Mutual respect and equality cannot be sustained in such circumstances.

> There is a sense in which the researcher knows aspects of their world better than the oppressed groups themselves … there is a very real sense in which they (the researchers) engage in an act of 'colonisation' – that is to say, they take data about people and use it without any guarantee of return or dividend; nor do those about whom they write have any institutional mechanism for exercising control over those who 'write their world'. (Lynch 1999:28)

Although many of those who write do so as advocates of knowledge-as-emancipation, their work has to be seen as interpretative. They filter what is known by others and normalise it within constructs favoured by the dominant system. No matter how empathetic the writing is, it remains secondhand and by virtue of that fact, it is unauthentic and distorted.

While those who write may perceive themselves as confronting the dominant system, and may as part of the research process utilise participatory methodologies, the continuing exclusive nature of the knowledge and skills of academic writing to which they have access, positions them as 'insiders' and positions those who do not have access as 'outsiders'. As such the power to decide what is important and noteworthy is located in those who could be seen as having a vested interest in the system by virtue of the exclusiveness of their skill.

This is a reality that aggrieves grassroots activists. They see themselves and their work as fodder for academics who write 'about' them, but seem unable, or unwilling, to facilitate them to acquire the skills needed to write about themselves and to insert that knowledge into the academic knowledge base.

The challenge posed by Santos (1999) to find ways to give voice to those who have been silenced demands that this barrier be dismantled. Until participative and mutually beneficial processes of writing are devised the task of democratising knowledge will remain incomplete.

Conclusion

Higher Education occupies a pivotal position within the entire education system. Its status as a repository of 'valued knowledge' and its remit to train the teachers who work at all levels of the educational system, afford it a decisive role in shaping the educational agenda. As the Higher Education sector becomes more active globally its influence extends well beyond the confines of national boundaries.

The degree of importance attributed to the democratisation of knowledge depends on whether education is viewed as an entitlement or a commodity. When viewed as a commodity, accountability is restricted to a provider's capacity to be cost effective and responsive to existing demand. However, when viewed as an entitlement, the needs of those who are poorly served or excluded from the current provision and the complex manifestations of peripherality are to the fore.

Within the Higher Education sector to date there is evidence of a marked preference for maintaining the existing educational delivery system and little evidence of a willingness to critique the knowledge base that informs this system. Participation in the system is conditional on conformity to predetermined truths and dissent is suppressed. In these circumstances engaging with learners who have experienced peripherality is tantamount to intellectual colonisation.

Successful experiments in entitlement-based educational provision have shown that inclusiveness necessitates radical changes in how education is delivered and in how 'knowingness' is perceived. The distinguishing characteristics of these endeavours have much in common with the principles that underpin community education.

To date these initiatives have been afforded the status of 'gap fillers' or appropriate alternatives to accommodate those who are excluded from mainstream provision. There is now an opportunity, even an onus, on community education to broker a dialogue between Higher Education and those who are excluded. A dialogue that (1) is premised on education as a right and (2) calls for a knowledge base that is informed by a plurality of perspectives and experiences has the potential to rejuvenate education's capacity as a force for development.

To rise to this challenge community education has to engage with the formal education system. Informed as it is by radical adult education, community education often defines itself in terms of how it differs from mainstream education. Although a separatist stance calls attention to the distinctiveness of this kind of provision, precisely because it 'has the radically democratic development of knowledge at its heart' (Barr 1999:71) adult and community education cannot afford to be isolated from the broader mainstream educational system. A number of key contemporary education commentators, including Mayo (1999), Thompson (1997) and Walters (1997), have highlighted the need to engage with the broader educational system in order to reveal and create change in the systemic and structural forms of domination in which mainstream education is embedded.

Notes

1   An example of this kind of initiative is BRAC's Non-Formal Primary Education programme in Bangladesh (Ryan and Taylor 1999). Since its inception in the mid 1980s this programme, which targets poor children and adolescents, especially girls, has grown rapidly and now has a network of 34,000 schools in rural and urban areas. 'BRAC's education programme has attracted attention because of its capacity to reach relatively large numbers of children (in excess of two million have benefited), maintain an even standard of provision across the country in a variety of settings, and perhaps most significantly it is noted for its capacity to enroll and retain a high proportion of girls' (Ryan and Taylor 1999:17).
2   ORAP (Organisation of Rural Association for Progress) has one million members.
3   The Rural Development Programme of BRAC (Bangladesh Rural Advancement Committee) reaches 2.23 million.

References

Barr J (1999) 'Women, adult education and really useful knowledge', in Crowther J, Martin I and Shaw M (eds), *Popular Education and Social Movements in Scotland Today*, Leicester: NIACE (pp 70–82)

Blunkett D (2000) Speech by Secretary of State for Education and Employment, at Greenwich Maritime Museum, 15 February

Caracostas P and Mulder U (1998) *Society, The Endless Frontier: a European vision of research and innovation policies for the 21st century*, Strasbourg: Office for Official Publication of the European Community

Clancy P (1999) 'Education policy', in Quin S, Kennedy P, O'Donnell A and Kiely G (eds), *Contemporary Irish Social Policy*, Dublin: University College Dublin Press (pp 72–107)

Department of Education and Science (1998) *Adult Education in an Era of Lifelong Learning: green paper on adult education*. Dublin: Stationery Office

Easton P (1997) *Sharpening Our Tools: improving evaluation in adult and nonformal education*, UIE Studies 4, Hamburg: UNESCO Institute for Education and German Foundation for International Development

Hanna D (1997) 'The organisation as an open system', in Harris A, Bennett N and Preedy M (eds), *Organisational Effectiveness and Improvement in Education*, Bristol: Open University Press (pp 13–21)

Illich I (1971) *Deschooling Society*, New York: Harper and Row

Korsgaard O (1997) 'The impact of globalization on adult education', in Walters S (ed), *Globalization, Adult Education and Training: impacts and issues*, London: Zed (pp 15–26)

Lynch K (1999) *Equality in Education*, Dublin: Gill and Macmillan

Mayo P (1999) *Gramsci, Freire and Adult Education: possibilities for transformative action*, London: Zed

Ryan A and Taylor B (1999) 'Non-formal primary education, phase II (1996–1999): final evaluation', unpublished report presented to the BRAC Donor Consortium, Dhaka 11th August 1999

Sachs W (ed) (1992) *The Development Dictionary: a guide to knowledge as power*, London: Zed

Santos Boaventura de Sousa (1999) 'On oppositional postmodernism', in Munck R and O'Hearn D (eds), *Critical Development Theory: contributions to a new paradigm*, London: Zed (pp 29–43)

Thompson J (1997) *Words in Edgeways: Radical Learning for Social Change*, Leicester: NIACE

Wagner A (1999) 'Adult education in an Era of Lifelong Learning: trends, developments and issues from an OECD-wide perspective', unpublished paper delivered at the National Adult Education Forum, Dublin, 22 September 1999

Walters S (ed) (1997) *Globalisation, Adult Education and Training: impacts and issues*, Leicester: NIACE

Webster K (1996) 'The Secondary Years', in Huckle J and Sterling S (eds), *Education for Sustainability*, London: Earthscan (pp 72–85)

4 Common goods: beyond the new work ethic to the universe of the imagination

Tom Steele

Three currents of nineteenth-century education

Is there still a role for independent radical education in the era of 'mass' and 'universal' higher education or is adult education, conventionally understood, merely a hangover from the days of university scarcity when higher education was a finishing school for a small elite? Was adult education, then, ever more than an imperialism of knowledge deployed by liberal academics in pursuit of an inclusive national identity for the potentially disruptive lower orders?

Raymond Williams, in his seminal essay *The Common Good*, noted that the three dominant educational tendencies in the nineteenth century were, roughly, those of the Old Humanist, the Industrial Trainers and the Public Educators. The old humanists defended an elite education for those designated largely from birth as governors of society and the guardians of the culture, where education was no so much *for* anything but an ineffable spirit that wrapped its supplicants in the embrace of benign tradition. However, shuffling their feet in the anteroom to the academy, the new breed of entrepreneurial industrialists could not see how this kind of education gave them the kind of skilled workers they needed. They decided to set up their own schools to train skilled working men, one important outcome of which were the mechanics institutes. This industrial trainer tendency led to the passing of legislation for the state provision of technical education and eventually further education colleges and polytechnics (Fieldhouse *et al* 1996). A third tendency that addressed those whose class, like that of Hardy's Jude, was largely inadmissible to the academy, was that of the public educators. This tendency included radicals who were not convinced that the achievements of liberal humanism should remain the inheritance of a decaying aristocracy or be plundered by an avaricious capitalist class. Many, like Carlyle and Ruskin, promoted this message through public lectures and popular journalism. They celebrated the dignity of labour and often the rude health of working-class culture. Ruskin and his followers were convinced that the working class should be encouraged to achieve a political maturity and to project a kind of society that reflected their own culture, not merely that of their 'betters'. It is this latter tendency that fostered much of the radical tradition of British adult education, its feet planted uneasily in both the academy and the soil of working-class consciousness. Associated with this tendency but in polemical opposition to it was the domestic Marxist tradition of the labour colleges and the Plebs League.

This chapter argues that instead of finding a new synthesis of this educational triad, modern mass Higher Education is largely driven by the industrial trainer tendency, suitably disguised as 'vocationalism' but a vocationalism of 'transferable skills' and ephemeral 'competencies'. The old humanist is now a rare breed but he can still be found defending his elite (and well-endowed collegiate) corner against the monstrous regiments of feminist critics, cultural studies heretics and postcolonial upstarts who have hacked away at his pretensions to spiritual enlightenment and revealed the flimsy ideological bases upon which he stands. Nevertheless, around half the students he will educate will be recruited from the private and independent sector, which caters for only 7 per cent of the school population.

So what has happened to the public educator? He was also a male with vested interests in a version of 'class' that often disguised its own subordinates and minorities. The slogan 'the personal is political' meant little to Ruskin and 'commonality' might reinforce a division of labour where women remained the 'angels of the hearth'. He may also have believed that the 'coloured' races were children in dire need of Christian redemption and homosexuals a species of Wildean deviant (or 'pervert' as the Scottish cardinal so quaintly has it) that should be firmly closeted. Commonality did not necessarily imply difference and certainly not heterodoxy. In *After Strange Gods*, T S Eliot (1934), an admirer of Ruskin and a sometime university extension lecturer for Oxford and London Universities, could imagine nothing worse than bands of 'free thinking Jews' roaming the urban spaces and undermining Christian orthodoxy. H G Wells, in *Modern Utopia*, believed that the 'yellow and brown' races would inevitably die out and proposed eugenics as a solution to those born physically and mentally handicapped. He added that, for modern democracies, it was 'foolish and dangerous' to sustain linguistic differences and 'all sorts of foolish and irritating differences between their various citizens' (Wells nd:336).

Things have moved on and in the last half century especially with terrifying speed. However, if a genuinely participatory mass democracy, with meaningful employment for all, and an active toleration of cultural and sexual difference is to be achieved, some new educational synthesis needs to be attempted. Adult education, I believe, has a vital role to play in this.

Widening participation and the liberation of time

As workers in adult education, we find ourselves in a cleft stick. We have worried away at the elitist and disciplinary-based university, which contented itself with educating a small, class-based minority of the population, for long enough. Are we ungenerous then, to be suspicious of the intentions of a government that now not only seems to agree with us but apparently makes widening participation a strategic element in its educational programme? There are reasons to be cautious. This form of widening participation has not taken the form of paid educational leave, reinstated maintenance grants or continued access to benefit for adults to receive periods of full-time university immersion. While many over the age of 21 are indeed in full-time higher education, older adults and especially women are most characteristically found in 'flexible' entry, part-time qualification routes, mostly in a 'new' university or The Open University (Robertson 1997). Government policy, indeed, largely equates widening participation with part-time access to sub-degree qualification in further education colleges or a new university.

The dominance of the Government's rhetoric of the workplace – upgrading skills, new and improved competencies, expanded portfolios and so on – positions the learner in a very restricted way, namely as a potential worker, so that she or he is encouraged to choose a course of study that will lead to some sort of vocational qualification. Martin Ryle notes that 'Today, the primary goal of education is said to be to equip individuals with skills which will allow them to participate in a modern economy...It is the Prime Minister's insistent aspiration that Britain may have "the best educated *workforce* in the world"' (Ryle 1999). In his forward to *The Learning Age*, the Government's discussion document on lifelong learning, David Blunkett notably qualifies this approach by insisting that 'As well as securing our economic future, learning has a wider contribution. It helps to make ours a civilised society, develops the spiritual side of our lives and promotes active citizenship'. Although Blunkett bows to cultural development and social purpose, there is no doubting that the central purpose of lifelong learning is vocational: 'To achieve a stable an sustainable growth, we will need a well-educated, well-equipped and adaptable labour force'.

Education therefore is increasingly tied to the disciplines of work rather than the needs thrown up by cultural and personal circumstances or what Andre Gorz calls 'the sphere of autonomy' (Gorz 1989).

But is there some incoherence in the Government's emphasis on identifying the potential 'lifelong learner' as a lifelong worker? Andre Gorz contends that 'work' as we understand it is really an innovation of modernity, or more exactly of industrial capitalism (Gorz 1994:53). 'Work' as regular, undifferentiated, paid employment carried out not so much for its intrinsic or immanent value but simply as means to generate income, assumed its present meaning only as commodity production and consumption gained dominance over production for self. Under late capitalism, this kind of 'work' occupies a decreasing amount of socially necessary time and the amount of permanent productive work, especially that with a meaningful 'vocational' content, is declining. This is not to romanticise medieval toil. However, satisfying, well-paid secure employment will be available for a smaller and smaller proportion of the population. The so-called period of post-Fordism and globalisation signify that the former staple jobs of the Western industrial states are increasingly relocated in low-wage economies elsewhere in the world. (It does not preclude the fact that should wage rates fall and state inducements rise in the former industrial sector than the new that manufacturing will not relocate back. The location of Japanese, Korean and Taiwanese electronic companies during the last decade in Scotland is an example). Clearly while the manufacture of consumables is still escalating, associated employment in the West is not. Instead, a new 'servant' culture, according to Gorz, is creating a new kind of work. These jobs in everything from paid housework, office cleaning and nannying to serving in fast food joints are low-paid, largely temporary and non-unionised. The major shifts in contemporary employment patterns include the intensified employment of women in service occupations and the low-skilled assembly line. Associated social problems include a now generational culture of unemployment among unskilled young men, exponential drug-related crime and the weakening of the ability of national governments to effect permanent solutions.

As a consequence the customary division between skilled and unskilled labour, which resulted in the often-disabling craft-demarcated unionisation of the nineteenth century (or organised *dis*-unity of the working class) is, according to Gorz, now generating an even more severe social division in the twenty-first:

> *In a context in which there can no longer be stable full time jobs for all*, this extolling of maximum effort and glorification of employment as a source of social identity and national wealth and greatness will succeed in clouding the political waters by disconcertingly overturning the previous system of allegiances; as a result the class of skilled wage-earners with stable jobs will be induced to behave as *jealous proprietors* of that rare commodity, employment, and to ally with the traditional middle classes and the modern employers to defend their jobs and wages against the pressure from a growing mass of unemployed workers. (Gorz 1994:19 author's italics)

The growing mass of unemployed – and underemployed – may well prove to be a decisive political configuration in the new century. As the Seattle world trade convention riots and earlier demonstrations against 'capitalism in the City' of London in 1999 graphically displayed, not only have the old alliances for a kind of cultural stability or political settlement been decisively broken. Indeed the creativity of the demonstrators in using new technology communications and carnivalistic methods of protest are profoundly disconcerting to the political establishment. They can be seen as a sophisticated extension of the carnival culture of the New Age travellers and motorway, eco-warriors of the 1980s. Significantly, a common thread uniting the various groups in these *ad hoc* and volatile alliances is a distaste for 'work' as conventionally conceived (both the 'stress-related work' of those in secure employment and the 'Mac-job' drudgery of those on the margin). At its most thoughtful, it signifies a concern for global deep ecology, sustainable growth, fulfilling life and common fellowship.

However, in its more extreme manifestations, amounting almost to a religious fundamentalism, it can be a kind of mindless tribalism, violently anarchic and fascistic in its treatment of opponents.

A common theme in sociological analysis is that the break down of older patterns of socialisation associated with the high employment, industrialised society of the post-war decades is generating increasing social fragmentation. As a consequence, education, which was formerly an essential sector of the State's ideological apparatus for creating consent and social solidarity, has become a severely troubled area. The erosion of the autonomy of the educational sector in the last 20 years is indicative of the Government's lack of confidence in educators to deliver the goods. This dates from the early 1980s when, as Minster for Employment, Norman Tebbitt's use of the Manpower Services Agency to colonise the further education sector, while simultaneously cutting funding, was one of the first indications that new disciplinary forms were required. The plethora of job creation schemes and youth training opportunities that cascaded down during the Keith Joseph years as Minister for Education signified both the intensified role vocational training was taking and at the same time a restructuring of the post compulsory sector. Many will remember the ending of liberal studies funding to continuing education, the break-up of Her Majesty's (far-too-liberal) Inspectorate and introduction of OFSTED in its place and finally the merging of the ministries of education and employment. Thus while the unit of resource (and relative pay) in education was dropping rapidly and bureaucratic intensification of work was growing, a reserve army of privatised trainers was being steadily marshalled. Under the new audit culture, which was borrowed from conservative corporations like IBM, the desired outcomes of the new edu-training were no longer the fuzzily defined 'citizens' or well-rounded individuals of the post-war period of democratic optimism but willing and flexible employees, whose loyalties were to the company and the ethic of self-promotion. The Durkheimian ideal of 'society' was being replaced by that of Edward Heath's Selsdon Man (and given teeth by Margaret Thatcher).

However, since none of this 'job creation' actually moved the country back to stable high employment but only appeared to increase the numbers without permanent full-time work to levels not seen since the 1930s, the questions had to be asked: what was it all for?

One answer was that what was really happening was a new form of social disciplining. The older, Durkheimian, form of educational socialisation had stressed the need for social solidarity across class and religious boundaries, through a secular educational system, in favour of a 'religion' of humanity, scientific engagement with reality, meritocratic reward, citizenship and an ethic of welfarism on the part of the wealthy to be collected in the form of income tax. All this was a way of steering the working classes away from revolutionary alternatives and gaining their consent to incorporation within the dominant system of exploitation and social inequality. It worked so long as American and

European imperialism secured enough surpluses from the rest of the world, to raise wages and supply basic welfare (and women were content to be used as unpaid labour in the home). When this 'liberal humanist' settlement started to break up the 1970s it was clear some other mechanism of socialisation would be needed.

In effect the ratcheting up of the work ethic *without at the same time an increase in available worthwhile work* became a new form of social disciplining, or what Foucault called a 'technology of the self'. Forget the gobbledegook of humanity and society and get real about the self – no worry that the 'self' was now, apparently, multiple. By subordinating the liberal humanist curriculum and focusing on technical competencies learners were encouraged to see themselves as warriors in the urban employment jungle. Upskilling, retooling, flexible multi-tasking, problem solving and performativity became the new code for the goals of education. Learners were also encouraged to believe there was no alternative to this way of thinking. Thus, in effect, two of the three tendencies of education – personal and cultural development, and social understanding and engagement – were strictly subordinated to vocational training with the consequent diminishing of the larger sense of self and social relations.

But, Gorz notes, during this period the patterns of work changed dramatically and contradictorily and, in particular, the rise of youth unemployment, the difficulty of finding genuine apprenticeship places or even any sustained training (as opposed to brief injections of low-level competencies) increasingly randomised occupational choice. 'Vocation' in the classic sense of 'life-project' or calling became rare outside of certain restricted-entry professions.

There was another side to this, however. Culturally, Gorz continues, life changed significantly and not necessarily in the ways that the disciplining process has required: adolescent behaviour was prolonged late into life; the rejection of routine, experimentation, change and the desire to go on learning and extend horizons are more common features of life. The loosening of social constraints and increased sense of individuality has increased the desire for personal fulfilment, openness and availability. While this new sense of 'human' possibilities might be the obverse of the mobile and flexibly focused worker, it can create such discordance within the individual that mental instability and breakdown frequently result. In Sartre's phrase we are 'condemned to be free' or are 'forced into autonomy' and the very process of coming to terms with that autonomy without falling back into a kind of religious fundamentalism or desire for authoritarian solutions, has huge educational implications. The truth is that work can no longer supply the social identity that formerly glued society together and generated a sense of role fulfilment. The economy no longer requires all men to devote themselves to specific paid occupations and while women are encouraged to take up part-time, low paid occupations it has not created the means for them to escape their traditional family roles. Women have too much to do and men have too little.

The recipe for chaos implicit in this situation may force many into a nostalgic desire for order and authority, much in the way that in the former Soviet Union, instead of withering away, the spectres of communism and czarist imperialism remain desirable options haunting a demoralised democracy. Other forms of political and religious authoritarianism may seem attractive to those for whom work offers no settled identity. Nostalgia for the welfare state of 1950s, while signifying the genuine losses of social care, nevertheless masks the frustration felt with bureaucratic delay, corporate dullness and sexual repression. There is, moreover, little left of that alternative working–class culture, that nursed the collectivities of the co–operative movement, trade unions and Old Labour, the high mindedness of the chapel and the puritanical devotion to public service. Nor can it be reinvented.

The lack of an alternative social–communitary order means that more than ever the burden of ethical autonomy has to be shouldered without recourse to legitimated authority. The intense complexity of modern industrial societies makes it increasingly difficult for individual and social identities to be reconciled. Gorz argues that 'in complex modern society the differentiation of spheres of activity brings with it a differentiation of the dimensions of existence and prevents the subject from seeking his or her unity in any of them' (Gorz 1994:24). Under this pressure a unified conception of the self, especially an ethical self that can be a responsible social agent, is increasingly fragile. Yet some such notion of ethical agency has to be regained.

Late capitalist society has become a kind a Nietzschean cripple, that is to say a system which is massively overdeveloped in one faculty and only negligibly in others, such that the one faculty dominates all the others. This faculty is, according to Gorz, that of 'economic rationality': the logic of production has been allowed to dwarf all other rational forms. It is not rationality *per se* which is at fault but the subordination of all other forms of rationality to that of the rationality of the market. Socially, therefore, the dominance of economic rationality has to be circumscribed and other forms of rational and emotional activity – ecological conservation, creative expression, nurturing children, developing multiple skills, active democratic engagement, enjoying discussion and conversation, engaging in scientific experiment, playfulness, cultivating cultural difference – the list can go on – have to be encouraged to flourish. The end of work, therefore offers the opportunity for the 'liberation of time'. For Gorz this means the completion of modernity not its termination. The role of education, that other invention of modernity, must be instrumental in both containing the monster that the market system created and enabling the flowering of multiple rationalities, cultural identity and individual potentialities.

This requires self-governing individuals capable of rich and rewarding lives, who can generously respond to need and disability in others and take on ethical responsibility for their actions. In this way Gorz follows Habermas in arguing that only then can the balance between 'autonomous self-organised public spheres' governed by voluntary, freely given time and 'the domains of action regulated by money and administrative power' be altered in favour of the former. The latter domain can, of course, never be eliminated so long as useful goods and services have to be made and distributed fairly. But the overwhelming dominance of that sector over the other means that *useless* goods will continue to be massively overproduced to the detriment of the environment and services will never be adequate to needs. Education's most urgent tasks are to enable learners to understand, evaluate and remedy this imbalance of spheres.

The task of a liberatory education is therefore at base an ecological one, both holistic in the sense that it regards it as a reconstitution of human wholeness but unlike some versions of enlightenment man, it regards this non-gender specific human as in harmony with nature rather than mercilessly exploiting it. This is not to argue for some form of mystical balance in nature or to assert that in some pre-lapsarian time human societies lived in perfect harmony with other animals and vegetables, as has been argued about Native Americans.

The point is rather different. In the first place nature as a construct is largely a Romantic idea which seemed in some respects to stand in for the then discredited idea of a benign deity when, under the pressure of rational enquiry, such an idea could no longer be sustained. The kind of pan-theism which gripped poets like Wordsworth was a kind of god in green clothing as experienced by rich imaginations liberated from orthodox theology.

In the second place, the version of the whole human cannot be confused with the 'harmonious *man*' of the Enlightenment period. This richly conceived individual stood in his wholeness (holiness) quite apart from society in monadic glory, the marbled David of perfect feature and form. The 'whole human' of the dawn of the third millennium is unlikely to be so gracefully formed, beatifically conceived or, gladly, unequivocally male. Time is out of joint with such 'perfection'. While some postmodernist versions have drawn on the classic works of modernism to reject the idea of the human being in its entirety and to celebrate the pluralistic multifaceted identities of contemporary life, it could be argued that, in reality, such lifestyles are probably only found among the more well-heeled inhabitants of the Californian coast. Postmodernism, while properly noting that the bourgeois humanist ideal of the individual has had its day, then oversteps the mark in claiming the end of human beings as such.

The whole person, then, can no longer rely on spontaneous spiritual harmony, the rule of perfect reason over irrational desires or assumed species superiority over the natural world. Rather her and his ability to live with themselves, with others and with 'nature' will be, of necessity, a kind of *work*. They will have to work at it. It will require a great deal of reflection and understanding of themselves, their relations with others and the natural world. What is lost for good and all is that these things can be achieved by instinct alone (although) this has to be listened to, or by some reference to a supernatural authority (although some notion of 'the Good' has to be agreed upon).

The feminist insistence on *difference* is also crucial to the kind of self-understanding required. While the human being or 'man as such' so valued by the Enlightenment has not survived the division of labour under *laissez-faire* capitalism and the failure of European imperialism, under the pressure of gendered, sexual and cultural differences, the differentiation of individuals survives. Equally, despite the Thatcherite assertion of the end of society, a truly universal characteristic of these individuals is that they are still social animals – Aristotle's *zoon politikon*. Human beings tend to stick together, in groups, families, tribes, as adherent to religious faiths, as members of voluntary associations, trade unions or professional groupings, as citizens of political units such as nation states, as supporters of football clubs. While examples of individuals who exist outwith some form of social group are not unknown, it is significant that the most familiar form of punishment is still social exclusion.

It is unfortunately necessary in a brief chapter to make substantial leaps in the argument and hope they will be pardoned. The leap here is to assert that the bourgeois individual of the Enlightenment has perforce had to give way to some notion of the 'social individual' – not the 'Socialist Man', who has already joined the Neanderthals as a flawed prototype, or the primitive communalist – but the educated intelligent reflective being who realises that the state of her or his well-being relies implicitly on the health of the societies to which they belong. The founding insight of the classical sociologists such as Durkheim was to understand that modern societies could no longer lay claim to the pre-conscious solidarities of religious or culturally based tribalism but had to construct considered collectivities, based on mutual respect and obligations.

For Durkheim, it was the function of education to foster national solidarity through the development of morality. School teachers were to become a secular priesthood. By the late nineteenth century Durkheim was installed in the first chair in sociology (and education), in Bordeaux. His *De la division du travail social* (1896) argued that the social fabric of the country was crumbling due to an excessive infatuation with individualism and the weakening of the bonds of religion and the family. He argued not only that a new morality was needed to solidify a new social organisation based on *professional* associations. Jacques Donzelot noted that, 'Durkheim sees the concept of solidarity as encapsulating a general law of social development'. This was further elaborated in his notion of 'organic solidarity' which, 'at once reinforces and overlays the unity which arises from similarities with the interdependence created by the increasing division of labour and the resulting tendency for people to identify themselves as individuals' (Donzelot 1991:172).

The new solidarities required by modern industrial societies would have to be achieved by other means. These would be secured largely by conscious and rational associations which made a virtue of friendship and fellowship voluntarily entered into, mutual tolerance, respect for the subjectivity of others, some notion of honouring contracts and responsibilities socially required, backed up by legal sanction, and a (limited) commitment to some form of social justice. There had also to be some notion of allegiance to a larger totality or totalities. This larger collective was the nation state, which in turn relied on a healthy domestic capitalist economy. Unlike Marx, Durkheim believed that class harmony could be achieved within such a system so long as the State made provision for the poor, sick and aged. The means to this was a system of taxation. Durkheim believe that the wealthy discharged their duty to the State largely through taxation, which would finance the welfare state and an educated social conscience.

Durkheim then 'hailed' education as the means to the creation of solidarity around the new work-based society of the late nineteenth century. It was no accident that his chair was in both sociology and education as he saw his purpose fundamentally as educational and that his primary tool was the new 'science' of society. The laic system of education introduced by the French State was in many respects the high point of the move towards secular education undertaken by post-Enlightenment Europe and much emulated. Similarly the 'welfare' state was the classical third way taken by European social-democratic States to avoid both the extremes of *laissez-faire* capitalism and Bolshevik bloody revolution.

The welfare state achieved a social consensus throughout the industrialised world, with increasing urgency after the Russian Revolution of 1917 but especially in the reconstruction in the non-communist sphere after the Second World War. By the late 1970s this consensus was cracking and during the 1980s conservative free-market policies severely eroded the taxable commitment of the wealthy to the poor and scorned the ideal of public service, which Durkheim espoused. As we have seen these policies accompanied both a weakening of the commitment to social solidarity and scepticism about the liberal value of education.

Despite the great nostalgia for the golden age of the welfare state and the relatively stable social national settlement that accompanied it, welfarism produced its own problems. Gorz's associate, Kallscheuer, notes that the welfare state even contributed to the decay of sociability that it was designed to support, because it was in effect a form of 'asocial socialisation'. He argues that, because of the way it regulates poverty, the welfare state actually breaks down even abstract solidarities. Welfarism assumes the normative standard is 'those in work' and those who are not 'in work' are positioned according to their employability or non-employability rather than any other indicator of deprivation or need. Kallscheuer notes: 'The various classes of social poverty are ranked in descending order on the basis of their relationship to the work-based society's central category of the fully and permanently employed' (Kallscheuer 1994:120). A return to welfarism on the old model is therefore a return to the work-based model of social needs, which is no longer appropriate.

Nussbaum and the new curriculum?

What then is left of the modernist project of education and communal solidarity? As we have seen, the rough balance of the three analytically separate but practically related spheres of educational engagement namely: personal/cultural development, social/political understanding, and vocational preparation have, in mass education, been sharply reduced to the last of the three. Even the nature of this vocational preparation has atrophied into a kind of minimal functionalism with, for the bulk of those from what used to be called the 'working class', the loss of deep craft apprenticeships coinciding with the collapse, or robotisation, of older form of industrial production (Canning and Cloonan 2000). That this was almost entirely a male stronghold and frequently encouraged an often homophobic and misogynist culture is understood. Nevertheless, it championed the nascent women's movement at the turn of the century and joined the crusade for enfranchisement. At its socialist best, it nurtured a dream of the New Life, an alternative co-operative way of life, in which the ideal of work was dignified as craft rather than wage labour (for example in the work of William Morris and Edward Carpenter) and a whole range of liberal attitudes to education, family life, punishment and freedom of thought were openly debated. While undeniably Romantic and even medieval in many respects, this *socialist* facet of working-class culture bred many values which were admirable. Although second wave feminism is strongly critical of the period, the most advanced feminists of the period, like Isabella Ford, saw the liberation of women as a project within the broader working-class socialist movement (Hannam 1989).

However, the break-up of the old industrial base and its attendant male-dominated, working-class culture has the potential to release women from economic subordination to the breadwinning males of the household, as was radically demonstrated by the women's support groups in the miners' strike of 1984–85 (Rowbotham 1989). The downside is that most of the new forms of employment for women echo the worst of the early phases of industrialisation, long hours, low pay, tedious repetitive jobs, little security and, still, oppressive male supervision at work. More women than ever receive post-compulsory education and now comprise a slight majority of those in higher education. In universities the increase in women's numbers is largely to be found in the former polytechnics, the Open University and, especially for mature women, in continuing education. The elite universities, degree courses and cultural capital in the form of prestigious qualifications are still largely the preserve of white men from wealthier backgrounds.

Most women's employment prospects are limited to the lower paid 'caring' professions and junior administrative positions. Few make it through to the top jobs and those that do have often to emulate the less commendable characteristics of their male competitors – aggressively calculating, self-promoting approaches, combined with elevation of career goals over mutual relationships with family and friends and disregard of civic virtues.

Vocationalism is then still an issue for women and cannot be ignored. Some form of strong vocational preparation is still needed alongside the necessary institutional reform of employment opportunities. Moreover, the curriculum which was so powerfully developed in the women's studies movement of the 1970s is by no means no longer relevant. Indeed the relative depoliticising of the women's movement in the 1990s makes it even more important, not the least aspect of which is for the re-education of men.

The rebalancing of the curriculum must draw on the strengths of women's studies and indeed postcolonial studies if it is to make any sense in the world Gorz describes. As Martha Nussbaum argues, there can no simple return to 'the gentleman's model' of liberal studies with its patrician, white, male, unreflectively Eurocentric orientation (Nussbaum 1997:297). Vocationalism has not been the answer to this discredited elitist tradition, as some progressive educators who went along with the new direction in the early 1980s believed. Nussbaum's illuminating commentary on liberal arts colleges in the US regrets that many institutions that call themselves liberal arts colleges, turned increasingly to vocational studies, and in doing so curtailed humanities requirements and cut back on humanities faculty. In a time of funding scarcities initiated by conservative administrations, and the critical deconstruction of the old humanities curriculum, this turn was to an extent understandable. But, notes Nussbaum,

> they sell our democracy short, preventing it from becoming as inclusive and reflective as it ought to be. People who have never learned to use reason and imagination to enter a broader world of cultures, groups, and ideas are impoverished personally and politically, however successful their vocational preparation. (Nussbaum 1997:297)

In effect the new curriculum for mass higher education has to generate a new type of intellectual, not the traditional conservative intellectual described by Gramsci in the *Prison Notebooks* (it is assumed that this group will still be produced in the elite institutions that will become increasingly privatised). Instead, in a truly *popular* higher education – 'popular' resonates better than 'mass' – the goal is something corresponding to Gramsci's idea of the 'organic' intellectual but now bereft of the 'collective intellectual' of the revolutionary political party and the olde form of working class culture. It is this much larger group drawn largely from the subaltern classes and rarely to be found in the elite universities that is the 'natural' constituency of adult and continuing education.

The desired goals or outcomes of the popular HE curriculum could be adapted from the traditional liberal and vocational curricula and grouped in the triad outlined above. The weighting of the balance would be up to the individual learner. Each element within the three focal groups should resonate across the other groupings. A rough sample of outcomes might be as follows:

1   *Personal and cultural development*:
    ● morally autonomous judgements based on understanding of ethical
      principles and enquiry
    ● critical rational enquiry based on understanding of conventions of
      argument and consensual resolution
    ● spontaneous and generous relationships, based understanding of ideals
      of friendship and solidarity
    ● tolerant and reflective attitudes, based on understanding and ability to
      empathise with cultural difference, traditions of belief and personal
      disability – to see the 'normal' as socially dysfunctional
    ● artistic creativity based on understanding of and confidence in playing
      with literary, audio and visual form, dramatic interaction and technical
      competence.

2   *Social and political understanding and engagement*:
    ● generation of the 'world citizen' and global interdependency
    ● concept of pluralistic centres of power, as described by Foucault
    ● origins and transcendence of structures of privilege such as class, caste,
      gender and (dis)ability.
    ● concept of participatory democracy and its relation to authoritarian
      structures
    ● concept of social justice, civil rights and cultural difference as base line
      for the 'human'
    ● principles of communal and social action in pursuit of consensual aims
    ● rules of dissent and agreement.

3   *Vocational preparation*:
    ● understanding of economics and global employment patterns
    ● highly developed communication and listening skills including: clear
      jargon-free presentation, reading, recognising rhetorical tropes and
      persuasive forms
    ● problem solving individually and in groups
    ● IT proficiency and critical understanding of IT limitations
    ● developing a specialist range of 'deep proficiencies', select technical
      expertise and professional skills
    ● cultivating creative intuitional responses and rationally assessing them
    ● learning reflective practices.

None of this is very new, I guess, but should be seen as a reformulation of a kind
of classical education of which the end in view is no longer the formation of a
governing elite, but the creation of a very broad class of *popular* intellectuals,
capable of leading generous, fulfilling lives, actively contributing to just and stable
democracies and local communities at many levels and with the ability to do

the necessary work to provide the goods for these societies to flourish. It's utopian, of course, but the consequences for not developing such individuals would have to be increased levels of exploitation, crime, intercommunal violence, personal neurosis and ill health on intensified levels, higher levels of family dysfunction, sustained unemployment or underemployment for the bottom third of society, little genuine *recreation* for those in employment and cultural impoverishment. Not perhaps a revolutionary agenda, but possibly a radical one.

References

Canning R and Cloonan M (2000) 'Revitalising "work-based" education: the Scottish apprenticeship framework', discussion paper, Institute of Education, University of Stirling

DfEE (1998) *The Learning Age: A Renaissance for a New Britain*, CM3790, London, Stationery Office

Donzelot J (1991) 'The mobilization of society', in Burchell G *et al* (eds), *The Foucault Effect*, London: Harvester, (pp 169–179)

Durkheim E (1964) *The Division of Labour in Society*, translated from the French by G. Simpson, London: Collier Macmillan

Eliot T S (1934) *After Strange Gods*, London: Faber

Fieldhouse R and associates (1996) *A History of Modern British Adult Education*, Leicester: NIACE

Gorz A (1989) *Critique of Economic Reason*, London: Verso

Gorz A (1994) *Capitalism, Socialism, Ecology*, London: Verso

Hannam J (1989) *Isabella Ford*, Oxford: Basil Blackwell

Kallscheuer O (1994) 'Afterward: will there be a European Left? Theoretical and political queries', in Gorz A *Capitalism, Socialism, Ecology* (pp 118–42)

Nussbaum M (1997) *Cultivating Humanity, a classical defense of reform in liberal education*, Cambridge MA: Harvard University Press

Robertson D (1997) 'Growth without equity? Reflections on the consequences for social cohesion of faltering progress on access to higher education', *Journal of Access Studies*, Vol 12 No 1, Spring, 1997

Rowbotham S (1989) *The Past is Before Us: feminism in action since the 1960s*, London: Penguin

Ryle M (1999) '"Relevant provision": the usefulness of cultural studies', in Aldred N and Ryle M (eds), *Teaching Culture: the long revolution in cultural studies*, Leicester: NIACE

Wells H G (nd but probably 1907) *A Modern Utopia*, London: Thomas Nelson

Williams R (1993) 'The Common Good', in McIlroy J and Westwood S (eds), *Border Country: Raymond Williams in Adult Education*, Leicester: NIACE

5 Concepts of self-directed learning in Higher Education: re-establishing the democratic tradition

Richard Taylor

Self-directed learning and contemporary policy

The learner and his or her interests, involvement and empowerment lie at the heart of the British Government's policy development for the whole of the post-compulsory field. David Blunkett, in his passionate and memorable introduction to *The Learning Age* (DfEE, 1998) articulated this centrality, within a broad humanistic framework:

> The Learning Age will be built on a renewed commitment to self-improvement and on a recognition of the enormous contribution learning makes to our society. Learning helps shape the values which we pass on to each succeeding generation. Learning supports active citizenship and democracy, giving men and women the capacity to provide leadership in their communities.

In the same document there is practical articulation of this principle through the proposal to introduce individual learning accounts (ILAs) whereby – on a pilot basis in the first instance – learners can exercise direct control over their own learning. The beginning of a restructuring and simplification of the post-compulsory system (excluding, for the present, higher education), as outlined in the Learning and Skills Bill (2000) is further evidence of the Government's intent.

These examples could be extended. The point here in this introductory section is to emphasise the perceived centrality of the learner, and the accompanying rhetoric of self-directed learning, in the contemporary policy context. The argument in this chapter is, however, that this masks a deep dichotomy between the democratic tradition of self-directed learning and learner empowerment, and contemporary, particularly New Labour, articulations of such concepts. As always, these differences reside neither in language and linguistic flexibility, nor in changed context *per se*; rather, they stem from sharp ideological difference. The concepts and their articulation thus reflect differing political objectives, differing ideological frameworks and indeed conflicting views on the purposes of education itself.

The argument here thus begins by delineating the traditions of democratic, self-directed learning as developed pre-eminently in adult and continuing education. This 'tradition' was itself complex and contested, but, in my view, at its radical best it provides at least the basis for a revitalised, socially purposive move to learner empowerment (Taylor 1996).

Over and above adult and continuing education – historically marginal, however worthy and significant – mainstream Higher Education has undoubtedly changed fundamentally in recent decades in virtually all developed societies but perhaps particularly in the United Kingdom. These changes have been described and analysed at length in a number of studies (Scott 1995, 1998; Barnett 1990, 1999, 2000; Schuller 1995; Smith and Webster 1997; Coffield and Williamson 1997).

Many of the characteristics of these changes impact upon the theme of self-directed learning. As the system changes from elite to mass, and from linearity to modularity, so flexibility and thus learner choice increases. Let me take the university in which I work as a fairly typical example: the University of Leeds, which in the 1970s had approximately 10,000 FTE students in mainstream undergraduate and postgraduate programmes, had by the late 1990s over 23,000 FTE students and more than 3,000 modules. While modular choice for the learner is by no means open, there is clearly a considerably increased degree of student choice. Similarly the rapid increase in open and distance learning technology and the growth of flexible modes of study through part-time degree development provide far greater student choice.

Perhaps most important of all, traditional subject disciplinary assumptions and the epistemological perspectives which underpinned them have come under persistent attack. Both postmodernists and the advocates of a more 'relevant', vocational higher education have struck at the very roots of traditional approaches to the academy (for example, see Smith and Webster 1997; Scott 1995; Jessop 1991; Edwards 1991; Usher and Edwards 1994). This again, almost by default, empowers the learners, and other 'stakeholders' as the tyranny of established disciplinary canons disintegrates. This argument should not be overstated: two key aspects of current bureaucratic systems – the Quality Assurance Agency's methodology, and the 'units of assessment' structure of the Research Assessment Exercise (RAE) – are based entirely upon traditional, conservative disciplinary divisions. Moreover, 'stakeholders' of a different kind to learners – most notably, business and global capitalist culture – exercise an increasing influence.

Even with these caveats, if the New Labour policy stance, and the dynamics of change in the higher education system itself, are working in unison to create a mass, more porous and more flexible system, characterised by self-directed learning among other things, where do the difficulties lie? Where is the dichotomy referred to above?

The democratic tradition of self-directed learning

In a 1968 lecture, E P Thompson (1968) referred to the symbiotic relationship, in adult education, between the worlds of life experience and work, and the abstract theorisation and historical knowledge of the academy:

> All education which is worth the name involves a relationship of mutuality, a dialectic: and no worthwhile educationalist conceives of his material as a class of inert recipients of instruction. But, in liberal adult education, no tutor is likely to last out a session — and no class is likely to stay the course with him — if he is under the misapprehension that the role of the class is passive. What is different about the adult student is the experience which he brings to the relationship. This experience modifies, sometimes subtly and sometimes more radically, the entire education process ... To strike the balance between intellectual rigour and respect for experience is always difficult. But the balance today (1968) is seriously awry ... (I wish to redress it a little) by reminding us that Universities engage in adult education not only to teach but also to learn.

The learner in this context is not simply an individual recipient of received knowledge and wisdom. This is far from a simple, one-way process of transmission. When the process works (and all of us who have worked in adult education can testify that it does *not* always work!) the learning is a collective as well as an individual experience. The empowerment, self-confidence and understanding that flow from interaction is just as valuable, often more so, than the specific knowledge attained. All this is common pedagogic knowledge and applies of course to settings other than adult education, though it is perhaps more pronounced here given the life experience that adult learners bring, their initially often low levels of self-confidence and their previously negative experience of the educational system.

However, the democratic tradition of self-directed learning in adult education is about far more than this. As the quotation from E P Thompson implies, learning in this context has at least three other key characteristics when operating ideally: it values highly the lived experience of the learners and regards that experience as a key element, in all its varied forms, in the construction of genuine, socially relevant knowledge (the 'really useful knowledge' concept); second, and following from this, curriculum content and specific syllabus construction take place through collective discussion, facilitated by the tutor but always a consensually agreed, but *negotiated* process; and finally, the learning process is seen explicitly within a context of social purpose.

Historically, adult education has been a part of a social movement — or rather a series of interlocking social movements. (The most obvious examples are the labour movement, linked to trade union day release provision and wider industrial and political education; and the women's movement linked *inter alia* to New Opportunities and Access programmes.) In the past, this was rooted in the strong belief in the liberatory power of education: 'Knowledge is power', and the political centrality of attaining equality of educational opportunity for a succession of labour movement activists – from William Lovett and the moral force Chartists through to revisionist social democrats such as Anthony Crosland and Shirley Williams.

These characteristics combined to produce an inextricable and dynamic mix of education, social purpose, individual enlightenment and politics. An important side issue, as far as this discussion is concerned, is the extent to which 'committed' education of this type is legitimate within the liberal parameters of most Western systems. How far is it appropriate for the tutor/facilitator to express his or her ideological perspective in this 'negotiating process'? The traditional liberal view – that whereas Marxist perspectives or variants of it were unacceptably biased, those of social democrats or liberals were somehow objective – is clearly untenable (see Fieldhouse 1985a). Rather, the purposes of the educator, working in conjunction and partnership with the group, should be to enable the student 'to find his (*sic*) own way to his own conclusions' (Hodges, cited in Fieldhouse 1985b). Tom Lovett and others have written at length on this issue in the particularly problematic context of community education, arguing that a commitment to and full empathy with the disadvantaged communities concerned does not preclude the open-ended, rigorous but explicitly political approach advocated by Fieldhouse and Hodges (Lovett 1975, 1983; Ward and Taylor 1986). The keynote of the rigour here must be methodological rather than ideological, and based on the intellectual scepticism embodied in the twin approaches of all questions being *open* questions and, in the word of Marx's favourite dictum, 'Doubt all things'.

However, though clearly relevant to a dynamic and symbiotic relationship between tutor and students (or facilitator and learners), these are, as noted, second-order issues in this context. The substance of the approach reflects the broader concern with the 'seamless robe' perspective on democratic process: in terms of mode, content, and broader political purposes.

Social purpose and the 'liberal tradition'

All this is to paint a general and rather too rosy picture of the learner empowerment and social purpose perspective as central to the liberal tradition of adult education. There are two large caveats: the complexity, and arguably inadequacy, of the 'political commitments' noted; and the fractured, highly contested nature of the wider liberal tradition. On the first issue of political commitments there is of course a whole literature on both the theory and the historical practice of the political movements of the left. In the British context, radical adult education has been largely aligned to left labourism (or democratic socialism, as its advocates would prefer). Even this, though, is a huge generalisation: and the commitments were often, anyway, more implicit than explicit. Many adult educators, and adult learners, were aligned to very different perspectives – predominantly, until the 1970s, Marxist or marxisant in emphasis. While some from this perspective exemplified the very best of democratic practice, including learner empowerment, many were committed to the educational equivalent of democratic centralism, where the emphasis was much more upon the centrality than the democracy. Needless to say, those committed to more democratic practice tended to be aligned in their broader politics to either the moralistic socialism of the Labour left or to the more libertarian of the breakaway movements from Communist Party hegemony. The prime examples in this democratic category are Raymond Williams and E P Thompson (Goodway 1996; Croft 1996). Those espousing a more centralist, even authoritarian, view were to be found largely in the NCLC and in many trade union education settings (Millar 1979; McIlroy 1985, 1990, 1991, 1995; Simon 1990).

Within the mainstream labourist tradition, though, commitment to learner empowerment was at best patchy. The shifting orthodoxy of labourism was very evident, particularly in the cold war years from the 1940s onwards (Fieldhouse 1985b, 1996). Too often the learner-centred, social-purpose approach was blocked at one level or another because of a conservative insistence on both established bureaucratic practice and ideological orthodoxy.

From the 1970s, though, radical adult education also reflected the explosion of new social movements, and the challenging of hitherto established orthodoxies, both educational and political. In particular, the women's movement had a profound influence on adult education policy and practice – and this was concerned centrally both with the 'lived experience' of women and its impact upon curriculum and pedagogy, and with the need to establish a democratic process of learning (with of course strong social purpose motivations) (Thompson 1983).

Self-directed learning, within a radical democratic tradition, has thus characterised radical adult education, but only intermittently. But there is a long and continuous history stretching, as J F C Harrison, for example, has graphically described, from at least the eighteenth century onwards (Thompson 1963; Harrison 1961). Others have described, analysed and celebrated more contemporary articulations of this tradition (Thompson 1983; Mayo and Thompson 1995; Ward and Taylor 1986; Lovett 1983; 1988; Johnston 1997). Education has been a key element of emancipation and radicalisation, albeit with very different ideological orientations in different periods.

However, radical adult education has been situated in a liberal tradition – a liberal theory and a liberal practice – which is far from wholly democratic and learner centred. Some analysts have gone so far as to characterise the liberal tradition as quintessentially elitist, conservative and instrumental. Robin Usher, for example, has written:

> It is actually possible to argue that liberal adult education is instrumental – not perhaps in a narrow sense, but in the sense of being directed towards the fulfilment of the project of modernity...Liberal adult education, particularly in terms of its emphasis on 'serious' academically based study, did not so much provide 'learning for its own sake' but a training for a certain kind of citizenship. It was an important instrument in the formation of the 'liberal' citizen. Individualistic, rationalistic, with a faith in benevolent progress through science and 'truth'. (Usher, in Usher *et al* 1997, p 11)

Others, such as Jane Thompson, have seen the liberal tradition as patriarchal and exclusive (Thompson 1983). From the other side, politically, others have seen the liberal tradition as anachronistic and a brake upon a more vocational professional approach (Jessop 1991).

The liberal tradition is certainly based upon the assumptions and perspective of the wider liberal world view. This is centred on individualism, largely *possessive* individualism, and upon the priority that should be given to freedom, socially and economically (Taylor *et al* 1985; Taylor 1996; Fieldhouse 1996; Coffield and Williamson 1997). At one level, then, this position places the individual learner at the centre of the system: it is his or her educational welfare and development that is the key measure of success (the key 'performance indicator' in today's parlance). However, there is an obvious tension here with the idea of a collective, group approach. Learners are seen, rather, as discrete individuals and the tutor as the arbiter and reconciler of different interests, levels of ability and so on. Add to this the acceptance of a whole series of assumptions about the linearity of knowledge, the educational process as a one-way transmission process, and the sanctity of disciplinary boundaries – and there is a conservatism in much of the traditional approach to adult learning. To a large extent this was mirrored too in the traditional mainstream practice of university Higher Education, as many analysts have recognised (Scott 1995, 1998; Barnett 1990, 1999, 2000). There is also the obvious and predictable empirical fact that the large majority of those attending liberal adult education provision are middle class, white and relatively well-educated. (The same applies historically of course to an even greater majority of those engaged in mainstream Higher Education.)

The liberal tradition is thus both pluralistic and contested. I have argued at length elsewhere that, despite the validity of many of the critiques, a revitalised liberal tradition can serve as the basis for a radical reorientation of not only adult education but of higher education at large (Taylor 1996; Watson and Taylor 1998; Taylor 1999). This is a theme I return to below in the concluding section of this chapter, where the specific place of self-directed learning in this framework is discussed.

'New Labour' and self-directed learning

How then does this complex of social purpose and the liberal tradition relate to New Labour perspectives on self-directed learning? New Labour ideology, as articulated from the later 1990s, is notoriously difficult to tie down. Part of its attraction is its packaging of being all things to all people, and its relentless modernism (or rather postmodernism). It is, in some ways, the contemporary articulation of McLuhan's 'the medium is the message'. Nevertheless, certain characteristics are clear, many of them in tension with each other.

There is, first, a genuine aspiration to humanism, reflected in the educational context by the quotation from David Blunkett cited earlier. Similarly, there are Christian Socialist roots to Tony Blair's perspective, as proclaimed in a variety of interviews and speeches. The old ILP tradition of labourism, though in so many respects an anathema to New Labour, also drew upon Christian Socialism, and argued for social equality on essentially non-conformist Christian grounds (Pritchard and Taylor 1978; Beer 1959, Nairn 1961).

More important than these influences, though, have been the directly political legacies of Social Democratic Party (SDP), social democratic ideologies, drawing not only on contemporary politicians like Roy Jenkins and Shirley Williams but on their more weighty ideological precursors, particularly Anthony Crosland and Hugh Gaitskell (Williams 1979; Crosland 1956).

The ideological amalgam, stripped of the hype, the spinning and all the rest, is clearly a variant on the 'caring capitalism' theme. This was first articulated in the cold war environment by revisionist social democrats who argued, following James Burnham, that the managerial revolution had changed fundamentally the old class structure. Ownership and control were held to have become separated, through economic and organisational development, thus rendering redundant traditional Marxist and neo-Marxist class analysis.

Anthony Crosland, in particular, argued forcefully in *The Future of Socialism* and many other writings that socialism had to be re-articulated and refocused, with the achievement of social equality as the keynote of future policy (Crosland 1956). This analysis was combined with economic arguments to the effect that neo-Keynesian policies had resolved the previous 'boom and slump' tendencies of market capitalism. Continued growth could therefore provide the resource base, and the industrial as well as economic stability, to move forwards to a more prosperous, equal and socially just society. The validity or otherwise of this position is not an issue for discussion in this context, though it is worth noting both the catastrophic economic slump in the 1970s throughout the Western world, the consequent eruption of the extreme market oriented ideology of Thatcher and Reagan and the subsequent intellectual demolition of this whole edifice by Ralph Miliband and others (Miliband 1969, 1994).

New Labour politics, in my view, essentially replicates this social democratic ideology. The 'third way' championed by Tony Blair and his acolytes (including

Anthony Giddens in his 1999 book of that title (Giddens 1999)), is a cruder, glitzier and modernised version of Crosland's original blueprint. The terminology, incidentally, is politically ironic, given the origins of third way concepts in both radical pacifist and New Left thinking from the 1940s to the 1980s (Taylor 1983, 1988; Thompson 1960, 1981).

Of course, by far the most significant change in this context, between the 1950s and 1960s political climate in which Crosland *et al* were writing and the New Labour period of the 1990s and beyond, has been the collapse of Soviet Communism, the discrediting of Marxism-Leninism and the consequent undermining of the whole socialist project and its accompanying ideology. (For socialist analyses of the 'new situation' see Alexander 1995; Miliband 1994.)

This has shifted the whole spectrum of the political debate. 'Revisionist' socialist ideas of the past, which found their main reference point in one or other of the variants of socialist class analysis, are now contextualised in an almost unchallenged, hegemonic free market system.

How does New Labour ideology impact upon the particular, microcosmic concerns of this discussion? Self-directed learning, within New Labour thinking and practice, is defined primarily, I would argue, in three ways. First, there is a genuine commitment to cultural change in the educational context, so that learners should have a real say in that learning process. Learners are 'stakeholders', and have a right to negotiate and, to an extent, to choose, what, when and how they study. The strong impetus is to make education and learning more relevant to the perceived needs of learners. There is also a principled commitment to enabling far more people to have the opportunity to study and enjoy the arts, and to engage in 'citizenship activity'.

These positive attributes are often overlooked but, having noted these commitments, it has to be emphasised, second, that they are greatly overshadowed by the priority given to skills training and competence-based education. At all levels in the education system (including schools, though this lies beyond the scope of this discussion), the key objective is to enhance the skills base of the workforce to produce a more efficient and thus competitive economy for the UK. The learner is thus conceptualised largely within this 'economic' framework. This reflects the neo-liberal market orientation of New Labour. This follows on *directly* from the somewhat crude reconceptualisation of education by Thatcherism as being worthwhile only in so far as it enhanced economic performance and the entrepreneurial spirit. This has been modified only marginally by New Labour. Market capitalism is held to be not only a given, but also to be both permanent and, potentially at least, beneficial. (All talk of 'socialism', and still more of structural change to remove the power of capital, has been effectively removed from New Labour's political vocabulary.)

Within this pervasive market context, then, the learner is seen as a customer, a consumer of learning in the marketplace (Robertson 2000). Self-directed learning is thus seen as a process in which the learner should be able to shop around to find the best buy to meet his or her requirements. Learning is thus commodified; buying learning is no different from buying a car, or a packet of cornflakes. Implicitly, the criteria against which the educational experience should be judged are instrumental: 'What is the most cost effective level of investment in learning which will yield the greatest return in terms of earning potential?' Of course it is never formulated in these terms, but it is hard to interpret the roots of New Labour ideology in any other way. All this, incidentally, reflects too postmodernist views of contemporary education and its social context (Usher and Edwards 1994).

It is primarily within this context, in my view, that innovations such as ILAs should be seen. The influence of other stakeholders, in particular business and private capital generally, complements the Government's ideological stance. It is not a coincidence that business studies is now clearly the most popular degree programme in higher education, and that discussions of the 'university and the community' tend to assume that the latter is defined largely in terms of the business community – another Orwellian use of language.

The third important element in New Labour's definition of self-directed learning complements the second. New Labour's ideology, like that of Labour's social democratic wing, which became in the 1980s the SDP, is fundamentally individualist rather than collective. There are deep historical roots for this stance: the early Labour Party *was* more influenced by Methodism than Marxism, as the old examination question has it. The Liberal (as well as liberal) inheritance of the Labour Party was always dominant, as numerous analysts have argued convincingly (Miliband 1973; Coates 1974, Nairn 1961). In the past Labour was always a broad church, with both the Fabian, neo-utilitarian and collectivist perspectives and the radical egalitarian and largely non-conformist Christian ILP, both influential (Nairn 1961; Beer 1959). Marxism of any description, after a brief initial flurry of activity by the Social Democratic Federation in its early years, was always a marginal force, politically, in the Labour Party (though its ideological influence was arguably rather greater).

This longstanding, individualist perspective has had profound consequences for labourist social analysis and, in the context of this discussion, for educational policy specifically. Moreover, now that Labour's broad church has become virtually a single, centralist creed from which little or no perceived deviation, however mild, is tolerated (consider Ken Livingstone *et al*), this individualist focus has become more pronounced. The result, in the context of this discussion, is to exclude consideration of the collective, the group needs. This of course stems from the basic a *priori* reference points for differing ideologies; to put it rather over-schematically for the socialist, it is the *class* (since the 1970s complemented by other collective definitions – gender, ethnicity, etc); for the liberal, and the social democrat (and indeed the Christian – but that is, in part, a rather different story), it is the *individual*.

This is no mere abstraction. The policy and its implementation articulate this perspective clearly: the Higher Education Funding Council's welcome initiatives in the late 1990s on Widening Participation, for example, are focused almost entirely upon the *individual's* accessibility and progression (HEFCE 1998, 1999).

Putting these three elements together, then, produces a version of self-directed learning sharply distinct from that of the democratic tradition: in New Labour's framework, self-directed learning is in part inspired by liberal humanism, but largely by a consumerist, individualistic conception of the learner, operating within the marketplace and assumed to be motivated by uncritically accepted free market ideology.

Self-directed learning: myth or reality?

From the perspective of radical educators, do we then have to dismiss self-directed learning as yet another concept and practice that has been captured by the right, and must therefore be opposed? Certainly not. It is an old and valid socialist precept that no social processes of any significance are monolithic. This is no exception.

Just because the cultural forces of capital – in this context, New Labour or the preponderant 'voice' of New Labour – have redefined a good, democratic concept in unacceptable ways, does not mean that this is the end of the matter. There are difficult issues to confront – apart from the obvious one that New Labour conceptions are powerful and exercise considerable influence. How far, for example, is the self-directed approach open ended? In a society and culture dominated by market capital, it is certain that many individuals and groups will opt for instrumental and/or conservative learning experiences (see the popularity of business studies). Are 'access' and self-directed learning *a priori* desirable, without qualification? Or are they rather means to an end, and judgement on their desirability dependent upon the assessment of the end in question?

These are, as I have noted, difficult issues, and it ill behoves those in secure professional positions to dictate to learners what they should and should not study, and to decry 'materialist' motivations. However, these are not new problems – they have been present for community educators, for example, for many years and have been analysed in some detail (see, for example, Lovett 1988; Ward and Taylor 1986.)

There are, as always, contradictory or conflicting tendencies at work in this social process. The role of the radical educator is to encourage and support the democratic and progressive articulation of self-directed learning and to oppose the more reactionary and negative perspectives. This is of course easy to state and difficult to implement, and there are always grey areas. But then that is the nature of socialist praxis.

References

Alexander J C (1995) 'Modern, anti, post, neo', *New Left Review* 290, March/April

Barnett R (1990) *The Idea of Higher Education*, Buckingham: SRHE and Open University Press

Barnett R (1999) *Realising the University*, Buckingham: Open University Press

Barnett R (2000) 'Reconfiguring the university', in Scott P (ed), *Higher Education Reformed*, Brighton: Falmer Press

Beer S H (1959) *Modern British Politics*, London: Allen and Unwin

Coates D (1974) *The Labour Party and the Struggle for Socialism*, Cambridge: Cambridge University Press

Coffield F and Williamson B (eds) (1997) *Repositioning Higher Education*, Buckingham: SRHE and Open University Press

Croft A (1996) 'Walthamstow, Little Gidding and Middlesbrough: Edward Thompson the literature tutor', in Taylor R (ed), *Beyond the Walls: 50 Years of Adult and Continuing Education at the University of Leeds 1946–1996*, Leeds Studies in Continuing Education

Crosland A (1956) *The Future of Socialism*, Cape

DfEE (1988) *The Learning Age: a Renaissance for a New Britain*, CM 3790, London: The Stationery Office

Edwards R 'The politics of meeting learner needs: power, subject, subjection', *Studies in the Education of Adults*, Vol 23 No 1, April, pp 85–97

Edwards R (1997) *Changing Places? Flexibility, Lifelong Learning and a Learning Society*, London: Routledge

Fieldhouse R (1985a) *Adult Education and the Cold War*, University of Leeds

Fieldhouse R (1985b) 'Objectivity and commitment', in Taylor R, Rockhill K and Fieldhouse R, *Adult Education in England and the USA: a reappraisal of the liberal tradition*, Beckenham: Croom Helm

Fieldhouse R and Associates (1996) *A History of Modern British Adult Education*, Leicester: NIACE

Giddens A (1999) *The Third Way*, Cambridge: Polity Press

Goodway D (1996) 'E P Thompson and the making of the making of the English working class', in Taylor R (ed), *Beyond the Walls: 50 Years of Adult and Continuing Education at the University of Leeds 1946–1996*, Leeds Studies in Continuing Education

Harrison J F C (1961) *Learning and Living*, London: Routledge

HEFCE (1998) 'Widening participation: special funding programme 1998–99', June 98/35

HEFCE (1999) 'Widening participation in higher education. Invitation to bid for special funds: 1999–2000 to 2001–02', May 99/33

Jessop G (1991) *Outcomes: NVQs and the emerging model of education and training*, Brighton: Falmer Press

Johnston R (1997) 'Adult learning for citizenship', in Usher R, Bryant I and Johnston R, *Adult Education and the Postmodern Challenge*, London: Routledge

Lovett T (1975) *Adult Education, Community Development and the Working Class*, London: Ward Lock

Lovett T (ed) (1998) *Radical Approaches to Adult Education*, London: Routledge

Lovett T, Clarke C, and Kilmurray A (1983) *Adult Education and Community Action*, Beckenham: Croom Helm

Mayo M and Thompson J (eds) (1995) *Adult Learning, Critical Intelligence and Social Change*, Leicester: NIACE

McIlroy J (1990) 'Border country: Raymond Williams in adult education part I', *Studies in the Education of Adults*, Vol 22 No 4, October, pp 126–66

McIlroy J (1991) 'Border country: Raymond Williams in adult education part II', *Studies in the Education of Adults*, Vol 23 No 1, April, pp 1–23

McIlroy J 'Adult Education and the role of the client – the TUC Education Scheme 1929–1980', *Studies in the Education of Adults*, Vol 16 No 2

McIlroy J (1995) *Trade Unions in Britain Today*, Manchester: Manchester University Press

Miliband R (1973) *Parliamentary Socialism* (2nd edn), London: Merlin Press

Miliband R (1969) *The State in Capitalist Society*, London: Weidenfeld and Nicolson

Miliband R (1994) *Socialism for a Sceptical Age*, Cambridge: Polity Press

Millar J P M (1979) *The Labour College Movement*, London: NCLC Publications Society

Nairn T (1961) 'The nature of labourism', in Anderson P and Nairn T (eds), *Towards Socialism*, London: Fontana and New Left Books

Pritchard C and Taylor R (1978) *Social Work: Reform or Revolution?* London: Routledge and Kegan Paul

Robertson D (2000) 'Students as consumers', in Scott P (ed), *Higher Education Re-formed*, Brighton: Falmer Press

Schuller T (ed) (1995) *The Changing University?*, Buckingham: SRHE and Open University Press

Scott P (1995) *The Meanings of Mass Higher Education*, Buckingham: SRHE and Open University Press

Scott P (1998) *The Globalisation of Higher Education*, Buckingham: SRHE and Open University Press

Scott P (2000) *Higher Education Re-formed*, Brighton: Falmer Press

Simon B (ed) (1990) *The Search for Enlightenment: The Working Class and Adult Education in the 20th Century*, Leicester: NIACE

Smith A and Webster F (eds) (1997) *The Postmodern University?* Buckingham: SRHE and Open University Press

Taylor R (1983) 'The British nuclear disarmament movement of 1958 to 1965 and its legacy to the Left', PhD thesis (unpublished), University of Leeds

Taylor R (1988) *Against the Bomb: The British Nuclear Disarmament Movement of 1958 to 1965*, Oxford: Oxford University Press

Taylor R (1996) 'Preserving the Liberal tradition in "New Times"', in Wallis J (ed), *The Liberal Tradition: the end of an era?*, Nottingham: Continuing Education Press

Taylor R (1999) 'A good man fallen amongst post-modernists': a response to Peter Scott's 'After Dearing', *Scottish Journal of Adult and Continuing Education*, 5(1), pp 99–103

Taylor R, Rockhill K and Fieldhouse R (1985) *University Adult Education in England and the USA: a reappraisal of the liberal tradition*, Beckenham: Croom Helm

Thompson E P (1960) *Out of Apathy*, London: A C Black & Sons

Thompson E P (1963) *The Making of the English Working Class*, London: Gollancz

Thompson E P (1968) *Education and Experience*, Fifth Albert Mansbridge Memorial Lecture, University of Leeds

Thompson E P (1981) *Writing by Candlelight*, London: Merlin Press

Thompson J (1983) *Learning Liberation: women's response to men's education*, Beckenham: Croom Helm

Usher R, Bryant I and Johnston R (1997) *Adult Education and the Postmodern Challenge*, London: Routledge

Usher R and Edwards R (1994) *Postmodernism and Education*, London: Routledge

Ward K and Taylor R (1986) *Adult Education and the Working Class: education for the missing millions*, Beckenham: Croom Helm

Watson D and Taylor R (1998) *Lifelong Learning and the University: a post-Dearing agenda*, Brighton: Falmer Press

Williams P (1979) *Hugh Gaitskell: a political biography*, Oxford: Oxford University Press

6 Social capital: a critique

Loraine Blaxter and Christina Hughes

Introduction

Our purposes in this chapter are to consider the concept of social capital within a frame that extends critical thinking about issues of social inclusion. In this exploration we aim to contribute to, and extend, the analyses of other UK Higher Education researchers (Field and Spence 2000; Riddell, Baron and Wilson 1999; Schuller and Field 1998). Their empirical work has demonstrated the usefulness of current conceptualisations of social capital and its limitations. For example, Riddell, Baron and Wilson (1999) comment that functionalist accounts of social capital do not take account of differential access that groups in society have to various capitals. Their work has demonstrated these issues in relation to people with learning difficulties. Schuller and Field (1998) similarly comment on the need to take account of issues of power and conflict within models of social capital. One can readily see the saliency of this perspective as their work has drawn on a comparative study of Northern Ireland and Scotland. Field and Spence (2000) have highlighted the significance, and the need to recognise, the nature and role of informal learning which is so easily forgotten within dominant discourses of formal education. Finally Edwards (2000) has noted that, while arguments about social capital can be useful in rebalancing debates in lifelong learning away from human capital, they can also constrain those debates because they inscribe the hegemony of economics.

The first part of this chapter is designed to introduce the concept of social capital. Here we focus on what might be described as its 'founding fathers'. It is mainly through the work of Bourdieu (1979, 1986, 1987, 1989) and Coleman (1987; 1988a; 1988b) that the concept has been imported into educational theorising. However, it should be noted that Bourdieu and Coleman are associated with different theoretical traditions. Bourdieu's interests lay with the ways in which social advantage and disadvantage were maintained. His explanatory framework uses a critical analysis of class relations and draws out the distinctions between social, human, cultural and symbolic capitals. Working within theories of functionalism and individualism, Coleman saw his work in terms of a convergence between economics and sociology that was underpinned by a rational choice model of human action. In this he sought to develop human capital theory by recognising the role of social relationships.

The focus on 'founding fathers' is as much a heuristic device as it is one of description. We highlight how it is the work of Coleman that has been most influential as a theoretical framework for analyses of social capital and the problems related to this. Thus, one of our concerns in this first part of the paper are to draw attention to some of the inherent dangers in taking up functionalist positions with regard to social capital. Our other concern is to note the lack of take-up of critical positions in relation to class that is a mark of the work of Bourdieu.

The second part of the chapter explores the saliency of social capital as a concept of its time. Our main purpose here is to explain why some conceptualisations of social capital appear to be fit for purpose. We set out the material, political and discursive conditions that have given rise to the take-up of social capital and note that fear of unbridled individualism and fragmentation, coupled with the demise of some forms of socialism, are associated with the re-emergence of communitarianism. We suggest that associated 'third way' positions offer amelioration rather than radicalism. We also suggest that this ameliorative agenda is one that is likely to contribute to the neglect of issues of class that we noted previously and, more generally, to the neglect of wider issues of power relations.

The focus that is given in this chapter on two different traditions in social capital theorising should not detract from the point that the term social capital has several shades of meaning. Indeed, it is a fuzzy or blurred concept and of the sort that leads students to feel that *they* are muddled and confused. Predominantly, social capital is a contemporary key word that has 'positive connotations across multiple Discourse communities' (Lankshear *et al* 1997:97). While, therefore, it is a term that is being used to convey the effects of, or is used as a substitute for, concepts that are found in everyday language, we should note that these terms have also been subject to intense academic analysis and debate in a variety of arenas.

Thus, the language of social capital includes concepts such as trust, connections, reciprocity, mutual aid, social support, social networks, norms, ethics, community and cultures. These terms are not solely the preserve of the social capital literature. They are also central to much feminist theorising. At first glance one might think that there is much to be valued in the social capital literature from a feminist perspective and we would not want to deny that the attention paid to issues of social relationship is not welcome. Nevertheless, the absence in this literature of any adequate attention to the micro-relations of power that exist within such social relationships is a serious issue. It is one that we take up in the third part of the chapter. Our major concern here is to remedy the gender-blindness in the literature on social capital. We provide the key elements of this literature in order to illustrate how this gender blindness is both derogatory to women's family and community work and how, if left neglected, it will contribute to the continuation of gendered oppressions in our daily lives.

Founding fathers

Riddell, Baron and Wilson (1999) indicate that there have been two main analytic frameworks that have been brought to understanding how social capital arises and the effects of this. The most dominant of these, and the most influential at public policy levels, is that of normative, functionalist theory. Here social capital is defined in rather positive overtones. As Riddell, Baron and Wilson (1999:55) note within this perspective social capital is

> the network of social and community relations which underpin people's ability to engage in education, training and work and to sustain a healthy civic community. Key conditions for the nurturance of social capital include reciprocity and trust, the imposition of sanctions when these fail, the existence of horizontal, not vertical, mechanisms for the exchange of information and support and the willingness of the community to take on responsibility for the provision of as many social services as possible.

This definition can be viewed in the work of Coleman (1987, 1988a, 1988b).

Coleman is associated with forms of methodological individualism developed by scholars in the Department of Sociology at the University of Chicago (Fine 1999). He is, as Fine points out, the intellectual partner to Becker, the founding father of human capital. Thus, as Fine notes, we might view social capital as the economic colonisation of social science discourse. Coleman's main concerns were to demonstrate how an individual's attainment of human capital, say in the levels of their examination and scholarly successes, were influenced by family and inter-family relations. By recognising the significance of family and household the explanatory framework that Coleman develops does take more account of the influences of social structures than is found in the explicit individualism of Becker's earlier work on human capital. Nevertheless, given the conceptual distinctions between family and household, it is a muted development of an individualistic discourse.

Coleman suggested that social capital is generated in two ways. These are within the household and between households. For example, an important source of social capital is the amount of time that parents spend with their children and one another. In this way, Coleman offered an explanation of why parents rich in human capital themselves might not pass this advantage of to their children. Their engagement in paid work, for example, meant that they had limited contact with their children and with each other. The result is a lack of necessary investment of time and energy in their children's potential human capital. In another example Coleman (1988a) recounts a situation in Asian immigrant households in the USA where mothers purchase two copies of school textbooks in order to help their children. Here Coleman argues that the social capital available for the child's education is extremely high while their human capital is low. This social capital, according to Coleman, is converted into human capital in the form of educational qualifications.

Despite Coleman's important recognition of the micro-relations that structure social capital, the essential functionalism in his perspective is replicated in those that follow him. The work of Putnam (1993) is salutary in this respect. Although Putnam builds on Coleman's work his use of social capital is different. Rather than treating social capital as a resource that works to assist individuals, Putnam treats it as a property of collectivities, such as groups and regions. In addition, rather than focusing on reciprocal relations within and between households, the indicators of social capital in Putnam's work are found in clubs and associations.

In Putnam's view civic action, through the work of clubs and associations, is a key source of regional wealth creation and good governance. His field of study originated in research on the institutional changes in Italy that had arisen from the introduction of decentralised regional government in 1970. Putnam argued that economic performance, and the performance of regional governments, was influenced by the form and intensity of networks of civic engagement. He argued, for example, that the north of Italy had prospered more than the south because of its history of vibrant horizontal networks that had fostered 'robust norms of reciprocity' (p 173) and had facilitated communication. In contrast, the south of Italy, with a history of amoral familism, fragmentation and distrust, and vertical social ties had been less economically prosperous. In this we can see how Putnam's argument illustrates a functional conception of social capital.

The less commonly cited and less dominant interpretation of social capital is that which arises from the work of critical theorists. Critical theorists are concerned, among other things, with a focus on power relationships. Here, their purposes are to expose hegemonic relations and their associated injustices. It is the work of Bourdieu (1979, 1986, 1987, 1989) that has been most influential in terms of critical analyses in the study of social capital. As a critical theorist, Bourdieu illustrates the lack of concern with conflict and oppression found in dominant positivistic theories and in forms of ethnomethodology. Bourdieu's theoretical viewpoint is explicit. Like positivist social researchers Bourdieu believes in social facts. Unlike positivists, for Bourdieu these facts are not neutral. They are brutal and concerned with inequality between social actors.

The basis of Bourdieu's work was to demonstrate how social advantage and disadvantage are historically based and maintained. In this he identified four forms of capital. These are economic, cultural, social and symbolic. Bourdieu refers to social capital as connections. He suggests that this focus on connections is useful in understanding the function of clubs and families as the main site of accumulation and transmission of social capital. There is little at a descriptive level to distinguish Bourdieu's definition from that of definitions of social capital more generally. Nevertheless it is the frame of analysis that marks a substantive difference. It is the interrelationship of these various capitals within relations of class (and we would add other social divisions) that inequalities are reproduced.

Further, Bourdieu's conceptualisation of capital was not in terms of a descriptor of empirical positions as found in functionalist accounts. The concept of capital is used as a metaphor to capture these differential interests and benefits of groups in society (Skeggs 1997). The differential values given to different groups in society means that these capitals are not tradeable commodities in relations of equality. As Bourdieu comments all forms of capital are accumulated labour, take time to accumulate and have a capacity to produce and reproduce themselves so that in society people are not equal and 'everything is not equally possible or impossible' (1986:241).

We cannot assume, therefore, that the conversion of social capital into other forms of capital, such as human, is accomplished within neutral space. And it is the issue of spatial positioning that is significant in terms of this form of critical analysis. This is illuminated in the work of Skeggs (1997) who extended Bourdieu's work on class inequalities to incorporate issues of gender. Skeggs illustrates how key social divisions frame our possibilities and our access to a variety of capitals, be they economic, cultural, symbolic or social. Her research is therefore a useful illustration of how social mobility is restricted because of the effects of spatial framing such as those of class and gender.

Skeggs (1997) notes how working-class women are framed by a variety of discourses that deem them as pathological, dangerous and threatening. The women in Skeggs' research refused to be fixed or measured by class and, in consequence, sought to escape negative class identifications. However they were not successful in this. This is not simply because working class women have little access to human and cultural capital because of their inherited class position. It is also because 'the women constantly enter implicit trading arenas where their sexuality, femininity and respectability are judged in terms of value in which the rate is established by others' (p 12). These judgements maintain the denigration of these women's economic, cultural, symbolic and social value.

Skeggs' work illustrates how any position, whether it is economic, institutional, subjective or discursive, is not equally available. Her work also illustrates the potential of critical analyses to more fully explore the power relations of vertical, asymmetric, ties. Yet her research is not centrally concerned with social capital but rather is an analysis of cultural, symbolic and economic capitals. A more focused application of Bourdieu to the field of social capital can be found in Riddell, Baron and Wilson (1999). Their research considers the implications of social capital theory for people with learning difficulties.

Riddell, Baron and Wilson indicate that the transmission of class privilege is only partial for those with learning difficulties. Indeed, in their work the take up of a critical perspective is mainly viewed as an antidote to the dominance of functionalist theory that influences policy discourses in this area. In particular they dismiss the saliency of class as a specific way of developing critical analyses of social capital in relation to people with learning difficulties. This is because 'for this group the transmission of social capital is likely to be disrupted' (p 62).

This dismissal of class perspectives is illustrative of the more general minimal development of critical perspectives of social capital. It is to this that we now turn. We consider the conditions that have given rise to the take-up of social capital as a relevant theory for understanding issues of social exclusion and social inclusion in order to develop an understanding of how functionalist accounts of social capital can claim their 'truth'.

A concept for the times

We explore here how late 20th century Western societies held in place the material, political and discursive conditions that facilitated the emergence and take-up of social capital. In doing so we illustrate how dominant ideas about social capital reflect dominant ideas in society. In particular we explore a number of discourses of anxiety that are at the heart of social capital. These anxieties have occurred because old certainties or 'truths' have been called into question. We portray these discourses in terms of a binary of individualism and collectivism and suggest that social capital seeks to resolve the contradictions of this binary. Yet the resolutions that it offers continues to take insufficient account of micro-relations of power.

Our framework for this is an analysis of the key discursive formations around the role of social capital in combating social exclusion and non-participation. Discursive formations are combinations of discourses 'with different histories, but combined in particular relations of force, in process in the same place and time ... always being produced, always changing and internally very diverse' (Epstein and Johnson 1998:16). Our analysis illustrates the broad parameters of these diverse discursive formations.

There are several discourses of anxiety that mark the contemporary conditions that are often described as postmodern. These discourses are related to changes in communication and information technologies, the globalising processes of trade, migration and shifting national boundaries. They are also associated with the social and cultural transformations that arise from these changing conditions. On the one hand, these discourses are related to concerns about the effects of excessive individualism. They speak of the isolation, individualism and fragmentation that is a mark of the postmodern. They speak of a concern that this fragmentation is a threat to forms of established order in relation to the ties that bind (Hoskyns 2000). On the other hand, these discourses of anxiety are related to concerns about the effects of excessive collectivism. These arise, for example, from the demise of certain forms of socialism and the perceived illegitimacy, or redundancy, of certain social movements. Most predominantly are those related to trade unionism and feminism.

One place where a resolution to these anxieties is embodied is within a broader questioning of the proper role of the State in relation to capitalist markets. However, the responses to this questioning do not begin with a deconstruction of the binaries set up through concepts of individualism and collectivism. Rather they strive to create a balance between what are viewed as opposing forces or social facts. This resolution can be viewed in some forms of communitarianism. Frazer (2000:178) notes that communitarianism is a 'distinctive and time-specific' philosophy and politics. This is because communitarians see themselves as neither left nor right but as offering a 'third way' for political development. This 'third way' position is placed between government and market precisely because of the problems that are deemed to have arisen from either too much or too little state governance in the supply and distribution of welfare, education, health and so forth (Fine 1999). Communitarians, like some positions within feminism, seek to promote strong communities and active citizens while also recognising the place of the market. However, the critical focus in feminism of issues of power marks out the difference.

The philosophical roots of communitariansim are those of liberalism. We have to bear in mind that liberalism and capitalism are not monolithic but that there are many views and practices within each of them. Also the alignment between the two are many and varied. Nevertheless, Browning (2000) notes that liberalism is not only the most successful ideology in practice but is well suited to rapidly changing social and economic conditions. It is a political philosophy that is closely aligned to capitalism. These connections facilitate the hegemony of liberalism on a global scale. As Browning (2000:153) notes, 'Capitalism promotes consumerism and engenders calculating individualism on a global scale. These features of capitalism harmonize with core values of liberalism, such as individuality, rationality and freedom, and thereby facilitate the spread of liberalism across the globe'.

The concerns of communitarians are that 'calculating individualism' or 'amoral familism' will become too excessive and will lead to a loss of a sense of civic responsibility or care for others. Just as social capital adds a *social* face to human capital, communitarianism adds *collectivity* to liberalism. In this it seeks to soften the emphasis on rights and individuality found in liberalism through the reiteration of obligations and solidarity. Yet this view does not constitute a challenge to liberalism nor to the fundamental ways in which issues of rights and equality are conceptualised within liberalism. This can be seen when we examine a little more closely the issues of horizontal ties that are central to conceptualisations of social capital.

The discourses of social capital are those of supporting and integrating communities and active citizenship. Indeed, social capital is defined by, and is considered creative of, these features. While there are a range of foci that are brought to the analysis of social capital, horizontal ties are considered of utmost importance. For example, Wilson (1997:745) refers to social capital as 'inter-personal trust and community [and] patterns of mutual accountability and co-operation that enhance connectedness'. Within such a view it is the quality of relationships that builds social capital through, for example, membership of clubs and through co-operation. Field and Spence (2000:32) note that social capital is the 'existence of networks, norms and levels of trust that promote collective action between members of a given social group'. In measuring this in terms of Northern Ireland they highlight the institutional indicators of low divorce rates, high church attendance and a marked tendency to collectivism, albeit within strong ethnic-religious divisions. They argue, therefore, that Northern Ireland has high levels of social capital.

The notion that inter-group ties of reciprocity are beneficial, and indeed beneficent, can be seen in the contrasting ways that horizontal ties are viewed. For example, Putnam (1993) suggests that the exchanges associated with vertical ties contribute to the maintenance of poverty. While these forms of asymmetric reciprocity help the poor to survive they reinforce rather than undermine the inequalities between social groups. We take no issue with this. Such an argument confirms the view, though differentially theorised, of a range of critical theorists. Yet the relative neglect in the social capital literature of the asymmetric reciprocity that also marks horizontal social ties is deeply problematic. Such a neglect illustrates a considerable silence that the literature on social capital evidences of feminist perspectives of family and inter-household relations.

It is to these issues that we now turn. Our analysis highlights the wealth of feminist critiques that are salient to developing critical understandings of social capital. These illustrate that the exchange relations of horizontal ties are unbalanced in terms of family and community care. Yet we also want to highlight that the blaming discourses that mark the underside of social capital are not simply directed at regulating the usual suspects for social intervention. In addition to seeking to regulate what is viewed by some as an underclass, the blaming discourses of social capital are also directed at those women who have more fully taken up the liberalist discourses of success that mark full-time employment. These are middle-class women.

Putting gender in discourses of social capital

There is a gender blindness in accounts of social capital. For example, when we read of parents who do not spend enough time with their children, whom do we really mean? It has long been established within feminist scholarship that whenever the term parent is invoked the speaker really means mothers (Hughes *et al* 1991). Similarly when we discuss the poor we should note that the majority of the world's poor are women (Payne 1991). When we argue for the bonds of collectivities to be strengthened who do we think is already doing the bulk of this unpaid emotional and physical work? Feminist work around household divisions of labour has documented the scale and unending nature of the caring and servicing tasks of household labour undertaken by women. This is both a lifetime commitment through the care of partners, children and subsequently parents and is consistent across a range of changing family situations.

Further, when we read of the importance of social connections for help in crisis (OECD 1999) or that peer reciprocity is associated with young families (Micheli 1996) who do we think is providing that help or exchanging those services? A gender sensitive piece of research funded by the World Bank and carried out by Moser (1996) is illustrative here. Moser's research built on her previous research where she had identified the triple roles of reproduction, production and community management that women undertook. In her study women, united by a struggle for land, established the organisations and the reciprocity conducive to the development of norms and networks. As Moser demonstrates, economic pressures and government policy can both undermine or reinforce the development of such connections. When one lives in an area of increasing crime and burglary the necessary trust between neighbours that is required is easily severely eroded.

More generally within the field of community studies, feminists have illustrated how 'community' care is built on the work of women (Bornat *et al* 1993; Corti *et al* 1994). In addition, and although women are tremendously time poor because of their caring responsibilities for others, this has not prevented them from taking up opportunities for further education and lifelong learning. One needs only to consult the literature on women in higher education for evidence of this (see for example Blaxter and Tight 1994; Blaxter, Hughes and Tight 1997; Merrill 1999).

Moreover, despite ideas that relationships between women and men are becoming more egalitarian, this appears to have led to little change in household divisions of labour. For example, women in dual-income families continue to retain the major responsibilities for childcare (Lewis *et al* 1992). And even when women experience divorce they are still required to exercise certain kinds of responsibility for others. Piper (1993) indicates how post-divorce mothers are viewed in mediation and conciliation services as responsible for the maintenance of good relationships between themselves and their ex-partner. In other words, there are strong expectations that they will continue to do the necessary work in managing and facilitating relationships between themselves, their ex-partner and their children. There is also strong evidence that these expectations are lived practices. Divorced women do take on the major tasks of such work (Silva and Smart 1999).

In all, it is clear to us, that through their levels of commitments and sense of responsibility to others, women *are* the main producers of these aspects of social capital. That the social capital literature is silent on these issues is of great concern. Nevertheless, to suggest that the regulating discourses of active citizenship are, in consequence, directed at men would be a mistake. Certainly there are concerns around male participation in adult education and training (McGivney 1999) which echo other moral panics about boys' 'underachievement' at school (Raphael Reed 1999). Yet these concerns relate to men and boys who are of a certain class and race. By and large the discourses of participation are not concerned to address themselves to middle-class white men whose access to, and participation in, employer-based development is well documented (McGivney 1999) – and some of whom, in addition, are conspicuous and visible through their active 'community' engagement in associations such as the Rotarians and Masons. We might, in contrast, note that men's social action as trade unionists has not always been viewed as positive or 'functional'.

Moreover, it would be too easy to suggest that the regulatory discourses of social capital are simply concerned to discipline the poor, the black and the working class of whatever sex. Women of all classes, for reasons other than individualist self-regard, are in paid employment. Nevertheless, it is the rise of white women's employment in the last two decade that is significant. Women now represent nearly half of all employees in the paid labour force (Pilcher 1999). Historically, black women have always had to undertake paid work in the labour market (Anthias and Yuval-Davis 1993). This is also the case for lesbian women who do not have access, via partners, to the 'male wage'. This has not been the situation of white heterosexual women and particularly those of the middle class. Here we find that, for these groups of women, a lifetime involvement in paid labour is a more recent phenomenon.

Walby (1997) notes that it is women in higher economic groups who have the highest rates of economic activity. Middle-class women are able to maintain their attachment to the paid labour force even when they have dependent children because the are able to pay for the necessary childcare. Middle-class women are, therefore, most likely to maintain their position as full-time employees. White heterosexual women of lower social classes, in juggling their commitments, are more likely to be found in part-time, casualised forms of paid employment.

This increase in women engaged in paid labour has not happened without a range of concerns being raised about women's perceived absence from their 'traditional' parenting work. Here we find further discourses of anxiety around motherhood and care (Kaplan 1992). These discourses tell stories of neglected children left with untrained or unscrupulous childminders. In social capital speak they tell of parents who neglect to transmit their human capital to their children. They produce guilt in women and concern in policy makers. The question 'Who should be caring for those who need care?' is subsequently raised.

It is often assumed that this question is concerned with equitable divisions of labour between women and men. In an egalitarian age this would be an obvious reading. This is not the issue at the heart of this question. The question 'Who cares for others? is a question with a moral intent. As the feminist literature has long demonstrated, a woman's moral nature is seen as based in her capacities for care of others. Motherhood is the epitome of this. To fail to mother, or to fail to care for others, is to fail to be a moral woman. Indeed, to fail to become a mother is to fail to be a woman at all.

When we read, as in Coleman's (1988a) work, that parents are not investing enough of their time and energy with their children, we are reading a disciplinary discourse directed at perceptions of women's moral failures. Certainly, as they have always been, such discourses are also directed more generally at the poor, the black and the working class all of whom are most at risk of being viewed as the 'non-respectable'. Nevertheless, when we hear the discourses that lament the absence of social capital in the family and the community we also need to be mindful that the rise of paid employment has included that of middle-class women. We might, then, hear the disciplining discourses of those who deal in social capital as directed generally to all those groups in society who are viewed as morally wanting. But more particularly, we should note that it is a discourse directed at those women who share the class positions of those who are privileged to produce the intellectual discourses of social capital. These are the women of the middle classes.

Conclusion

During the 1990s the concept of social capital was imported into the applied social sciences in the United Kingdom. The take up of this concept can be associated with three main reasons. First, as its name suggests, *social* capital offers a way of recognising the social relations inherent in the production of human capital. In this way social capital modifies the arrogant individualism of human capital theories that suggest that people act primarily with concern for self in terms of how much investment they will make in their education and training. Indeed, the cynical might say that the addition of the concept of social makes such individualistic theories more palatable.

Second, and again as its name suggests, the concept of social *capital* is in accord with profit, loss and accumulation as dominant ways of understanding social relations. Within such understandings the social world is primarily ordered around market-based individual exchange. In this way social capital does not challenge the hegemony of economics but rather contributes to its maintenance.

Third, social capital is an inherently cause and effect model and so lends itself to those who must primarily seek solutions to problems. Social capital, then, appears a useful tool for governments and policy makers with an agenda to tackle social exclusion and new poverties by promoting active citizenship and lifelong learning. Overall, it is an economic model with a community face. Most fitting, we might say, in the UK for 'New Labour' and 'third way' policies.

This chapter has selected issues that offer a way to reflect on social capital from a critical perspective. We turn in our final conclusions to indicate how this criticality might be further developed. In particular we shall focus on the question of horizontal ties that are central to discourses of social capital. We believe that the attention that social capital theorists pay to horizontal ties of social relation is welcome but can be judged insufficient or seen as a new imperialism. It is welcome because the discourses of social capital insert into economically powerful discourses a necessary regard for inter-relationship and connection. These issues have long been at the heart of feminist perspectives of the social. In addition, the concept of social capital carries the potential of making visible the economic worth of forms of labour that mostly go unnoticed and therefore uncounted. These include housework, relationship building, trust, reciprocity, care and emotional labour. Again, these have been important sites for feminist politics and their recognition in mainstream educational theorising in the field of lifelong learning is significant.

There is, none the less, much that remains to be done in building a critical agenda on social capital. This agenda would begin by deconstructing the concept of 'horizontal ties' within a framework in which other ties are hierarchical. The literature on social capital posits such ties as beneficent and democratic. The discourse uses the language of trust, reciprocity, mutuality, support and community to convey this rosy glow of social relations. Within an 'us and them' model of power these are contrasted with the vertical ties of society to convey how vertical social relations are detrimental to the development of social capital.

In shifting our gaze away from such dominant, and more obvious, power relations we are encouraged to shift our gaze away from power relations altogether. Yet a critical agenda would take as central a recognition that the horizontal ties that exist between and within communities are not comprised of equal relations, however these are conceptualised. Nor we might add are they necessarily mutually beneficial. They are, rather, embedded within matrices of power, struggle and resistance through which people come to know their place and their possibilities. A view of social capital that incorporates such an analysis would contribute to the productive nature of social capital not simply in terms of economic worth but of how other use values may be produced or destroyed. It would also contribute to an understanding of how social capital produces the subject and subjectivities.

To take up this agenda it is not only necessary to use an analytic framework that places power and resistance at its centre. It is also necessary to critically engage with how key terms within the social capital literature are conceptualised. It requires a measure of conceptual literacy that builds on more general concerns within the critical literacy literature (Hughes 1999 and forthcoming). Of course much of what we say in this conclusion speaks against the true of dominant economic and bullying discourses that value a person by their capacity to produce 'capital' in any form and in any way. As the work of Field and Spence (2000) and Coffield (2000) illustrates, such discourses evidence their disrespect for each and all of us through the ways that they chastise and denigrate those that are not visibly participative and productive in terms of such economic discourses. By providing solutions without even asking they also evidence more fully their low regard for the worth of those people whose voices are silenced in discourses of social capital and for whom social capital purports to liberate. Our message to those who seek to 'stretch the academy' is one that challenges dominant interpretations of social capital through the incorporation of feminist perspectives. But it is also one that requires a radical deconstruction of the concepts that lay at the heart of these dominant perspectives. We might ask, is the academy up for this degree of stretching?

Acknowledgements

Our thanks go to Richard Edwards, John Field and Malcolm Tight for their perceptive and welcome comments on an earlier draft of this chapter. Any inadequacies, of course, remain our own.

References

Anthias F and Yuval-Davis N with Cain H (1993) *Racialized Boundaries: race, nation, gender, colour and class and the anti-racist struggle*, London: Routledge

Blaxter L, Hughes C and Tight M (1997) 'How adults relate their learning to their work, family and social lives', in Sutherland P (ed), *Adult Learning: a reader*, London: Kogan Page, pp 135–47

Blaxter L and Tight M (1994) 'Juggling with time: how adults manage their time for lifelong learning', *Studies in the Education of Adults*, Vol 26 No 2, pp 162–79

Bornat J, Pereira C, Pilgrim D and Williams F (eds) (1993) *Community Care: a reader*, Basingstoke: Macmillan/Open University

Bourdieu P (1979) 'Symbolic power', *Critique of Anthropology*, Vol 4, pp 77–85

Bourdieu P (1986) 'The Forms of Capital', in Richardson J (ed), *Handbook of Theory and Research for the Sociology of Education*, New York: Greenwood Press, pp 241–58

Bourdieu P (1987) 'What makes a social class? On the theoretical and practical existence of groups', *Berkeley Journal of Sociology*, Vol 32, 1–17

Bourdieu P (1989) 'Social space and symbolic power', *Sociological Theory*, 7, pp 14–25

Browning G (2000) 'Contemporary liberalism', in Browning G, Halcli A and Webster F (eds), *Understanding Contemporary Society: Theories of the Present*, London: Sage, pp 152–64

Coffield F (2000) *The Necessity of Informal Learning*, Bristol: Policy Press

Coleman J (1987) 'Norms as social capital', in Radnitzky G and Bernholz P (eds), *Economic Imperialism: the economic method applied outside the field of economics*, New York: Pragon, pp 133–56

Coleman J (1988a) 'Social capital in the creation of human capital', *American Journal of Sociology*, 94, pp 945–1558

Coleman J (1988b) *Foundations of Social Theory*, Cambridge MA: Harvard University Press

Corti L, Laurie H and Dex S (1994) *Caring and Employment*, Research Series 39, Sheffield, Department of Employment

Edwards R (2000) Editorial: 'The subject of citizens: developing social justice', *Studies in the Education of Adults*, 32, 1

Epstein D and Johnson R (1998) *Schooling Sexualities*, Buckingham: Open University Press

Field J and Spence L (2000) 'Informal learning and social capital', in Coffield F (ed), *The Necessity of Informal Learning*, Bristol: Policy Press, pp 32–42

Fine B (1999) 'The development state is dead – long live social capital?', *Development and Change*, 30, pp 1–19

Frazer E (2000) Communitariansim, in Browning G, Halcli A and Webster F (eds), *Understanding Contemporary Society: theories of the present*, London: Sage, pp 178–90

Hoskyns C (2000) *The Feminisation of Politics? From Virginia Woolf to the network state*, inaugural lecture, University of Coventry

Hughes C (1999) *Border Crossings: responsible women, relational subjects*, BERA Annual Conference, University of Sussex

Hughes C (forthcoming) *Key Concepts in Feminist Theory and Research*, London: Sage

Hughes C, Burgess R and Moxon S (1991) 'Parents are welcome: headteachers' and matrons' perspectives on parental participation in the early years', *International Journal of Qualitative Studies in Education*, Vol 4 No 2, pp 95–107

Kaplan E (1992) *Motherhood and Representation: the mother in popular culture and melodrama*, London: Routledge

Lankshear C with Gee J, Knobel M and Searle C (1997) *Changing Literacies*, Buckingham: Open University Press

Lewis S, Izraeli D and Hootsmans H (1992) *Dual-Earner Families: international perspectives*, London: Sage

McGivney V (1999) *Excluded Men: men who are missing from education and training*, Leicester: NIACE

Merrill B (1999) *Gender, Change and Identity: mature women students in universities*, Aldershot: Ashgate

Micheli G (1996) 'Downdrift: provoking agents and symptom formation in the process of impoverishment', in Mingione E (ed), *Urban Poverty and the Underclass: a reader*, Oxford: Blackwell

Moser C (1996) *Confronting Crisis: a comparative study of household responses to poverty and vulnerability*, EDS Monographs Series 8, Washington: The World Bank

OECD (1999) *Overcoming Social Exclusion through Adult Learning*, Paris: OECD

Payne S (1991) *Women, Health and Poverty: an introduction*, London: Harvester Wheatsheaf

Pilcher J (1999) *Women in Contemporary Britain: an introduction*, London: Routledge

Piper C (1993) *The Responsible Parent: a study of divorce mediation*, London: Harvester Wheatsheaf

Putnam R (1993) *Making Democracy Work: civic traditions in modern Italy*, Princeton: Princeton University Press

Raphael Reed L (1999) 'Troubling boys and disturbing discourses on masculinity and schooling: a feminist exploration of current debates and interventions concerning boys in school', *Gender and Education*, Vol 11 No 1, pp 93–110

Riddell S, Baron S and Wilson A (1999) 'Social capital and people with learning difficulties', *Studies in the Education of Adults*, Vol 31 No 1, pp 49–65

Schuller T and Field J (1998) 'Social capital, human capital and the learning society', *International Journal of Lifelong Education*, Vol 17 No 2, pp 226–35

Silva E and Smart C (eds) (1999) *The New Family?*, London: Sage

Skeggs B (1997) *Formations of Class and Gender*, London: Sage

Walby S (1997) *Gender Transformations*, London: Routledge

Wilson P (1997) 'Building social capital: a learning agenda for the twenty-first century', *Urban Studies*, Vol 34 No 5–6, pp 745–60

7 Women's community education in Ireland: the need for new directions towards 'really useful knowledge'

Anne B Ryan and Bríd Connolly

Introduction

Community education has woven itself into the lives of thousands of women in Ireland over the past 20 years or so, and has contributed to the development of content and methodology in a vast range of educational initiatives. From small beginnings in community centres, disused schoolrooms, church basements, and kitchens this movement became a highly significant force in education. It is important to understand the threads that went into weaving this tapestry, to examine the layers and textures that characterise the work and to trace the impact that it has had outside itself.

The trend, which we now see as women's community education, started in a very politicised way, in the early 1980s. It was characterised by the attributes associated with Freire's (1986) principles of praxis and conscientisation but came from feminist sources. Although the founder members of women's daytime community education may not have been very familiar with Freire, they did identify with and found themselves helping to build the ideas of the women's movement as these ideas percolated through Irish society. Women's community education set itself in opposition to schooling (Gilligan 1999; Kiely *et al* 1999; Quinn, 1999; Rath 1999) and to the traditional routes in community activity.

A number of factors combined to bring about early examples of daytime adult education classes. In the late 1970s and early 1980s, Irish women were beginning to experience the legal and social changes which were set in train by the report from the Commission on the Status of Women in 1970. The work of women like Mary Robinson,[1] particularly in the constitutional challenge to the prohibition on the sale or distribution of contraception, reinforced these changes. In addition the work of the Well Women Centres, Rape Crisis Centres, Women's Aid and certain media and print journalists, raised awareness about issues that were central to women's lives. However, for women with children, there were very few public gathering places. Because of declining family sizes, the individualisation of housework and the growth of suburban living, women and children experienced unprecedented isolation. Many turned to adult education, which had always been an acceptable way for women with children to spend their time (see Barr 1999).

A number of strands combined to make adult education women-centred:

- the influence of key women in local areas who mobilised their communities
- the availability of space in, for example, unused schoolrooms or community centres for crèche facilities and for classes
- the co-operation of some VEC adult education organisers (AEOs);[2]
- the development of academic-type courses such as Women's Studies and Social and Human Studies, in educational institutions such as Maynooth College
- the availability of models, such as the Boston Women's Health Book Collective (1978) or Anne Dickson's (1983a, 1983b) work on assertiveness and sexuality.

These classes began to answer the needs that women felt when they expressed the urgency to 'talk about something interesting, rather than talking about babies all the time' (Connolly 1989). This contrasts with the observation of Jane Thompson, writing in 1980, who commented that women's education in Britain before feminism was much more about traditional roles or children or communities, rather than women's own educational needs.

By the mid-1980s daytime adult education groups existed in many suburbs of Dublin, in a few rural areas, facilitated by a small number of AEOs and clustered around some universities. Two central characteristics featured in this new phenomenon. First, the subjects were very different to the subjects offered in evening adult education and, second, the pedagogical approach was different. Traditionally, evening adult education provided courses which reinforced women's traditional roles as homemaker or hostess, such as sewing and knitting, cookery and home maintenance. In the early days the subjects on daytime adult education courses, selected, organised and run by the participants themselves, were social studies, women's studies, history, creative writing, and were soon to be joined by assertiveness, personal development and parenting skills – thereby bringing together the academic and personal. This reflected the experience of women at this time in history. There were profound changes taking place as a result of the women's movement, but the status and esteem of women was very low, in spite of the rhetoric attached to the contribution women were said to make to the common good and enshrined in the Irish Constitution of 1937. The subject matter increasingly engaged with the political changes in Irish society via the women's liberation movement and the personal impact of these changes. These strands, which have had a deeper significance and which will be looked at later, brought to the fore the need to develop a feminist pedagogy. An engaged, feminist pedagogical approach was developed to subvert the traditional hierarchical relationship between tutors and participants, all of whom were free to adopt these new approaches in both academic and experiential learning situations.

Key characteristics of the emerging women's community education

The provision of adult education in the daytime provided one of the clearest contrasts with traditional adult education. This was mirrored in the names of some groups: MADE: Maynooth Adult Daytime Education; CAME: Clondalkin Adult Morning Education; Lucan Daytime Classes.[3] The provision of classes at times that suited women was the first characteristic that indicated a women-centred approach. Care was available for their young children who were not in school. This means of organising also suited the ways in which women's social status and socialisation had taught them to operate, via co-operation, shared leadership and nurturence.

The second key characteristic was the women-centred content: they explored the history, sociology and psychology of women. They took on board many of the topics that women's studies academics were introducing into the in the academy, and began to see themselves in significantly different ways. This involved consciousness raising and addressed cognitive, psychological and experiential processes (Connolly 1997).

The women also owned the classes, in that they organised them, they fund-raised to pay for the crèches, they selected the subjects and the tutors, they organised the spaces to suit themselves and they engaged with outside agencies to provide certification and payment for tutors and premises.

Finally a common characteristic was the development of a feminist, engaged, emancipatory pedagogy based on humanistic group work. Tutors in community education were committed to their own growth and development as well as that of their participants (see hooks 1994:15). While this has been considered more fully elsewhere (see Connolly 1999), the point made here is that the women-centred, emancipatory, feminist pedagogy was crucial, both to community education and ultimately to stretching the academy. It ensured that the method valued the participants and tutors, it challenged them to look at their assumptions about their place in the world and it provided them with analytical tools. The effects of this method in the 'private' lives of the participants indicates the strength of community education as a feminist force for change. Participants often recalled that their husbands and children did not like what was happening as a result of their classes (Connolly 1989).

The thinking that underpinned the first stages of women's community education was probably intuitive and eclectic, centring on the lived experiences of women, within the context of a changing Ireland. It was supplemented by feminist scholarship on the one hand and on the other by the growth of personal effectiveness and communication skills. It drew on the available discourses of feminism and change. The founding members were generally women who had not had third-level education, but they employed tutors who had. In order to be employed by educational institutions such as Maynooth College tutors had to have a primary degree and some understanding of the principles of adult education. Tutors in the VEC system had to have a track record, again with knowledge of the principles of adult education. A dynamic curriculum, linking personal awareness and academic scholarship, developed from the drive of the early activists, their desire for an alternative to schooling and for women-centred learning. This was particularly pertinent in working-class areas, where women's experiences of school were largely negative (see Kiely *et al* 1999) and from the tutors' and outside agencies' experience and thinking. The underlying philosophy of the women's community education sector was created by doing it, in a dynamic process of practice and reflection. By the late 1980s and the early 1990s the principles underpinning a coherent women's community education had emerged (see Bassett *et al* 1989). By now these principles drew on Freirean ideas in adult education about learning as a process for radical social change, but at the same time went beyond Freire's weaknesses around gender by insisting on the understanding of sexual divisions in the analysis of oppression.

Reflections on women's community education

The achievements of women's community education can be said to include:

- enabling relatively poor and working-class women to understand and analyse society from a gender perspective
- demonstrating that childcare is a prior requirement for the participation of women
- raising awareness about issues that are now part of public consciousness
- highlighting and condemning violence against women
- uncovering some recognition of child sexual abuse, which had been long hidden
- challenging the power hierarchy within the household
- fostering a self-help approach to health by offering reflexology, aromatherapy, yoga as a challenge to the dominant medical model of health, particularly women's health
- encouraging women's participation in community development in ways that were enjoyable and which they found useful and productive
- becoming highly significant in building cross-border links
- feeding into national politics in a few clearly identifiable ways, particularly in the election of Mary Robinson and the support for Marion Harkin[4] and Monica McWilliams.[5]

By and large many of these groups could be characterised by what Echols (1983) calls 'cultural feminism', that is the tendency to equate 'women's liberation with the development and preservation of a female counter-culture' (cited in Alcoff, 1988:412). As such the political effects of cultural feminism have been positive in insisting on viewing traditional feminine characteristics from a different, affirmative point of view (Eisenstein 1984; Alcoff 1988; Weedon 1997). The achievements of women's community education groups have combined to give Irish women a voice as a recognisable collective voice. This has been valuable, and has enhanced the lives of many women and their families and communities. However, this kind of thinking also reproduces dominant cultural assumptions about women while giving them a new, positive value, and it is difficult to see how this can be useful in the long term for radically challenging the ways that gender is organised in society. Moreover its development has led to a constraining feminist ideology for some (Gallop 1988) since not all women recognise themselves in the ideal of womanhood which cultural feminism promotes. For example, it fails to represent the variety of differences between women, as well as between women and men, so that 'caring, which is represented as a fundamental female quality' might be better understood in 'relational terms, as a way of negotiating from a position of low power' (Hare-Mustin 1991:70).

Equally, such a perspective has been situated, for the most part, in approaches to social change which take an either/or approach. It assumes either that change will happen as an amalgamation of personal change on the part of several individuals, or that it will happen through the change to social structures. This has led to two continuing standoffs: first, between women and men and, second, between the structuralists and the personalists.

Falling into dualism: a barrier to change and radicalism

Over time two strands developed in women's community education, one concentrating on self-esteem and personal development, the other concentrating on structural and social analysis. In some cases women's daytime education concentrating on social analysis was accused of making women dissatisfied and of isolating them from their communities. Personal development was seen as less threatening to the status quo, for the most part. We suggest that both strands are motivated by a belief in the differences between women and men. Structuralist analysis – as a way of understanding gender differences – has argued to incorporate female values and to give women more material and economic power. The more personalist approach has argued to preserve female culture in a separate sphere. At first the curriculum of women's community education offered both personal development and social analysis, though at the time it was simply a menu of courses from which participants could select their preferences. The weighting towards the personalist side may have had very practical origins. Women's community education at this time had to be self-financing, and a VEC tutor was paid about half that of a tutor from a university. It is more likely that the university tutors would have concentrated on the social analysis courses than the VEC tutors. The latter were more likely to provide courses aimed at personal development, such as assertiveness, communication skills and parenting skills. And of course women's community education was quite speedy in providing its own tutors.

However, a central tenet in liberal humanist personal development work is the assumption that a person can change only herself, thereby making social analysis somewhat futile. The concept of changing people by changing social structures also seems very crude to many people who are committed to the human relations psychologies which inform most approaches to personal development. These problems contribute to the rift which has developed between the idea of change as originating within the individual or, alternatively, within social structures. Those taking a social analysis perspective, recognising the importance of consciousness raising, exhort those concentrating on the personal to move on from it and to tackle the structures that lie beneath it (see Aontas Women's Education Group 1991; Mulvey 1995). This divide typifies the dualism inherent in many approaches to change, which are unable to overcome the personal/structural divide.

This agency/structure, or individual/society, dualism is widely recognised in sociological and educational theory. While it appears clear-cut in theory, and in the exhortations that structuralists make, it is also true that it is not so clear-cut in practice. Frequently, explanations rooted predominantly in one discourse reach their own explanatory limits: an individualist may not be able to explain a phenomenon by drawing on liberal-humanist discourses of change, and may turn to structural explanations. Similarly a structuralist may be aware of the need to attend to structures of cathexis, or emotionally charged relationships (Connell 1987; Hollway 1994) which in turn are underpinned by psychological investments in positions that confer power. Unfortunately mainstream psychological discourses of the person do not allow for the constructed nature of knowledge, seeing it instead as a discovery. Neither do they allow that many of the most subtle political battles are power struggles played out in the arenas of subjectivity and the interpretation of experience, in 'the capillaries of the structures' (Beckwith 1999). We suggest that both individualist and structuralist approaches to change need to take on board some feminist poststructuralist ideas about subjectivity, meaning and change, in order to overcome the impasse into which they have fallen. In so doing, the individualist focus on the personal can be radicalised and challenges can be made to the ideas about essential gender identities with which they work. Structuralists perspectives must be encouraged to take into account the more subtle and discursive operations of power and to examine the assumptions they make about the person. In the process both can find more common ground. In the discussion that follows we outline some of the ideas that inform feminist poststructuralism. We select subjectivity and experience as areas that need to be given critical attention in women's community education and go on to outline the challenges for the academy in making these ideas accessible to a wider constituency of students.

Brief outline of feminist poststructuralism

The feminist poststructuralist epistemological stance is based on a variety of theoretical work and practice influenced by, for example, post-Sausurean linguistics, marxism (especially Althusser's theory of ideology), Lacanian psychoanalysis, the feminism of Kristeva, the deconstruction of Derrida, the ethnomethodology of Garfinkel (1967) and Kessler and McKenna (2000), and the work of Foucault on power, knowledge and discourse. The poststructuralist ideas drawn on here are to be distinguished from postmodernism, even though they share postmodernism's questioning of the existence of fundamental truths and universal explanations (Lather 1991; Pritchard Hughes 1997). Poststructuralism has not been imported into a static feminist movement, however, but has come about in part because of feminism and the questioning of notions of essential femininity by feminists. (McLaughlin 1997, cited in Roulston 1999:8). The kind of feminist poststructuralism we put forward has avowedly political uses (see, for example, Jones 1993:158; Weedon 1997). It is capable of taking material conditions into account, so it is therefore compatible with the kind of socialist feminism advocated by Segal (1987, 1999). Importantly, however, it is also capable of taking into account the ways that people are positioned in multiple discourses and how this creates contradictions in experience. It is thus able to address resistance to structural change and complex emotional responses to structural changes.

Structuralist thought differs from feminist poststructuralism in that it sees the subject as socially constructed but static. The recognition of the ongoing nature of the constitution of self and of the non-unitary nature of self distinguishes poststructuralist theory from theory which is purely structuralist or social constructionist (see Davies 1990:xi). Feminist poststructuralism also allows that there are axes of oppression and domination which can exist alongside that of sex. Each person simultaneously occupies a range of positions in discourses of sex, class, race, age, ability and other social variables (Kenway *et al* 1994). This makes possible strategic alliances between feminist poststructuralism and other progressive social movements, and is central to its value for community education.

Feminist poststructuralism provides a radical framework for understanding the relation between people and the social world and for conceptualising social change (Davies 1990c:xi). The structures and process of the social world are recognised as having a material force, a capacity to constrain, to shape, to coerce, as well as to make possible individual action. The processes whereby individuals construct themselves as persons are understood as ongoing processes. The individual and the structural are dynamic mutual productions, both open to change (Mama 1995).

Subjectivity and experience

Radical adult education sees the human subject as the agent of change towards social justice, through the medium of praxis-oriented critical thinking. Most traditional adult education has relied on mainstream psychology for its theorisation of the subject, but psychology itself has been shown to be dominated by liberal humanist assumptions about the person (Fox and Prillentensky 1997; Henriques *et al* 1984). The term subjectivity is drawn from critical psychology to refer to a way of theorising the self which does not fall into an unproductive individual/society or agency/structure debate.

In direct contrast to humanist assumptions about the self, poststructuralism sees the subject as multiple, inconsistent and contradictory. It opposes the reification of individual experience as the arbiter of what is real or true about the world. It also denies the existence of an essential human nature – including essential female or male natures. In this it is in conflict with other kinds of feminism, which have based much of their theory and practice in the past on essentialist models of women and men. Liberal humanism, and feminisms situated within a liberal humanist approach, such as liberal feminism and cultural feminisms, often regard experience as unproblematic (Ryan 1999). Experience is seen as transparently reflecting reality. Similarly, language is seen as reflecting experience. 'As such, to speak "from experience" has almost unquestionable authority in much feminist discourse' (Gavey 1997:51). This approach to experience is also true of adult education. Discourse and language as important processes constitutive of subjectivity and experience are largely ignored. Feminist poststructuralism refuses to treat experience as authentic authority in the way that liberal humanist feminisms do, but insists that experience and subjectivity must be treated as outcomes of discourses and often of contradictory discourses. Therefore experience is something that needs to be scrutinised and explained, and seen as contradictory, dynamic and open to change. Experience is not assumed to be 'authoritative (because seen or felt) evidence that grounds what is known, but rather that which we seek to explain, that about which knowledge is produced' (Scott 1993:401, cited in Stephenson *et al* 1996:183).

In cultural feminist epistemologies, long taken for granted by women's community education, experience has been made the most reliable guide to reality. Experience, approached through description, tends to be reified as the most valid and most stable ground for knowing and for building an epistemology. To strengthen its achievements in asserting the importance of personal experience, feminist method needs to draw on poststructuralist theories and to *interpret* experience, not just *describe* it. It is a mistake to think that there is no theory or ideology behind 'plain description'. We need to combine the value of experience with Foucault's idea that truth is a historical product and therefore not absolute (Walkerdine 1989:40).

Feminist poststructuralism contends that experience must not be taken as the indicator of an essence, or an essential truth about, a person. Rigid categories of 'female experience' or 'male experience' are of limited educational usefulness. An exclusive feminist concentration on the special validity of women's experiences also suggests that if one has not had a woman's experiences, one cannot be a feminist or a pro-feminist, one is outside the 'circle' (see Said 1986). It puts the responsibility for 'progress' towards gender justice on women alone, since 'men can't understand'. In addition, it reduces women to their experiences as women and does not allow for overlapping experiences of class, race, ability, age, ethnicity and other social variables.

Challenges to the academy

Women's and men's different gendered experiences need to be included in community education, but as starting points for developing less rigid gender hierarchies, not for showing the true nature of women and men. The academic grounding of practitioners needs to provide them with the resources to scrutinise experience and to generate new knowledge out of this scrutiny. Practitioners need a good understanding of discourse, of emotional responses, and of their multiple uses and manifestations. And be able to draw on these resources in pedagogical situations. They need to take accounts of experience as discursive productions and not as reflections (accurate, distorted or otherwise) of a 'true' identity or as revealing some essential quality of the person. In other words, we cannot assume an unproblematic, taken-for-granted link between experience and human nature as liberal humanist approaches do. We also need to understand that, as researchers and practitioners, our own readings of other people's experiences and accounts are 'controlled by our own location in various discourses – for example, scientific, humanist, therapeutic, feminist, and so on' (Gavey 1997:56).

The challenge is to create a changed conceptual framework for practices concerning gender, meaning and experience. Urging a straightforward turn to the structural conditions of life is not an adequate response to the very real problems of women's community education in Ireland. Awareness of material and economic structures is important, but not sufficient. Calling for women to move 'on' from the personal implies that there is a hierarchy of moves which can lead to liberation, starting with the personal and moving on to higher forms of conscientisation such as the structural. All levels of power have to be tackled at the same time; not an easy task but an essential one. For feminists and educators committed to social transformation, it is not enough to say that a course of action can emphasise one aspect only. This means that all choices for action have limits which must be recognised. Neither is the solution to abandon spiritual development or individuation or the awareness that liberal humanism has created of individual human needs. However, if women remain preoccupied with introspection, essentialism and 'women's ways of knowing', people with vested interests in retaining the status quo will get on with that task (see Inglis 1995:4).

How can attention to the personal and to experience work if it is based on a deconstruction of the categories 'female' and 'male'? Again drawing on Hall (1988a, 1988b), Wetherell (1995:141) calls for a

> politics of articulation ... that is, a politics which tries to combine two contradictory movements – opening and closing. Closing in the sense that effective political action involves putting, at some point, a stop to talking: in feminist terms it involves defining a community of women, and an identity from which to act. But also opening – in that this community of women must not be taken for granted; the way it is constructed must be continually open to question. (see also Gallop 1982)

Wetherell (1995) advocates feminist psychology as a model of this new method of politics. A self-consciously feminist adult education praxis could also provide such a model. Within it, feminist poststructuralist concepts could be introduced and reflexively developed. Women's community education is, after all, where many women make the first contact with adult education and feminism. Such a model involves laying bare the power dynamics of different discourses of femininity and feminism, openly questioning the formulation of dominant discourses about women and pushing forward subordinated and barely formulated alternatives to rigid gender identities

The knowing subject of such a model of pedagogy will take on board the poststructural lesson *par excellence*, which is to be suspicious of authority and authoritative versions of who we are. Kiely (2000) describes the experiences of a group of lone mothers who were visited by a public health nurse who lectured them in a way that was clearly based on a notion of them as deficient, both as people and as mothers. This contradicted their experience of themselves as competent. Kiely, the facilitator, encouraged them to draw on other discourses about themselves that challenged the dominant one. In this way they were able to come to an understanding of how their experiences as women were also mediated by class and age, for example. As Weedon (1997:8) puts it:

> It is not enough to refer unproblematically to experience ... we need a theory of the relationship between experience, social power and resistance ... Theory must be able to address women's experience by showing where it comes from and how it relates to material social practices and the power relations which structure them.

It is important that feminist teachers can somehow make accessible to learners the various theoretical tools that are available for doing this, but it is equally important that such teaching does not take the form of an initiation into feminist theory as a disembodied form of knowledge. Feminist teaching projects must devise ways of teaching students about the various feminist perspectives in ways that focus them on students' everyday personal, intellectual and political dilemmas (Middleton 1993:31) and provide positions from which to act effectively for political change.

> Much of the unfamiliarity and strangeness of poststructuralism recedes when applied to everyday life. Work, relationships, beliefs, skills, and we ourselves are not identical from one day, or even one moment, to the next or from one place to another. There are always differences ... What we do in everyday life is negotiated, compromised, contingent, subject to miscalculation, and flawed. (Cherryholmes 1988:142)

Cain (1993:83) claims that once a concept is discursively arrived at in feminist theory, women recognise it. The role of the intellectual in this is facilitative, clearing the roadblocks, from the standpoint or site of the group of women engaged in producing knowledge. If we fail to incorporate practices surrounding the personal into our politicised and critical educational theory, then we leave open space for others to construct – either implicitly or explicitly – theories of the person and of experience that are not liberating in their effect.

It is important that intellectuals get involved in the 'arenas of practice' (Hollway 1994:268). Otherwise, dominant assumptions about experience and subjectivity will be reproduced unchanged. For many intellectuals and deeply committed radical feminists, this entails a possibly difficult 'reconciliation of radical political commitment with an appreciation of the shades of grey in the social world' (Cocks 1989: publisher's introduction). It also involves taking a close look at our own powers.

Feminism is a massive pedagogical project (Faith 1994:61). Generating new theoretical perspectives from which the dominant can be criticised and new possibilities envisaged is especially important. The concept of pedagogy draws attention to the process through which knowledge is produced. Lusted's (1986) concept of pedagogy is appropriate for a feminist poststructuralist pedagogical project because it recognises the relational nature of teaching, learning and the production of knowledge. 'How one teaches is therefore of central interest but, through the prism of pedagogy, it becomes inseparable from what is being taught and, crucially, from what one learns' (Lusted 1986:3). Feminism and pedagogy converge at the point of intersection between personal experience and commitment to transformative politics. As an instrument of social change, a truly transformative pedagogy requires the embodiment of a subjectivity conscious of her own subordination (Lewis 1993:54) and of her successful resistances. But if our understanding takes us only as far as pinpointing the construction of femininity and oppression, then it is inadequate for a transformative pedagogical practice. The social transformation of gender identities and experience must be an explicit concern of feminist pedagogy.

We are so attuned to the idea that fundamental truths exist that most people look for reductionist explanations in all walks of life. So, when they find an explanation that seems to fit their experience, they tend to stop there and to ignore the limitations of the explanation or where it fails to take contradictory experiences into account. If women consider that an essential femininity explains all of their experiences, this can operate to perpetuate the current power status quo. If they consider that the only way to emancipation is to tackle social structures, it can have the same effect because the personal is left untheorised in a politicised manner and the assumptions of a liberal humanist perspective are taken for granted. Foucault shows truth, reason and goodness as ideas produced inside a mode of life in order to ratify it (see Hollway 1991a). He exposed distinctions operating between rational and irrational as operating for power's sake (Cocks 1989:18). Distinctions between the personal and the structural can operate in the same way.

The concept of multiple and contradictory discourses, powers and subjectivities can act as a resource for women (and for men) who want to make changes. Radical self-reflection can create awareness of how all of these positions and discourses overlap in the same person, that is, how the person is multiply constructed. Awareness of this is profoundly liberatory in its potential, especially insofar as it has the effect of freeing people from guilt about not being consistently or 'adequately' politicised.

While the desire for change in their everyday lives motivates many women to attend community education courses, for feminists there exists an additional concern which is to disrupt prevailing gender regimes. No matter what kind of feminism is in play, the scrutiny of gender provides both opportunities and possibilities for change. What then happens will be influenced by the discourses which are drawn on, where the boundaries between discourses become blurred, by the explanatory limits of discourses and how feminist women approach resistance and the transformation of society.

Brookes (1992:156) cites Williamson (1981), suggesting that it makes relatively little difference what we teach as long as it leads to questioning of the assumptions which inform our social practices. The production of emancipatory forms of subjectivity is a practice which can be taken up immediately, in any classroom, including the personal development classroom, without devising a whole new curriculum (Brookes 1992:156). This is in contrast to work which suggests that we need to devise a special curriculum for women. (Jones 1993:158). Of course, feminists and educators cannot afford to ignore political economy and material conditions and some issues are more conducive than others when it comes to developing critical and emotional intelligence. To paraphrase Kessler and McKenna (2000), when a woman is abused, she is most likely to need a doctor or a lawyer, or money, than to need a gender theorist. But that is not sufficient reason for failing to theorise gender for failing to realise that meaning has material effects.

The alternative which we suggest is that it is possible to integrate a feminist perspective into students' reflection on everyday experiences and dilemmas. In this way it is possible to create a dynamic educational practice where different subject positions are available, supported by some theoretical understanding about the social construction of selves and the reproduction and transformation of society (see Stephenson *et al* 1996:184). In this way the classroom can become both a site of struggle and a focus for practice.

Part of the process of critically analysing discourses is to pay attention to the broader socio-cultural context in which discourses are generated and are reproduced (Lupton and Barclay 1997:5). This analysis includes exploring the political context. These types of questions can be asked no matter what the subject matter:

- whose interests are served by the use of specific discourses?
- how do elite groups, institutions and social structures shape discourses and favour some discourses over others?
- how are power relations sustained and justified by discursive choices?
- how are the interests of the powerful most often reflected in dualistic accounts of gender and change?
- what types of resistances and alternative discourses are generated in response to dominant discourses?

Conclusion

One challenge for both feminism in Ireland and for critical adult education seeking to stretch the academy – especially where these come together in women's community education – is to find a praxis adequate to the discursive construction of experience and subjectivity. The requirement of the pedagogy is that it can provide a framework where women can develop accounts of their experience which go beyond dualisms. We suggest that interrogating subjectivity is specifically ideological work which needs to be taken on board by all feminists, and that academics have a responsibility to make such ideas accessible and to develop them in dialogic relationships with community activists.

The conditions under which such ideas could be taken up in the classroom include the following resources:

1 *Personal resources, including:*
   - access to personal skills, including practical work-oriented skills, as well as the building of self-esteem
   - the desire to create social and gender justice, that is, a sense of self as being someone who can and should work towards change of this kind.

2   *Social resources; including:*
- access to other people who are striving for gender justice, so that collectivity can be fostered
- access to people different from oneself in terms of gender, age, class, race, etc, so that knowledge can be produced and questioned by drawing on diverse perspectives and experiences.

3   *Theoretical resources, including:*
- the ability to recognise which mode of gender action is appropriate to a particular situation.
- understandings of the individual which offer a range of alternative ways of being and which are not fixed in traditional ideas about what it is to be female or male, so that current definitions of masculinity or femininity are not seen as inevitable
- understandings of the individual as actively constructing meaning, via discourse, in concert with other people
- understandings of structures as cathectic, as well as material and economic.

In all these respects the terms 'woman' and 'women' are the basis of the political and conceptual framework of women's community education, and they are terms which must not be rejected. One option is to simultaneously use and reject the terms, and to act strategically in this. For example, we need to ask: 'When and how is it helpful to treat woman as a single category?' and 'Where and how is it important to focus on differences among women?'.

Of course, there are difficulties inherent in focusing upon differences between women, and on power as uneven and fragmentary, rather than monolithic and centrally held. This conceptualisation can all too easily be co-opted by anti-feminists to demonstrate that men suffer from a range of disadvantages in the same way as women, and that if you cannot talk about women as a homogeneous group, then there is no point in talking about them as a group at all. But the other position is equally dangerous in that some renowned misogynists are not averse to using essential differences between women and men as an excuse for defending the status quo. The old dichotomies based on essential differences led to clear-cut explanations and bases for action. But we cannot go on ignoring what we know about gender, subjectivity and experience being produced and multiple and open to change, or what we know about discursive power and the dangers of dualisms. The challenge is to take these complex ideas and use them as the spark for a continued movement towards gender justice. This is where the universities have a role. Intellectuals must act to help dismantle what is involved in engaging with these ideas – which are widely regarded in communities as too hard to understand, or too complex to be useful, or even, anti-feminist – and make them available to all in the pursuit of new kinds of 'really useful knowledge'.

Notes

1 Mary Robinson was president of Ireland, 1990–1997. She has been a feminist activist since the early 1970s.
2 Vocational Education Committee Adult Education Organisers (VEC AEOs) have a statutory obligation to provide adult education.
3 These are towns in the suburbs of Dublin.
4 Marion Harkin was an MEP candidate in the European elections. She is a community activist.
5 Monica McWilliams is an Assembly Member of the Northern Ireland Assembly, for the Women's Coalition.

References

Alcoff L (1988) 'Cultural feminism versus poststructuralism: the identity crisis in feminist theory', in *Signs*, 13, pp 405–36.
Aontas Women's Education Group (1991) *From the Personal to the Political*, Dublin: Aontas
Barr J (1999) *Liberating Knowledge: research, feminism and adult education*, Leicester: NIACE
Bassett M, Brady B, Fleming T and Inglis T (1989) *For Adults Only: a case for adult education in Ireland*, Dublin: Aontas
Beckwith J B (1999) 'Editor's Introduction: power between women: discourses within structures', in *Feminism and Psychology* Vol 9 No 4, pp 389–97 (Special Feature: *Power Between Women*)
Boston Women's Health Book Collective (1978) *Our bodies, ourselves: A health book by and for women*, Harmondsworth: Penguin
Brookes A L (1992) *Feminist Pedagogy: an autobiographical approach*, Halifax N J: Fernwood.
Cain M (1993) 'Foucault, feminism and feeling: what Foucault can and cannot contribute to feminist epistemology', in Ramazanoglu C (ed), *Up against Foucault: explorations of some tensions between Foucault and feminism*, London: Routledge
Cherryholmes C H (1988) *Power and Criticism: poststructural investigations in education*, New York: Teachers' College Press
Cocks J (1989) *The Oppositional Imagination: feminism, critique and political theory*, London: Routledge
Connell R W (1987) *Gender and Power: society, the person and sexual politics*, Cambridge: Polity Press
Connolly B (1989) Lucan daytime classes: an evaluation, unpublished thesis
Connolly B (1997) 'Community development and adult education: prospects for change?', in Connolly B, Fleming T, McCormack D and Ryan A (eds), *Radical Learning for Liberation*, Maynooth: MACE
Connolly B (1999) 'Groupwork and facilitation: a feminist evaluation of their role in transformative adult and community education', in Connolly B, and Ryan A B, (eds), *Women and Education in Ireland*, Maynooth: MACE
Davies B (1990) *Frogs and Snails and Feminist Tales*, Sydney: Allen and Unwin
Dickson A (1983) *A Woman in Your Own Right*, London: Quartet Books
Dickson A (1983) *The Mirror Within*, London: Quartet Books
Echols A (1983) 'The new feminism of yin and yang', in Snitow A, Stansell C and Thompson S (eds), *Powers of Desire: The Politics of Sexuality*, New York: Monthly Review Press.
Eisenstein H (1984) *Contemporary Feminist Thought*, London: Unwin
Faith K (1994) 'Resistance: lessons from Foucault and feminism, in Radtke H L and Stam H J (eds), *Power / Gender: social relations in theory and practice*, Inquiries in Social Construction Series, London: Sage

Fox D and Prillentensky I (1997) (eds), *Critical Psychology: an introduction*, London: Sage

Gallop J (1988) *Thinking Through the Body*, New York: Colombia University Press

Garfinkel H (1967) *Studies in Ethnomethodology*, Englewood Cliffs, NJ: Prentice-Hall

Gavey N (1997, first published 1989) 'Feminist poststructuralism and discourse analysis: contributions to feminist psychology', in Gergen, M M and Davis S N (eds), *Towards a New Psychology of Gender*, London and New York: Routledge

Hall S (1988a) 'Minimal selves', in *Identity: the real me*. ICA Document No 6, London: Institute of the Contemporary Arts

Hall S (1988b) 'The toad in the garden: Thatcherism among the theorists', in Nelson C and Grossberg L (eds), *Marxism and the Interpretation of Culture*, Urbana: University of Illinois Press

Hare-Mustin, R T (1991) 'Sex, lies and headaches: the problem is power', in Goodrich T J (ed), *Women and Power: perspectives for family therapy*, New York and London: W. W. Norton and Co

Henriques J, Hollway W, Urwin C, Venn C and Walkerdine V (1984) *Changing the Subject: psychology, social regulation and subjectivity*, London: Methuen

Holloway W (1991) *Work Psychology and Organizational Behaviour: managing the individual at work*, London: Sage

Holloway W (1994) 'Separations, integration and difference: contradictions in a gender regime', in Radtke H L and Stam H J (eds), *Power / Gender: social relations in theory and practice*, Inquiries in Social Construction Series, London: Sage

hooks b (1994) *Teaching to Transpress: education as the practice of freedom*, New York: Routledge

Inglis T (1997) 'Empowerment and Emancipation, in *Adult Education Quarterly*, Vol 48, No1, 3–17

Jones A (1993) 'Becoming a "Girl": post-structuralist suggestions for educational research', in *Gender and Education*, Vol 5 No 2, pp 157–66

Kenway J, Willis S, Blackmore J and Rennie L (1994) 'Making "hope practical" rather than "despair convincing": feminist post-structuralism, gender reform and educational change', in *British Journal of Sociology of Education*, Vol 15 No 2, pp 187–210

Kessler S J and McKenna W (2000) Afterword: retrospective response', in *Feminism and Psychology*, Special Feature on *Gender: an ethnomethodological approach*, Vol 10 No 1, pp 66–72

Kiely L (2000) 'A feminist critique of the concept of empowerment', paper presented at Women's Studies Seminar, University College Cork, 18 February

Kiely E, Leane M. and Meade R (1999) '"It's all changed from here": women's experiences of community education', in Ryan A B and Connolly B (eds), *Women and Education in Ireland*, Vol 1, Maynooth: MACE

Lather P (1991) *Feminist Research in education: within / against*, Geelong: Deakin University Press

Lewis M (1993) *Without a Word: teaching beyond women's silence*, London and New York: Routledge

Lupton D and Barclay L (1997) *Constructing Fatherhood: discourses and experiences*, London: Sage

Lusted D (1986) 'Why pedagogy?', introduction to a special issue on pedagogy, *Screen*, Vol 27, pp 2–14

Mama A (1995) *Beyond the Masks: race, gender and subjectivity*, London and New York: Routledge

McLaughlin J (1997) 'Feminist relations with postmodernism', in *Journal of Gender Studies*, Vol 6 No 1, pp 5–15

Middleton S (1993) *Educating Feminists: life history and pedagogy*, New York: Teachers College Press

Mulvey C (1995) *Women's Power ... for a Change: a report on a conference of women's networks in Ireland, 'Women, Leadership and Change'*, Dublin: AONTAS

Pritchard Hughes, K (1997) 'Feminist pedagogy and feminist epistemology: an overview', in *International Journal of Lifelong Education*, Vol 14 No 5, pp 214–30

Roulston C (1999) 'Feminism, politics and postmodernism', in Galligan Y, Ward E and Wilford R (eds), *Contesting Politics: Women in Ireland, North and South*, Boulder, CO and Oxford: Westview Press

Ryan A B (1999) 'Sources for a politicised practice of women's personal development education', in Connolly B and Ryan A B (eds), *Women and Education in Ireland*, Maynooth: MACE

Said E (1986) 'Intellectuals in the post-colonial world', in *Salmagundi*, No 70/71, pp 44–81

Scott J (1993) 'The evidence of experience', in Abelove H, Barale M A and Halperin D M (eds), *The Lesbian and Gay Studies Reader*, New York: Routledge

Segal L (1987) *Is the Future Female? Troubled thoughts on contemporary feminism*, London: Virago

Segal L (1999) *Why Feminism?*, Cambridge: Polity Press

Stephenson N, Kippax S and Crawford J (1996) 'You and I and she: memory work and the construction of self', in Wilkinson S (ed), *Feminist Social Psychologies: international perspectives*, Buckingham and Philadelphia: Open University Press.

Walkerdine V (1989) *Counting Girls Out* compiled for the Girls and Mathematics Unit, Institute of Education, London: Virago

Walkerdine V (1999) *Feminism, theory and the politics of difference*, Oxford: Blackwell

Weedon C (1997, 2nd edn, first published 1987) *Feminist Practice and Poststructuralist Theory*, Cambridge, Mass: Blackwell

Wetherell M (1995) 'Romantic discourse and feminist analysis: interrogating investment, power and desire', in Wilkinson S and Kitzinger C (eds), *Feminism and Discourse: Psychological Perspectives*, London: Sage

Williamson J (1981) 'How does girl number twenty understand ideology?', in *Screen Education*, No 40, pp 80–87

8 Friendship, flourishing and solidarity in community-based adult education

Keith Hammond

Different men want different things. I happen from boyhood to have set my heart on a certain possession, in the same way as other men want to own horses, or hounds, or wealth, or to hold high position. I feel quite lukewarm towards these things; but towards the possession of friends I feel most passionately. I would rather acquire a good friend than the best fighting-cock or quail in the world, and, I assure you, even the best horse or hound! And – yes, by Gad, I think I'd far rather have a comrade than the wealth of the King of Persia – such a lover of friendship am I! (Socrates to Lysis and Menexemus – Plato)

[Adult] education is not an addendum to life imposed from outside. It is no more an asset to be gained than is culture. To use the language of philosophers, it lies not in the field of 'having' but in that of 'being'. (*An Introduction to Lifelong Education* – Paul Legrand)

This chapter starts from the premise that Aristotle's philosophy has a central relevance to adult education today. Of course Aristotle is not an infallible guide in all our concerns: he was clearly wrong, for instance, in his thinking on both women and slavery. However, his position on women and slaves is not necessary to the structure of his thought. Thus dropping this part of his thinking does not mean the rest of his philosophy is impaired or that it has to be similarly rejected. The relevance of Aristotelian thought to contemporary practice in adult education remains. This is so because Aristotle's 'practical' philosophy – his ethics and politics – is primarily concerned with human flourishing (*eudaimonia*) – surely the aim of community-based adult education, no matter what Tony Blair says about education being 'the best economic policy we have' (Blair in Ecclestone 1999). It is because of this eudaimonic aim that Aristotle's thought echoes loud and clear in the early concerns of adult education. It is expressed in documents like the 1919 Report and articulated in the language of 'personal development' arising from 'the desire for knowledge', the desire for 'self-expression' and the wish to satisfy 'intellectual and aesthetic spiritual needs'. Here consumerism and exploitation are considered completely incommensurate with the long-term aim of improving the quality of life for the working class, as many non-material needs, like the need for friendship and shared interests, cannot be transformed into needs for commodities. Aristotle would have had great sympathy with the 1919 Report in as much as he thought the project of humans lay in learning to be human and not necessarily in learning to become efficient producers of surplus value. The basic task of humans, he thought, was to live a life of well-being and constructing a community of the same, and from its first beginnings right up to recently many of the aspirations of adult educators seem to have followed roughly in this vein (for early statements of these aspirations see Morris in Ree 1973). This of course is not the case now (see Fryer 1997; Kennedy 1997) though there is perhaps even more of a need for an adult education focused on personal development. Human flourishing or well-being cannot be reduced to a matter of economic policy. It is far more social and therefore far more complex.

In what follows I look at the way Aristotle's practical philosophy informs a community-based adult education project in and around the city of Glasgow. The project in question is the Outreach Pre-Access programme, organised by the University of Glasgow's Department of Adult and Continuing Education in collaboration with the community education services of various local authorities. As each Pre-Access course begins, the aim of promoting and encouraging flourishing is spelled out and it social nature made clear. Flourishing in the Aristotelian sense cannot be realised by individuals in isolation, no matter what their competencies. A consequence of this is that the self-sufficiency of one person is connected to the self-sufficiency of others. How this actually works itself out, of course, is down to the students and the way the project develops in the conditions of any particular locality. But on the Pre-Access programme the idea of flourishing is never left in the background. This is not the same as talk of 'inclusion', a term which is avoided simply because it implies the existence of its opposite and must entail some sort of integration procedure whereby someone must get left out, otherwise the idea of inclusion would be meaningless.

So in the first classes the tutor refers to the aim of well-being and flourishing. The Pre-Access students are almost all women and this perhaps makes the application of Aristotle's political ideas unusual since women in Aristotle's day would not have been considered 'suitable' for the project of human flourishing. They would have been tied to managing the household efficiently. Citizenship would most certainly have been out of the question. But the warp and weft of the Pre-Access is Aristotle's thought and this comes out subtly in the lives of the students and their communities as they become far more interconnected and far less atomised. For example in one area some of the students set up a credit union while others took up tutoring work in basic literacy. In another area a women's writing group was set up, producing a regular pamphlet, *Women's Words*, which contained not only poetry and other creative writing but also essays pitched against the local council on things like their housing policy and inadequate child-minding facilities. Even the poetry to some extent articulated the needs of that community. In another area one particular student researched the rundown of the Hydepark and Atlas engineering plants in north Glasgow as part of her essay on Aristotle. She had been impressed by the importance Aristotle placed on humans needing to know where they were going in life. This student made the point that 'the distinctive mode of activity' defining workers and the character of the area had disappeared and a plethora of social problems had emerged. However, she did not leave her reading of Aristotle at that. Along with others, she then acted on her findings and established a community flat that now accommodates various education and health projects. All this is completely in line with the Aristotelian idea of good function where the good for the human living in a certain neighborhood is not separate from the good of that neighborhood or community and friendship, as a fundamental bond is incredibly important here (see Whiting 1998).

The Outreach Pre-Access

The Outreach Pre-Access was set up as a collaborative project involving the University of Glasgow's Department of Adult and Continuing Education and Strathclyde Region Community Education Services in 1994. When the regional authority was abolished in 1997 the community education services of the various new local authorities took over responsibilities from the region. The project was based in areas of multiple-deprivation, now referred to as areas of social exclusion. In 1997 the Pre-Access course was the first collaborative project of its kind, organised by a university, to gain funding from the European Union (Director General V). The European input of cash helped the project grow considerably while its organisation and aims stayed fundamentally the same. It has always had the aim of giving students the chance of beginning classes in their own neighborhoods and of moving through access routes into the academy. The Pre-Access's success is due in no small part to the organising principles of the project which neutralise the barriers in first step provision that inhibit or hold students back from moving on to more formal study. Travel costs, for example, are avoided by the classes being located in the community. Crèche facilities are provided in the same building as the classes. The timing of the classes is such that it does not compromise dropping children off and picking them up from school or visiting job centres.

Class tuition on the course purposely avoids academic jargon and technical terms, and brings in personal experience in open dialogue around the books and compilations of reading that are put together by tutors and provided by the university. These include Chinua Achebe's *Things Fall Apart*, Kate Chopin's *Awakening*, Aristotle's *Nichomachean Ethics*, Plato's *Republic*, anthologies of poetry and standard texts in sociology and psychology where students are encouraged to look at the question of social organisation critically; as well as readings on social history and the nature of science. Quite deliberately, students are directly introduced to primary texts – in history they look at eighteenth-century parish records – and are not given predigested summaries. In this way the programme is ambitious, but students rise to it. Problems that have been encountered have never been about challenging the students too much but always of underestimating their aspirations once they become involved in the work of the course. The subjects of study are put together in such a way that they work as a whole rather than as a collection of individual units. Meeting weekly, the classes span three 10-week terms, corresponding again with local school terms; and in each term two subjects are covered, one in the morning and another in the afternoon. In each subject study skills are built into the course; they are not handled separately. One-to-one help and guidance is made available with a variety of reading: book boxes go out to every Pre-Access class. Discussion is a strong feature of each class and is a significant aspect of the tutoring. In dialogue the course material is linked to the student's experience and so made more rich and real. There is no formal assessment involved in the project but essays are written and individual tuition helps students consider the strengths and weaknesses of their written work. Frequently, informal study groups are set up by members of the class. Here they can explore the peculiarities of a text in their own way, and this is encouraged. Lunch is arranged between the morning and afternoon class. Tutors, students and their children all eat together as informal discussion continues and friendships develop. As in the case of study groups, the recognition and acknowledgment of these bonds has become increasingly central and necessary to the project. These are not relationships that just happen.

Aristotelian flourishing

In many ways adult education debates of the last decade have reflected debates in social and especially political philosophy that in Scotland can be traced back to the Enlightenment and the emergence of industry along the Clyde. The political themes at work in Scotland now connect with the current concerns of devolution and accountability, which inspire an outlook of 'stakeholders' similar to that of stockholders in a business. This is an outlook which often parallels the rigid posture of contracts and commercial law. Value is only recognised as value when it is located in the impersonal, the impartial and in that which claims objectivity, as though the variety and richness of human values must be reduced to contractual arrangements if they are to count as anything of worth. But, as in most conditions of employment, in which contracts favour the party with the stronger hand, so contractual arrangements in themselves guarantee little in terms of equality or fairness. The feminist Rossana Rossanda (Gutman 1985) makes some good points here:

> The political sphere stands accused by the feminist campaign of being an arena with essentially masculine, essentially productivist parameters, and hence parameters which are competitive and war-like, which take no

account of the body, reproduction and the emotions ... the body, sex ... powerfully resisting legal abstraction, resisting that *reductio ad unum* which denies dyssymmetry and is the basis of masculine culture and power.

Shaped by the contours of work, adult learning is increasingly framed in ideas of contracts and learning accounts, where provision has to be justified in terms of national prosperity and international economic competitiveness. The dialogue dominating current adult education is thus about building portfolios, as though the adult learner should be considered as a kind of myopic broker, touting for trade in the city. This is not something which corresponds with the real situation of those who take part in adult education, where often the very ordinary aim is that of getting to grips with a full and interesting life. Those who come to class simply want to improve the quality of their lives and meet others wishing to do the same. They rarely come to class for reasons related to employment. This notion is ignored in policy debates which see education solely in vocational and economic terms. Aristotle's notion of flourishing is very different. Ontologically, flourishing is an activity, an actuality or kind of getting on with something. This is not to say that it is the same activity for everyone. It is normative but it does not in any way inhibit personal autonomy and in fact flourishing does the opposite. It encourages autonomy. The same cannot be said of projects that shamelessly see education as something only to be justified in vocational terms. In *The Times Higher Educational Supplement* ('Letters & Opinions', 24 March 2000) one writer comments that 'it is probably the humanities focus of so many access courses that reduces the interest of mature males who often have family responsibilities'. Are these responsibilities, then, of a certain kind that can only be honored through participation in vocational aims? This seems to be the message, but for Aristotle the foremost responsibility of a human is to live well and flourish, encouraging others to do the same. On this point Ackrill (in Rorty 1980) notes that

> [Aristotle] certainly does think that the nature of man – the powers and needs all men have – determine the character that any satisfying human life must have. But since his account of the nature of man is in general terms the corresponding specification of the best life for man is general. So while his assumption puts some limits on the possible answers to the question 'how shall I live?' it leaves considerable scope for a discussion which takes account of my individual tastes, capacities, and circumstances.

In saying that the Outreach Pre-Access encourages students to consider the Aristotelian idea of flourishing there is no one sort of life being promoted or one line of educational progress envisioned. As for learning outcomes: the Pre-Access can lead in many different directions, as indeed can the idea of flourishing. The outcome of the course is down to the student's desires and aspirations, and the way these are expressed in choice. But again choice is exercised in a social context and often it is political in that women choose areas of study they feel 'their class' and 'their kind' have been denied or discouraged from thinking about. Again this is often done in groups. This is in keeping with the aims of the Pre-Access in that it tries to open up ground. But policy that ties adult education exclusively to the world of employment in some way or another can never be compatible with this idea of flourishing simply because flourishing is built on choice. In Aristotelian terms, the life of flourishing is the most choiceworthy life, and this is not because someone chooses it but because it is a life of inherent value and therefore a life most worthy of being chosen. This seems complicated but it is not. Choiceworthyness is simply about gaining a handle on the best sort of life. If this is seen as plausible project then it follows that adult education should contribute something to this process of making some good life choices. The Pre-Access is formed in such a way that it opens up new and broader choices for students. It opens up different educational activities with the aim of improving the quality of life. Political activities may be required for this: these might involve gaining access to local accommodation for meetings, study groups or readings, which in turn might demand access to community printing facilities. Similarly they might mean lobbying local agencies for more nursery provision to coincide with the timing of adult education classes. This kind of activity is specific to humans and is the activity Aristotle had in mind when he described humans as political animals. All this indicates that flourishing is dependent on human agency and this is at the forefront of the Pre-Access work.

Human flourishing is what human conduct is all about. But flourishing is not just an end in itself of inherent value. It is a preparation for going further. With this in mind the Pre-Access has been put together in such a way that students find it valuable in itself and valuable as a preparation for further study. Flourishing is made up of generic goods – for instance the acquisition of life-skills, health and friendship, creative achievement, pleasure, integrity, temperance, knowledge and education. All this emerges in the reading of Aristotle and sometimes in literature too, where someone admires and emulates a character in a story or novel. Sometimes it is the qualities found in fictional characters that a student may find inspiring and which might influence the student's idea of human flourishing. Aristotle's idea of flourishing involves qualities like 'courage', 'autonomy' and 'integrity' that often describe these fictional characters and these may be extremely necessary in reality for a women who has to discontinue an abusive marriage and separate from the husband while having three young children to rear and a life to live. Aristotle expresses the 'inclusive' and non-instrumental nature of flourishing; that includes a number of different aims where education figures centrally – as follows:

> What is always chosen as an end in itself and never as a means to something else is called final in an unqualified sense. This description seems to apply

to *eudaimonia* above all else; for we always choose *eudaimonia* as an end in itself and never for the sake of something else. Honour, pleasure, intelligence, and all virtue we choose partly for themselves – for we would choose each of them even if no further advantage would accrue from them – but we also choose them partly for the sake of *eudaimonia*. (*Nichomachean Ethics*, 1097bff)

Human flourishing is both individualised and diverse. There is no blueprint of the good life but this does not make it relative. If flourishing were relative then solidarity in the project would be impossible and this simply is not so. There are universal features at work in flourishing because students are in similar situations and share interests – as well as anxieties! Yet to a certain extent flourishing is dependent on *who* as well as *what* a person is: for in reality no two cases of flourishing can be exactly the same. Though there are generic potentials, the actualisation of one person's potential is always going to be something that is unique simply because there will always be potentialities that are more important to one person than they are to another. Rasmussen (Paul *et al* 1999) states:

It is only when the individual's particular talents, potentialities, and circumstances are jointly engaged that these goods and virtues become real or achieve determinacy. Individuals thus do more than locate human flourishing in space. Human flourishing exists neither apart from the choices and actions of individual human beings nor independently of the particular mix of goods that individual human beings need to determine as being appropriate for their circumstances.

The Outreach Pre-Access gives students a chance to experience (frequently for the first time) the study of Greek philosophy, psychology, sociology, literature and history. It also introduces students to the way science works and the way it gains application in technology. Different qualities are encouraged in the study of different subjects because different disciplines employ different modes of enquiry and students find themselves taking to one area of study rather than another. This often surprises them. One-to-one help and guidance is made available which in turn means students are less likely to drop out of subsequent studies, since they have become acquainted with their own interests and intellectual inclinations. They work out the parameters of their own potential. This makes flourishing something that is agent relative: always and necessarily involved in the well-being of some person in *particular*. As Rasmussen (Paul *et al* 1999) explains:

It is not that flourishing merely happens or occurs within some person's life, as if a person were simply a placeholder for this ultimate value. Rather, the relationship between flourishing and a person's life is much more intimate. The status of human flourishing *as the ultimate value* arises within and obtains only *in relationship to* some person's life. That is to say, its value is found in and exhausted by those activities of a person that constitute that persons flourishing. Further, human flourishing involves an essential reference to the person for whom it is good as part of its description. Human flourishing is thus neither a *tertium quid* nor a value-at-large.

Based, as the Pre-Access is, mainly in large housing 'schemes' around the city of Glasgow, the ethnic and cultural differences amongst people who participate on the Pre-Access are highly relevant to the project. The fact that values held by one person may be of no significance to others in the class does not make those values meaningless. On the Pre-Access this kind of value is regarded with nothing but respect and this encourages, strange as it may seem, a sense of solidarity that is based on an appreciation of difference as well as similarities. The Aristotelian point of view focuses on the human and takes it that people are more than a cluster of culturally specific passions and desires making up the internal life of a person. It takes the view that there are shared potentialities and needs that spread across all cultures. Thus it does not violate the particulars of culture that often characterise who and what a person is, just as it does not abandon shared ground. This means that the agent-relative nature of human flourishing is not in any way incompatible with it being objective. Again Rasmussen (1999) makes the point that agent-neutrality is not necessary for upholding either the value-objectivity or the choiceworthiness that are at the heart of human flourishing. He says:

> Agent-relativity should not be confused with egoism. To say that human flourishing is agent-relative does not mean or imply that flourishing cannot involve concern for others or that acting for the welfare of another could not be a value or reason for one's conduct. Acting for the sake of another could be only good-for-you and not necessarily anyone else. Parents sacrifice for *their* children, or friends helping and nurturing one another, are among the many examples of how flourishing can be agent-relative and nonetheless involve authentic concern for others.

Human flourishing is a self-directed activity. It cannot be attained through factors that are beyond each person's control. So flourishing cannot just be the possession and use of needed goods. Flourishing has to be the result of an individual taking charge of their own life. But for some women living along the Clyde in the old shipbuilding areas this is not easy because traditional domestic arrangements centred on supporting the man and his work still endure even though the shipyards no longer exist and the work simply is not there. Breaking from this kind of ossified tradition is difficult for many women who come on to the Pre-Access. However, Aristotle is clear when he says that flourishing is a way of being where three conditions have to be met. These are that (1) the agent must act in full consciousness of what she is doing (and not doing); (2) she must 'will' the actions of flourishing for no instrumental ends; and (3) these actions must not be temporary but fixed to a set course of flourishing. This makes flourishing anything but passive and it poses a great challenge to some women. But when a number of women take on this project together, and question and then break from their old routine in one of these old shipbuilding areas, they seem to find incredible strength in being about the very same task. Aristotle would say that these women were turning themselves towards good function. Whiting (1988) expresses what is going on in this aspect of Aristotle's thought when she writes:

> A heart which, owing to some deficiency in its natural capacities, cannot beat on its own but is made to beat by means of a pacemaker is not a healthy heart. For *it*, the heart, is not strictly performing its function. Similarly a man owing to some deficiency in his natural capacities, cannot manage his own life but is managed by means of another's deliberating and ordering him is not *eudaimon* – not even if he possesses the same goods and engages in the same first order activities as does a *eudaimon* man. For *he*, the man, is not strictly performing his function ... Aristotle's claim that *eudaimonia* is an activity of the soul in accordance with virtue shows that he thinks that *eudaimonia consists in* exercising rational agency.

So self-direction is the essence of flourishing. It is not simply one of the conditions of flourishing. For working-class women involved in oppressive relationships where they are financially dependent on a spouse, this raises some incredibly difficult problems. But human flourishing cannot be human flourishing if there is no kernel of self-direction. Rasmussen stresses the point that functioning as a rational agent, regardless of the degree of learning or intelligence that is involved, does not occur automatically. It is something that humans have to initiate and maintain themselves. It thus requires effort and energy in the use of intellectual capacities that really are just this exercise of self-direction. Here the responsibility of self-direction cannot be shared but it helps considerably if it is exercised in the context of other women being about the same thing as on the Pre-Access.

Friendship and the social nature of flourishing

In the *Nicomachean Ethics* Aristotle sets out to account for all the moral qualities that constitute the core of human flourishing and the aim of education then falls in line with this project of flourishing, interwoven as it is with the well-being of partners, children friends and other citizens. In this context the individual works towards the development and exercise of qualities of character and intellect of which a grasp of justice figures as fundamental. Having such importance, justice gathers all the moral virtues into one, as a collective capacity expressed in thought and action on 'the good of another' (1129b27–30). Justice is then closely aligned with friendship since they are both 'other regarding'. Aristotle makes the point that those who are basically just, in the way they go about their life, still need friends but in the relationship of real friends there is no need for justice. True friendship goes beyond justice. This creates a puzzle because friendship is one of the many virtues or excellences of character and justice 'is complete virtue ... in relation to another' (1129b25–27) and yet friendship goes beyond justice. Aristotle says that friendship renders justice unnecessary (1155a27). Putting this puzzle aside it is still easy to see what Aristotle is getting at in the way Pre-Access students help one another out in endlessly different ways that could not be given a systematic representation. This is rarely a matter of just doing the 'right' thing. Acts of friendship do not seem to work in anything like a dutiful sort of way. The actions involved in friendship give mutual benefit and pleasure. It is in this element of pleasure and reciprocity that those friendships become something necessary to the well-being of those involved in the relationship. It is also in the same reciprocity that justice is transcended, as spontaneous acts of friendship become something far more pleasant than the more impersonal acts of justice. All this makes friendship in both Aristotle and on the Pre-Access something that is not in any way self-denying. Yet having friends and living the best of lives are both social and communal achievements, requiring good 'household management and a constitution' (1142a9–17) that are both derived from a grasp of justice that is expressed in good politics. This means flourishing cannot in any way be atomistic. In Aristotelian terms, the life of any human is inevitably intertwined with the lives of others.

Friendship, then, is one of the major features of a good life and, according to Aristotle, it is essentially a reciprocal arrangement that can have three purposes: there can be friendship for *advantage*, friendship for *pleasure*, and friendship for *virtue* or *excellence of character*. Aristotle is not so stuffy as to think that pleasure and utility are completely absent from the later kind of friendship which serves the good, and by 'the good' he simply means that which is valued by those who are living good lives, which is to say those who are flourishing in life. Goodwill plays a role here in that it naturally inclines humans towards what they admire for one reason or another. Aristotle seems to say that goodwill is directed towards different qualities in different kinds of friendship and that this has something to do with the kind of relationship that follows. He makes the point that befriending another implies a need, a kind of thirst or hunger for something that cannot be satisfied by one individual alone looking in upon her own inner resources. However Aristotle is not to be read as echoing Aristophanes in Plato's *Symposium*, who defines the love of a friend as something that is about 'finding one's missing half'. Aristotle stresses the centrality of reciprocity in friendship, time and time again. From this it might be inferred that self-concern is never completely absent from his idea of friendship. In its fullest sense, friendship involves mutual enjoyment and common activity. Pleasure is important because 'most of all nature appears to flee what is painful and to aim at what is pleasant'. Current good practice in adult education bears this out. In periods of stress, the moments that no adult education course completely avoids, the longing for companionship becomes particularly strong. At these times Aristotle says good friends can make things easier and less painful for one another. On the Pre-Access, these times tend to be essay submission dates. Study groups are crucial here as everyone helps each other and Aristotle observes that in situations like this friendship requires equality or balance, so that each person is satisfied with what she gets out of friendships. The well-being of all parties in a friendship must be attended to, and attended to more or less equally. This means that if the good of each becomes part of the good of the other it is never the whole or even the heart of it, because then the good of either would suffice for all parties and this would clearly not be right.

Friendship and self-love

In Book IX of the *Nichomachean Ethics* Aristotle gives his fullest treatment of the relationship between friendship and self-love. Chapter IV begins as follows:

> The origin of relations of friends towards our neighbors, and of the characteristics by which we distinguish the various kinds of friendship, seem to be in our relations to ourselves.

Aristotle goes on to say that a friend is considered to be one who: (1) wishes for and does what is good or seems good for the friend in themselves; (2) wishes the friend to live for their own sake; (3) enjoys spending time with the friend; (4) enjoys or prefers [at least some of] the same sort of things as the friend; and (5) shares the sorrows and joys of the friend (1166a1–9). Aristotle then makes it absolutely clear that all these elements are found in the flourishing human's relationship with *herself*. He says:

> The excellent person is related to his friend in the same way as he is related to himself, since a friend is another self; and therefore, just as his own being is choiceworthy for him, the friend's being is choiceworthy for him in the same or similar way. (1170b6–9)

Brink notes (in Paul *et al* 1999) that Aristotle believed proper self-love required a proper conception of the self and what would be beneficial to that self.

Aristotle writes repeatedly about the human living a good life being the human who truly knows what is in their interest. He says:

> it is this [the virtuous person] more than any other sort of person who seems to be a self-lover. At any rate, he awards himself what is finest and best of all, and gratifies the most controlling part of himself, obeying it in everything. And just as a city and every other composite system seems to be above all its most controlling part, the same is true of the human being; hence someone loves himself most if he likes and gratifies this part. (1168b28)

When this is read out in the Pre-Access class older women are astonished. It is a point that is often difficult for some women to grasp simply because they may have spent most of their lives seeing to the needs of a spouse and family. Understandably, it is difficult for them to see a valuable life in any terms that are not self-abnegating or in terms that go far beyond this supporting role in the family. In this part of the *Ethics* Aristotle emphasises the importance of the intellect in self development. This is not a matter of everyone striving for exactly the same thing but it is a question of everyone having the same freedom and opportunity to be about the same sort of striving. It is in this striving not just to live life but to live a good life that Aristotle locates something that is particular to humans and is confirmed in a recent 'evaluation report' (unpublished) commissioned by Glasgow City Council Community Education Services (January 2000). While only 4 per cent of those interviewed said they took community-based learning courses for a qualification, a staggering 50 per cent of those interviewed took a course to 'gain knowledge/experience of a subject' with more than 31 per cent continuing to study at a higher level. While only 1 per cent of those interviewed said that after completing a course they had made 'financial benefits', a further 23 per cent mentioned benefits of 'increasing their ability/gaining more confidence/making new friends/sharing their learning/improving their health'. Given the present government- and business-driven preoccupations with accreditation and employability, this makes a strong case for the 'wider benefits' of learning that touch on the Aristotelian idea of flourishing.

Community-based learning is open-ended to the point that there are no *a priori* limitations on it or who may be friendly with whom while on a course. In principle, humans are open to an infinite variety of human relationships. These are necessary both for self-understanding and mutual well-being; and they invariably have political consequences. This point has never had to be made on the Pre-Access, as friendships of incredible variety seem to emerge. However, in the main they all seem to be based on approximate equality and mutual affection, interest and benevolence where the equality has something to do with personality, emotion and overall character. The mutual respect and balance at work in these relationships is summarised by Friedman (1993) as follows:

> One friend's superiority in one area, for example, in breadth of life experience, need not give that friend a privileged place in the relationship if it is balanced by the other friend's superiority in some other area, for example, in vitality of imagination.

Relationships that lack this balance do not constitute genuine friendships. They take on a master–apprentice or master–student quality. Tutors on the Pre-Access try to avoid this kind of relationship. Adult education is a privileged situation for the tutor in that friendships with students are not only possible, they are beneficial for all concerned, and according to Friedman (1993) where genuine friendships do emerge between tutor and student: 'It is likely that the formal inequality of social position is balanced by excellences in the student which inspire the mentor's respect and from which the mentor might *even learn something.*' The abstract individualism that often underlies liberal politics serves no such learning. It considers human beings as social atoms, removed from the life-world.

Conclusion

The argument of this chapter has been for outreach work. It has been an argument for community-based adult education that is shaped around Aristotle's thought. As well as furthering research and teaching, the university should play its part in promoting a healthy democracy, a democracy in which citizens take the initiative and create good lives for themselves and their communities. There cannot be anything more important to humans than living a life of flourishing, a life where humans are happy. This has been the traditional task of adult education since the end of the nineteenth century. This means that departments of adult and continuing education in universities have to be supported in organising non-vocational courses that balance the abundance of vocational provision in FE colleges and learning centres. The university cannot claim to have humanistic and egalitarian aims without being proactive and going out of the academy with these courses. The aim of this work cannot be narrow and must be supported by crèche facilities. It must be broad and lead into a number of different follow-on courses for those who wish to go on with study in a variety of different institutions. Current debates must take all this into consideration if society is to develop as a truly human society and not just an aggregate of atomised working individuals.

References

Ackrill J L (1980) 'Aristotle on Eudaimonia', in Rorty A O (ed), *Essays on Aristotle's Ethics*, Berkley: University of California Press

Aristotle (1980) *Nicomachean Ethics*, trans. Ross D, revised by Ackrill J L and Urmson J O, Oxford: Oxford University Press Aristotle (1958) *Politics*, ed. and trans. Barker E, London: Oxford University Press

Brink D (1999) 'Eudaimononism, love and friendship, and political community', in Paul E F, Miller F D Jr and Paul J, *Human Flourishing*, Cambridge: Cambridge University Press

Ecclestone K (1999) 'Care or control?: defining learners' needs for lifelong learning', in *British Journal of Educational Studies*, Vol 47 No. 4, December, pp 332–47

Friedman M (1993) *What Are Friends For?*, Ithaca: Cornell University Press, p 189

Fryer R H (1997) *Learning for the 21st Century: first report of the National Advisory Group for Continuing Education and Lifelong Learning*, London: Department for Education and Employment Gutman A (1985) 'Communitarian critics of liberalism', *Philosophy & Public Affairs*, Vol 14, summer

Kennedy H (1997) *Learning Works: widening participation in further education*, Coventry: Further Education Funding Council Rasmussen D B (1999) 'Human flourishing and the appeal to human nature', in Frankel P, Miller Jr F D and Paul J, *Human Flourishing*, Cambridge: Cambridge University Press

Paul E F, Miller F D Jr and Paul J (eds) (1999) *Human Flourishing*, Cambridge: Cambridge University Press

Ree H (1973) *Educator Extraordinary*, London: Longman

Rorty R (1980) *Philosophy and the Mirror of Nature*, Oxford: Blackwell

Whiting J (1998) 'Aristotle's function argument: a defence', *Ancient Philosophy*, Vol. 8, p 43

Wiltshire H, Taylor J and Jennings B (1980) *The 1919 Report – the final and interim reports of the Adult Education Committee of the Ministry of Reconstruction 1918–1919*, Nottingham: Department of Adult Education, University of Nottingham

9 Missionary and other positions: the community, the university and widening participation

Pat Whaley

North-east England provides the frame and the space for a critique of the problems and solutions addressed by the interrelated notions of widening participation and lifelong learning in Higher Education (HE). This chapter describes a joint initiative between the University of Durham and the Cleveland Community Enterprise Network to develop an accredited undergraduate programme in community development and enterprise. As a case study it can be used to explore the relationship between the university and its local communities, as it has developed in relation to a number of changes and to the widening participation agenda. In the process it analyses some of the myths and metaphors that have characterised the field of community education more generally, both inside and outside of the academy, as well as the links between those who occupy and inhabit it.

The analysis raises questions, issues and tensions about the concept of 'community'; the position of the university; the role of the HE and voluntary sectors in lifelong learning and community regeneration, demand and need, outreach and inreach, the use of experience, and at the heart of it all, widening participation.

So far as providers are concerned there has been an understandable concentration on what 'widening' means and the distinction between it and 'increasing', since the two are often conflated in quantitative and qualitative terms. Much less consideration has been given to 'participation'. Are we talking about extending access to the same old (excluding) curricula and systems? Offering a marginal (inferior) kind of provision? Creating opportunities in (not quite education but) training? Opening up different bits of the HE system to different kinds of students (university of excellence/university of inclusion)? Or do we mean participation in relevant, inclusive, challenging, transformative learning experiences? What is the nature of the participation? What is the education in which we want to encourage and effect participation?

The university and the community

If engagement between the university and the community means widening participation then the University of Durham has had a lot of practice. The university has, for over a century, worked with(in) the communities of North-east England. This work has taken various forms and been labelled and described in different ways. The department through which the university has focused its activities has variously been called Extra-Mural, Adult and Continuing Education (DACE), Continuing Education (DCE), and, currently, the Centre for Lifelong Learning (CLL). These name changes are a reflection (although not always by design) of wider changes in respect of university provision for local adults. The notion of a dedicated department is also illustrative of the provision in many older universities, and of the question – is this a distinct commitment to, or a structural marginalisation of, educational activity of this kind? It is, I think, 'both a compensatory and an alternative framework for Higher Education' (Taylor 1999). What can also be said about the University of Durham, at this point, is that for many years it has been a stable resource for collaborative provision, reaching out to local communities.

The various communities involved have in themselves undergone many changes throughout this time. The region, lying between the Pennines and the North Sea and encompassing the three great river valleys of the Tyne, Wear and Tees, has witnessed the triumphs and tribulations of industrialisation, with its mix of coal and chemicals, steel and shipbuilding. These have developed – and disappeared – alongside great tracts of agricultural land and rural emptiness. There are higher levels of deprivation than in most other parts of the UK. The University of Durham sits at the centre of the region, scattered throughout what Bill Bryson describes as 'wonderful – a perfect little city' (Bryson 1996:234). The University, one of the Russell group, prides itself on the Durham difference:

> the certain something over and above academic excellence that adds extra value to a Durham education. The Durham difference is hard to define, but easy to recognise, for Durham students also make their mark in sport, music, drama and the arts … In short, the Durham difference is encapsulated by the wonderful knack our students have, to constantly amaze us with their inventiveness, energy, creativity, talent and sense of purpose. (Vice Chancellor's address to Convocation 1999)

In 1992, the University established a second campus 20 miles to the south, on the banks of the Tees, in Cleveland County (created in 1974 following the abolition of the county borough of Teesside and subsequently abolished in 1996), replacing a terrace house in Stockton town centre and a premises shared with the Workers Educational Association for 25 years. University College Stockton (UCS), later renamed University of Durham Stockton campus, was built on the site of Prime Minister Thatcher's famous 1987 walkabout among the desolation and dereliction of defunct industry. Like many other urban areas whose prosperity and people depended largely on a single primary industry – in this case actually two, steelmaking and chemicals – it experienced a severe decline during the Thatcher years, with high levels of unemployment and social deprivation. In the 1980s and 1990s it became one of the country's poorest sub-regions. According to Cole and MacDonald (1990) 'Cleveland, perhaps more than any other area, has experienced the most dramatic consequences of economic recession and industrial restructuring (p 168). Unemployment rates were the highest in mainland Britain for part of the 1980s and in the early part of the 1990s were still around 11 per cent overall, with up to 26 per cent in some wards. Today, the official unemployment rate for the Tees Valley is 8.4 per cent, compared with 4.1 per cent for Great Britain as a whole (Tees Valley Statistics 2000).

Significantly, the take-up of Higher Education, participation in post-compulsory education generally and the proportion of graduates in the workforce are among the lowest in England, with half the national average for business start-ups. Even within the North-east, a region which shares many of these characteristics, the proportion of full-time students in HE is lower than on Tyneside or Wearside (19 per 1,000 as against 42 per 1,000) (University of Durham 1997a). Perhaps because of these features there have been a number of studies of the Teesside/Cleveland area (Beynon *et al* 1989; Hudson 1990; Beynon *et al* 1994) and various funded initiatives – City Challenge; Task Force; Teesside Development Corporation; and SRB. The Regional Development Agency (RDA), One North East and the four Learning and Skills Councils are expected to spearhead the economic and educational development in the region for the life of the present Government.

The partners and the project

At about the time that the University of Durham was establishing UCS, as a joint initiative with the University of Teesside, it also faced a major change in adult education funding. From 1994 HEFCE decreed that continuing education provision should be accredited. In DACE we faced the challenge of persuading a not altogether receptive local population of the value of dedicated, formally validated and assessed programmes to replace liberal adult education courses. The university was allowed to continue the specially funded provision for 'disadvantaged' individuals and groups, although this too was restructured into a Widening Provision Project, the result of a competitive bid (HEFCE 1997). Our bid responded to the Funding Council's aim to encourage 'HEIs to build partnerships with other organisations to widen participation in Higher Education' (HEFCE 1998). We also made a successful bid for some liberal adult education funding.

My role as the Director for Community Education has bridged both responsibility for the development of new accredited undergraduate courses and for developing learning opportunities for people in a variety of communities in North-east England. This latter brief had brought me into close contact with a number of significant individuals and organisations, including the Cleveland Community Enterprise Network (CEN). The Network was established in 1993 and is a Teesside-wide initiative to bring together a range of individuals, groups and organisations to identify needs, share common problems and ideas and to support each other. The Network is intended for all relevant organisations, from small groups just starting up, such as a mother and toddler group, to organisations such as a large community business. The Network is organised and developed by individuals from voluntary groups throughout the Teesside area. It represents something of the current Minister for Lifelong Learning, Malcolm Wicks' description of the voluntary sector as 'an extraordinary tapestry ... A significant sector for society as well as for the economy (Wicks 1999).

Just as the present Government regards grass roots organisations like the Network as important contributors to community regeneration, lifelong learning and combating social exclusion, the university also acknowledges its own role in this agenda in goal 4 of the UCS Mission statement: 'to pursue a partnership approach in order to provide mutual support and promote the regeneration of the region' (University of Durham 1997b).

CEN is explicit in its recognition that – drawing on a sense of community and identity – its members have an important part to play in building the future of their community and in to helping 'to shape developments that will benefit all residents' (CEN 1993). Far from needing persuasion as to the benefits of accredited programmes, CEN had been investigating the possibility of accrediting a training programme for paid and unpaid staff in the community and voluntary sector. Early in 1995 a working party, with members of the CEN executive and the department's administrator and myself, met to explore whether and how the university might provide an appropriate programme. A shared vision of community development and enterprise, and ways in which reflective practice might be embedded in and enhanced by academic scholarship, drew on the respective experience of both partners. The partnership between the University and CEN was made possible because of longstanding, dynamic links and networks between some of us in the academy and the community over a long period of time. It is debatable whether the initiative would have progressed at the pace it did without the solid foundation of these previous links and associations and the trust that they had created. Even so, it would prove to be a challenge to both partners: the old, traditional, established seat of learning and the new eclectic and evolving community organisation.

Widening participation is premised on the belief that an opportunity is being extended. Most academic institutions regularly assume that education is 'a good thing' and adopt something of the missionary position in taking the canon to the ignorant and unenlightened of the world. According to Mannion *et al* (1998), 'We could look at the characteristics of the university like this. The traditional university "believes in" objectivity, rational thinking, the disciplines as the options for "religious practice"; the need to be a member of an academic "tribe" which practises a particular "religion" (Mannion *et al* 1998:134).

Yet in the world beyond the academy there are some who view lifelong learning as a life sentence and learning as a poor substitute for gainful employment. A study of Consett, a County Durham town, following the closure of the steel plant, revealed a long-held conviction that manhood and education are oppositional, reversing the analysis that the working class are 'culturally deprived' and suggesting that the 'deficiencies' lie with the educated middle-class view of manhood (Holmes and Storrie 1995). Such views still prevail. The school of real life and hard knocks often serves people better than their own state education seems to have done and 'nobody volunteers for humiliation a second time around' (Mudie 1999).

For others, education is something finite. You learn and then you leave. A friend, born into a working-class family in Glasgow, told me of the bemused neighbour who, on being told by his mother that her 16-year-old son was going into the sixth form, asked 'Oh dear, is he no very bright?'

McGivney points to 'the profound ambivalence we have as a nation towards education in any form other than the purely vocational' (McGivney 1997:134) and which is reflected in the contradictions inherent in policy and the language of policy makers. As a consequence, 'If we who are in the educational world fail to make sense of these mixed messages, how can we expect traditional non learners to do so?' (McGivney 1997).

In the initiative I describe, both University and community organisation explicitly addressed the question of what kind of learning opportunity they were attempting to create, as equal partners. From the beginning the respective expertise of all members of the working party was recognised and everyone was given the opportunity to contribute to the discussions on curriculum, recruitment and development. Early in the process it was decided that this would not be a 'training course', but a new undergraduate programme, initially accredited at level 1 of a degree. We wanted to give students the opportunity to test theory against experience and use experience to inform theory; to provide them with sources and resources to develop a range of key professional and personal skills; and to develop critical thinking and analysis. It was also intended, in line with the aims of CEN, that the programme would enhance the students' capacity to help others in their own communities to make an effective contribution to social and economic regeneration – a central notion in the (subsequent) Labour Government's thinking. The Government 'want to develop local partnerships and build the capacity of local communities to take part in regeneration initiatives' (Department of Environment, Transport and Regions, 1997). We were confident that we were contributing purposefully to this agenda.

The programme

The programme developed as a modular arrangement, involving part-time study, validated by the university. The framework was drawn up through a series of regular meetings throughout 1995, with the departmental administrator providing essential knowledge of the University's systems and procedures through which our curriculum design would have to be steered. The process of curriculum development was far from straightforward and raised as many questions as it answered – but then this is a reflection of the programme itself, which encourages challenge, investigation and critical analysis.

As would the students themselves, the working party had to look critically at notions of 'community', 'development' and 'enterprise', to identify appropriate concepts and contexts, which would form the core of the programme. We found, as Raymond Williams (1976) indicated a quarter of a century earlier, a plethora of definitions, around which a number of positive images had grown. 'Community' – a word which continues to resonate through our everyday lives, a totem of how we would like our lives to be, as opposed to the less than perfect reality. The notion of community therefore retains an enduring appeal even though it becomes a somewhat empty vessel into which we can pour our images of the good life (Newby 1993:xi).

Similarly, we found an often uncritical, and somewhat high-minded view of community education:

> In the beginning was the word and the word was community education, and there arose many prophets willing to interpret the word, but few to deny its veracity. So that community education became a self-fulfilling prophecy, for its tenets were not written down on tablets of stone handed down from on high. And since no man knew what either community or education meant as separate creeds, when they were joined together their offspring multiplied exceedingly, offering diverse avenues to salvation. (Scottish Education Department 1977)

Six years on, it is clear that the overwhelmingly 'positive' connotations implied by these concepts, and the responsibility attached to them in practice, have tremendous significance in the rhetoric of the Learning Society and New Labour. In the words of Tony Blair:

> At the heart of my beliefs is the idea of community ... My argument ... is that the renewal of community is the answer to the challenges of the modern world ... with a new agenda of opportunity for all in a changing world ... the ever-turning kaleidoscope of change ... We take the best of the past but celebrate the new ... the old and the new together... Community cannot be rebuilt without opportunity ... shaped by the values of opportunity for all and responsibility from all. (Blair 2000)

In Tony Blair's now infamous speech to the Women's Institute in June 2000 he mentioned 'community' 18 times.

In the context of so much rhetoric – 'politicians talk continually of the magic word community. We must have more of one, we must be in one. We must strengthen a sense of community to cure all the assorted ills of society … [and] one person's idea of a blissful community is the next person's nightmare (Moore 1994) – we wanted students from local communities to critically examine these kinds of meanings in the light of their own experience and alternative visions, especially when community has come to mean 'the absence of'. 'So community development really means the absence of actual development; community councils are forums without any powers; community schools and community care betray the absence of proper provision – and community politics mean no identifiable policies' (McConaghy 1995). And when 'they can't bugger off' also illustrates a somewhat cynical definition of 'community roots' as supplied by more than one local activist (Pearce 1993:135).

The first challenge for our working party was to translate some of these ideas into the language and structures that the University would recognise, understand *and* acknowledge. I was not sure how the modules and the certificate framework would be received by the University's validation committees, given the substantive and methodological distinctiveness, but in the event all necessary approvals for a Certificate in HE were given. The validation process was completed in autumn 1995 and I invited the CEN members on the working party to sit on the management committee and examination board for the new qualification.

In the first year, students were all affiliated to and sponsored by CEN, but it was then decided to 'open' the programme to volunteers and paid workers from other community groups and projects, to community development officers employed by local authorities and to individuals interested in the ideas of community education and development and lifelong learning. For example, recruitment was particularly strong from a women-only women's studies programme I had established in 1994, which had originally been non-accredited and which was subsequently validated by the Regional Open College network – reflecting, I suppose, what providers like to define as 'progression'.

From 1995 to 1999 the modules in the 'CEN' pathway were linked to others at Certificate level (1) and Diploma level (2). For example, there were a number of modules focusing on women in society in historical and contemporary terms. There was also a Diploma in Adult and Community Education. Eventually, in March 1999, the programme was revised to form a new part-time BA with Honours in Lifelong Learning and Community Studies. By this time there were a small number of students ready to progress to the final degree level (3) modules.

However, in October 1999, a few weeks into the new term and the first year of the fully-fledged degree, the University announced unilaterally that the degree and its new sister degree, a part-time BA with Honours in Social Studies, would not, in the event, be offered. The programmes would be retained until the end of the academic year, when the Centre for Life Long Learning would also close as a teaching department. As I write, there is the possibility that parts of the programme will be incorporated into a new part-time degree, focusing on community work, offered by the Community and Youth Work section of the Sociology Department. The decision – unexpected and ill-timed – has left staff and students bewildered, upset and angry. The reasons which have emerged – in stages and with some ambiguity – centre around matters of quality assurance and the intention to transfer responsibility to mainstream departments. Only a tiny minority of departments has been prepared to accept this challenge. Among the many consequences is the perception of students that their achievements to date are not valued or recognised by the University. In the process the 'loss' of the past has been as painful to accept by those of us involved as the uncertainty of the future.

The lessons

So what are the lessons of five years of this initiative in widening participation? The course team learned a lot about teaching, learning and assessment in the context of widening provision and the lifelong learning agenda (Whaley forthcoming). Problematising the issue of experience – which has played such a fundamental role in the programme – offers insights into the contested notions of student-centred learning, the nature of knowledge and the relationship between pedagogy and practice (Whaley 2000a). Like 'community' and 'education', 'experience' is generally seen as 'a good thing'. The notion has been related to education in various ways and is now clearly attached to the agendas of lifelong learning and Higher Education. Certainly we saw it as being important in the programme in terms of admission, teaching and learning, and assessment. 'Experience' is often the currency of widening participation. But there's the problem. As we found, it is not the recognised currency of academia and there is rarely an equitable exchange rate. Furthermore, 'experience' is not just 'personal' – there are 'the lessons learned, sometimes much more painfully and tragically, from experiences that we are subject to as members of different cultural, economic and gendered environments … For those at the margins of political, economic and social power, the notion that they 'are what they have done' sounds more like a slap in the face than a term of encouragement' (Fraser 1995:xii).

The group – students and tutors – became, in some sense, an exemplar of the pedagogy and the discourse. We lived out some of the issues - which had the advantage of bringing relevant, current experience – including the decision by the university to close the course and close the department – to illuminate the conceptual and discursive and to face the challenge of using it in developing analytical frameworks. The distinction between education and training and the relationship with regeneration and social and economic change were played out in theory and practice (Whaley 1998). We engaged with the idea of 'really useful knowledge' – an important part of the participation question and one to which feminism has made a significant contribution (Thompson 1997; Barr 1999).

Although gender may no longer be widely regarded as a category denoting disadvantage in widening participation, gender remains a relevant analytical model and women are still demonstrably discriminated against as staff and students in HE (Whaley 2000b). Not only the treatment of women, but also 'Feminism still has something to offer us – something far richer than the simplistic gender-polarising polemic its opponents would have us see it' (Barr 2000).

The significance of the women's movement to the ideological development of continuing education is well documented (Thompson 1997; Benn *et al* 1998). Radical continuing education has always endorsed the link between popular education and social movements. The kind of feminist model of education, towards which so many of us in continuing education have been working, is perhaps best encapsulated by Smyth when she says it is 'open, empowering, co-operative, egalitarian and change-orientated – even in higher education' (Smyth 1998:11). The model is one that is both responsive and proactive.

Our initiative also demonstrated quite clearly that the issue of demand and need is often seen too simplistically. First, for need to become demand (for which educational institutions want to see hard evidence, before committing their resources) the provider has to *do* something. It is widely recognised that the missing link in many initiatives to widen participation and promote lifelong learning is the absence of sound, accessible, independent advice and guidance for adults. We did try to offer this, from open community-based information sessions, as a complement to the enquiry and applicant stages, and throughout the period of study. But what we could not do was to make an informed and secure pledge of future/continuing opportunities because of the continual reviews by the University of part-time provision and of the department's role. 'If you build it, they will come' represents an act of faith which unfortunately isn't easily realised outside of Hollywood.

Second, a needs-meeting perspective assumes that the appreciation and articulation of needs are somehow not distorted or precluded by previous educational experiences or the circumstances of class, ethnicity and gender. At its worst it is rooted in the belief that the meeters know best what is appropriate. We discussed this question often in the course modules as one of a number of tensions – as with 'student-centred learning' – which students contested, drawing on and applying it to their own experience.

From all of the evidence available to us we came to the conclusion that widening participation is about outreach *and* inreach. 'Departments of Continuing Education should play an important role in the development of equal opportunities in their university. Traditionally, they have reached out beyond the campus to ensure links with their local community, and have reached in to the university to influence the institution's responsiveness specifically to mature students and more generally to the local community at large' (UCACE 1990:7). As Leicester (1993) has pointed out in respect of anti-racist education, continuing education departments have significant experience of both inreach work across the university and collaborative outreach. This provides a potential 'richness of experience' which Chris Duke has described as 'a dowry that university adult education brings to its parent institution' (Leicester 1993:11). In practice it may be that adult and continuing education departments have been better at outreach in terms of impact and precarious sustainability than they have in inreach; the experiences that Duke (1988) identified as being about

> dialogue, negotiated curriculum, valuing and using students' experience; insights into the experience of curriculum renewal less restricted by the tramlines of departments and their disciplines, more open to other orderings of knowledge derived from life and work experience; a capacity for creating and sustaining external relationships via partnerships, networks, support systems and resource centres; flexibility and lateral thinking, in respect of time, place and mode of delivery. (Duke (1998):13)

are unwanted gifts, their quality questioned, their currency debased. In addition, the unsupported fear that such initiatives are a threat to quality has been given spurious legitimacy by the recent decision of the QAA to conduct a subject review. This has persuaded some universities to abolish continuing education provision altogether as being too difficult and different to manage and assure. It begs the question, of course, about whether the QAA foresaw this consequence, given their avowed interest in the kind of innovative development that continuing education has provided. While awaiting the answer I, like Smyth (1998)

> have learned that there is still serious ideological and systemic resistance, in terms of policy development and state funding mechanisms, as well as within academic institutions, to innovation in almost any sphere. However, resistance is particularly marked when it comes to understanding the meaning of the challenges posed by the pressure for fully validated Continuing Education programmes and increasing numbers of adult students. That challenge – to higher education values, structures, pedagogy and curricula – has repercussions for the ways in which people can live their lives, and it must be seriously confronted. (p 12)

Implicit in lifelong learning is the blessing of opportunity, and the burden of responsibility, for change which is placed on the learner. 'Innovation is demanded of individuals, whereas institutions are simply left to continue to behave as they always have' (Chisholm 1998).

Undoubtedly there is both a substantive and methodological challenge to universities from programmes like ours. Their interdisciplinarity sits uncomfortably with(out) the discipline framed system. The interrelationship of students' experience with institutional structures and values is one that will change both – a prospect that causes some universities to marshall the forces of resistance and some students to reject the risk of disjuncture and alienation from the familiar. But in order for widening participation to mean anything, there has to be change.

Change is also the focus of the learning society. But what, if anything, has changed by converting adult education and widening participation into lifelong learning? It seemed that the international shift in emphasis towards lifelong learning in the late 1990s was moving adults from the margins to the mainstream of educational policy (University of Surrey 1997). I was one of many adult educators who felt that our time had come. In fact it now seems to be more like the Dickensian version of the best of times and the worst of times. HE is not actually visible in much of the recent policy and rhetoric, which raises questions about the priorities for resources and resolve. The lifelong learning agenda has increased awareness of the learning divide between the educational haves and have–nots – in relation to adults as well as to children. It has also focused attention on 'young adults' between 18 and 25 years old, relatively few of whom have been involved in university adult education to date. And we now have a set of learning beatitudes, created by a new kind of missionary, the learning professionals (Longworth and Davies 1996:24):

> These are the new evangelists of learning who expatiate on the 9 'learning beatitudes'… these beatitudes are a set of worthy propositions which claim that 'learning pays', 'learning empowers' and 'learning civilises' etc … it is the safe middle class view of learning, propounded by those who have succeeded in our formerly elite system of education and whose learning has indeed paid off handsomely for them. But they tend to know nothing, for instance, of the 100,000 unemployed people who are studying on benefits in FE colleges (Kennedy 1997), a fifth of whom are forced each year to withdraw from their course to take short-term unskilled jobs. (Coffield 1997:3)

And yet I find myself wanting to believe that education can still 'make a difference' – in full awareness of the student who had to withdraw from our course because he was 'sentenced' – as he said – to three months sending off his CV at the Job Club; and of the women students who had to withdraw because they had neither independent income nor independent entitlement to financial assistance. I do believe … but not blindly. 'Continuing education (CE) has always been distinguished by and infused with a value system bearing something of the evangelical within it' (Law 1998:59). And, as Thompson suggests, if encouraging people to learn is posited against the continuing exclusion of reluctant and older learners which Chris Woodhead defends in terms of 'their free choice' to live in 'ignorance and squalor' – whose side would you take? (Thompson 2000:8).

It seems to me that the real issue is the way in which 'the discourse of lifelong learning has become disconnected from the discourse of social purpose adult education, despite the material reality of poverty and the evidence of continuing social polarisation in contemporary British society' (Martin 1999:181). I was struck in re-reading Midwinter's (1971) analysis of educational inequalities recently how little things have changed in 30 years:

> During the last few years it has been demonstrated over and over that equality of opportunity without equality of circumstances is largely a sham. The imbalance of educational attainment and social background is now well-documented … As it stands the educational system offers the same product to all. This is in trite terms, a ladder for all to climb, but as only a few obviously can reach the top, it is in part an education for frustration. … The rules of the game are indubitably the same for everyone; it's just that some of the participants are nobbled. This is like a football match with regulation size pitch and orthodox laws but between Manchester United and a team blindfolded and with its legs tied together. Even Manchester City could handle that kind of opposition. (p 2)

It is not enough to simply 'adjust' – or tweak – the education system here and there as a response to the needs of the disadvantaged. Instead there must be a real commitment to socio-economic change. 'Society has called the tune. It has embraced equality of opportunity as an ideal, but it has not accepted the socio-economic implications' (Midwinter 1971:7). Ideally, the lifelong learning agenda will incorporate this understanding, demonstrating that 'lifelong learning requires a holistic approach, organised from the students' perspective' (Wagner 1998).

So where does all of this leave us? I feel reasonably confident that the opportunities offered by the initiative we developed reached women and men living in local communities who were hitherto excluded from HE by all the well-documented barriers. Although our 'intervention' in their lives was brief, I hope the consequences will be positive, long term and radical for the students and for those with whom they share their critical thinking and informed practice. But did the programme and, importantly, the process that produced it penetrate the academy in any meaningful way? I am struck by the question Fraser posed in her foreword to *Empowerment Through Experiential Learning*, 'Is it possible that we practitioners may also be unwitting agents of the very oppression and limitations we seek to transcend by our good practice?' (Mulligan and Griffin 1992).

It is tempting – and defeatist – to feel that in raising and dashing aspirations, challenging the University to accommodate a difference too many, 'being successful', we became the means through which the academy reasserted its old position that 'anyone can participate in what we offer here' – so long as they can demonstrate their suitability according to the canon. So long as they accept the hierarchical nature of subject knowledge. So long as their progress can be measured by the book. Most significantly, so long as their diversity is expressed in 'appropriate' ways.

On the other hand, the issues raised by this initiative *have* now been articulated and, if politicians, Funding Councils, academics and practitioners are serious about widening participation in HE, they will continue to be so. In his speech to the Association of University Teachers about the role of the universities, the Secretary of State for Education spelt out (his) 'determination that the entrenched exclusion of large sections of the population from higher education must end and that the sector must become a force for social justice' (Blunkett 2000). But we will all have to take up the challenges that this involves. A fundamental question is the degree to which we should be trying to make systemic change in HE generally or simply trying to encourage small parts of the sector to adopt the social equity agenda. It seems to me that the only way the latter has any credibility is if the sector as a whole then accepts all parts with equity, foregoing the present hierarchical league tables of 'excellence' and the inflexible way in which this is measured. And this at a time when the super league is already in place. Durham is part of the Russell Group that seeks to set itself apart from the rest as 'selecting' rather than 'recruiting' universities. What then should we do? Bus the 'disadvantaged' out of our area, to the nearest university of inclusion?

There is also, I believe, a need to examine the relationship between academic freedom and accountability, because it seems to me we have accepted the former rather uncritically and avoided the latter when we could get away with it. It is vital that we retain the freedom to challenge and oppose, and should do so with vigour and commitment, when required: 'What is also important is that we, as adult educators and facilitators of learning, are agents of change, as well as the objects/victims' (Whaley forthcoming).

But this should be accompanied by a greater sense of the responsibility this imposes, and nothing of the god-like self-justification and detachment that ivory towers seem to produce. Widening participation has to be about justice, equity, opportunity and progressive social change. It is about changing the balance of power that rests with those who do the excluding, as well as allowing the excluded to come in. As such, it can only be achieved through partnerships and collaboration, based on mutual trust and respect, and some recognition that ideas can be contested and that practice can be open to negotiation. Among other things, 'a curricular focus within adult learning needs to take account of a lifelong learning process which takes place on multiple sites, acknowledges different identities, celebrates cultural diversity and makes room for all voices (Usher *et al* 1997:49).

Universities must be prepared to accommodate and learn from difference, to accept that diversity can coexist with quality; rigour with innovation, standards with equivalence, and that 'full-time equivalence' acts as a deficit model of HE which makes participation for part-time students very difficult. Widening participation is not just about individual opportunity but also about collective social change. Of course, it's also a question of power, and the university holds the trump card: it controls the HE validation process. But the community/ voluntary sector is far from powerless. Apart from the richness and diversity of culture, experience and expertise, it plays a significant part in central and devolved government policy and is often the crucial element in cross-sectoral funding bids (Whaley 2000c).

As well as access and participation, it is clear that quality and standards are also the engines of government policy. Politicians will have to address the tensions and antagonisms caused by the way these have been positioned as mutually exclusive – quality versus equality. They will also need to decide what role – if any – HE will play in non-award bearing courses. In moving from the margins to the mainstream there can be as much loss as gain. The danger is that in the process all that was distinctive about the provision may be lost, including the all-important questions about purpose, participation and power. Furthermore, the interstices, the creative spaces in organisations, can get reduced (Scott 1996); 'the cracks in the superstructures' (Thompson 1997) can become filled.

Those of us who are in a position to do so need to sustain, through research and critical commentary, a democratic view of education based on social inclusion, dialogue and the expectation of progressive social change and widening participation – to extend the boundaries of knowledge and understanding across the academy and the community; and to create spaces of opportunity.

And yes, I think I still do believe initiatives like ours can effect change, but keeping the faith has never been harder. Despite all of the evidence to the contrary we have not managed to persuade those with power and (vested) interests to defend that widening participation is not a dilution of the purity of quality. The message is powerfully persuasive and can lead to a kind of Marxist paradox (Groucho not Karl: who would want to belong to a club that lets me in?). You are not worthy: I am not worthy.

If raising the questions is the first part of a process of change, then there is real hope for the university and for the communities that embrace it. But what a long way there is still to go.

References

Barr J (1999) 'Women, adult education, and really useful knowledge', in Crowther J, Martin I, and Shaw M, *Popular Education and Social Movements in Scotland Today*, Leicester: NIACE

Barr J (2000) Letter to the Editor, *Adults Learning*,Vol 11 No 8 April, Leicester: NIACE

Benn R, Elliott J, and Whaley P, (eds) (1998) *Educating Rita and Her Sisters*, Leicester: NIACE

Benyon H, Hudson R, Lewis J, Sadler D and Townshend A (1989) '"It's all falling apart here": coming to terms with the failure in Teesside', in Cooke P (ed), *Localities: the changing face of urban Britain*, London: Unwin Hyman

Beynon H, Hudson R and Sadler D (1994) *A Place Called Teesside: a locality in a global economy* Edinburgh: Edinburgh University Press

Blair T (2000) Speech to the Women's Institute, 7 June

Blunkett D (2000) Keynote speech to the National Conference of the Association of University Teachers, 10 May

Bryson B (1996) *Notes from a Small Island* London: Black Swan

Chisholm L (1998) 'From systems to networks: the reconstruction of youth transitions in Europe', in Heinz W (ed), *New Passages Between Education and Employment in a Comparative Life Course Perspective* Cambridge: Cambridge University Press

Coffield F (1997) 'Nine learning fallacies and their replacement by a national strategy for lifelong learning', in Coffield F (ed), *A National Strategy for Lifelong Learning*, Newcastle: University of Newcastle

Cole B and MacDonald R (1990) 'From new vocationalism to the culture of enterprise', in Edwards R, Sieminski S and Zeldin D (eds), *Adult learners, Education and Training: learning through life 2*, London: Routledge in association with the Open University

Community Enterprise Network (CEN)(1993) membership form

Department of Environment, Transport and Regions (1997) press release 11, November

Duke C (1988) 'The future shape of continuing education and universities: an inaugural lecture', Papers in Continuing Education No 1, University of Warwick

Fraser W (1995*) Learning From Experience: empowerment or incorporation*, Leicester: NIACE

HEFCE (1997) report R/297

HEFCE (1998) circular 98/35

Holmes J and Storrie T C (1995) *Consett: A Case Study of Education and Unemployment*, Further Education Unit

Hudson R (1990) 'Trying to revive an infant Hercules: the rise and fall of local authority modernisation and policies on Teesside' in Harloe M, Pickvance C G and Urry J (eds*), Place, Policy and Politics: do localities matter?*, London: Unwin Hyman

Law C (1998) 'Accrediting women, normalising women', in Benn R, Elliott J and Whaley P (eds), *Educating Rita and Her Sisters: women and continuing education*, Leicester: NIACE

Leicester M (1993) 'Race for a change', in *Continuing and Higher Education*, Buckingham Open University

Longworth N and Davies W K (1996) *Lifelong Learning*, London: Kogan Page

Mannion G, Dockrell R and Sankey K(1998) *The University's Difficulty in Encouraging Community Partnership: a conversation about 'knowledge' and 'participation' as contested constructs*, Proceedings of the UACE 1997 Annual Conference

Martin I (1999) *Stretching the Discourse*, in Oliver P (ed), *Lifelong Learning and Continuing Education: what is a learning society?* Aldershot: Ashgate

McConaghy D (1995) Letter to the Editor, *Guardian* 17 February

McGivney V (1997) 'Adult participation in learning: can we change the pattern?', in Coffield F (ed), *A National Strategy for Lifelong Learning*, Newcastle: University of Newcastle

Midwinter E (1971) *Educational Priority Areas: the philosophic question*, Liverpool: Liverpool Educational Priority Area Project

Moore S (1994) 'Mooreover', *Guardian* 1 December

Mudie G (1999) Conversation between the Minister for Lifelong Learning and Professor Bob Fryer, cited by Fryer, CEDAR 8th International Conference, March 2000, University of Warwick

Mulligan J and Griffin C (eds) (1992) *Empowerment Through Experiential Learning: explorations of good practice*, London: Kogan Page

Newby H (1993) 'Foreword', in Crow G and Allan G, *Community Life: an Introduction to local social relations*, London: Harvester Wheatsheaf

Pearce J (1993) *At the Heart of the Community Economy: community economy in a changing world* London: Calouste Gulbenkian Foundation

Scott P (1996) *The Future of Continuing Education*, Proceedings of the UACE 1996 Annual Conference, University of Leeds

Scottish Education Department (1977) Community Education Occasional paper No 6, Edinburgh: HMSO

Smyth A (1998) *Moving Forward in Strength and Solidarity: forging links between university and community-based women's studies initiatives in Ireland*, Proceedings of the UACE 1997 Annual Conference

Taylor R (1999) *Lifelong Learning Policy in England*, UACE occasional paper

Tees Valley Statistics (2000) Tees Valley: Tees Valley Joint Strategy Unit

Thompson J (1997) *Words in Edgeways: radical learning for social change*, Leicester: NIACE

Thompson J (2000) 'Chris Woodhead! What is he like?', *Adults Learning* Vol 11 No 8, April, Leicester: NIACE

University Council for Adult and Continuing Education (1990) *Report of the Working Party on Continuing Education Provision for the Minority Ethnic Communities*, occasional paper no 2, Warwick: UCACE

University of Durham (1997a) Internal briefing document

University of Durham (1997b) University College Stockton mission statement

University of Surrey (1997) publicity leaflet – International Conference: Lifelong learning: reality, rhetoric and public policy, July

Usher R, Bryant I and Johnston R (1997) *Adult Education and the Postmodern Challenge*, London: Routledge

Wagner L (1998) 'How to generate that bigger picture', *Guardian*, 31 March

Whaley P (1998) '*Is training a valuable tool to fight against social exclusion?*', unpublished conference paper, L'Exclusion Sociale: Les Reponses Europeenes de l'Economie: La Formation en Question, Universite de Toulouse / Pole Universite Europeen de Toulouse, September

Whaley P (2000a) 'The problem with experience: living the issues and learning from each other', unpublished conference paper, CEDAR 8th International Conference, March, University of Warwick

Whaley P (2000b) 'Women and higher education: the good news and the bad news', in *Adults Learning*, Vol 11 No 7, March, Leicester: NIACE

Whaley P (2000c) 'Learning for Life: vision, value and the voluntary sector', RSA lecture, May 17, RSA North at Dean Clough

Whaley P (forthcoming) *The Experience of a Lifetime? A case study of theory and practice in adult and community education*, Proceedings of the 1998 International Conference of Lifelong Learning, University of Bremen

Wicks M (1999) 'Keynote Speech: Making it work: strategies for learning in the voluntary sector', RSA / Project 2001 Conference, 16 November, London

Williamson R (1976) *Key Words*, London: Fontana

10 Widening participation through Action Learning in the Community

Marjorie Mayo and Anan Collymore

Introduction

Adult educators have long contested that 'there is no such thing as a neutral education process' (Thompson 1980:26). So, by implication, far from representing an unproblematic programme for educational development and change, the 'widening participation' agenda raises a number of key questions, questions about who is to participate in what types of learning – and why. As Schuller (1998) has argued, in the face of the 'suspiciously unchallengeable' consensus which seems to pervade so much of the debate on the 'learning society' more generally, it is important to maintain a critical perspective (p 11). Within these discussions, as Edwards (1997) has pointed out, there are competing discourses, some of which are more powerful – and better placed to construct their discourses as truer and more valid than others (Edwards 1997).

In Britain, and indeed in Europe, official discourses have focused upon lifelong learning in general and widening participation more specifically as mechanisms for promoting economic competitiveness, 'putting jobs, skills and employability at the heart of Europe' (DfEE 1998). For individuals, this has been translated in terms of the importance of taking responsibility for his/her own education and training, to ensure each individual's future employability in an increasingly fragmented and casualised labour market. There are links here with New Labour agendas for welfare reform, from welfare to work, from dependency to individual responsibility.

While these have been the most powerful discourses, however, they have been and continue to be contested and challenged. Learning is not only to be valued in strictly economic terms. Even within official discourses, there have been wider interpretations. In his introduction to the Green Paper *The Learning Age* the Secretary of State, David Blunkett, reflected that learning was also to be valued for its wider contribution to active citizenship. As the Fryer Report had argued, support should be given to projects and initiatives which build capacity, strengthen voluntary organisation and contribute to social as well as economic regeneration, recognising the importance of critical reflection and creative initiative in strengthening democracy and promoting community development (Fryer 1997).

Effectively these arguments support the case for initiatives such as Action Learning in the Community (ALIC) – the subject of this chapter – initiatives which promote learning for active citizenship *as well as* for economic competitiveness, enhancing group learning and support *as well as* individual employability. ALIC's rationale is precisely that this is a social as well as an education inclusion project.

The chapter takes the form of a dialogue between the two authors – the project evaluator and the project worker – who have been working together on ALIC. In the first section the evaluator raises a series of questions about where and how to locate ALIC within the context of current debates and about how to take account of existing knowledge about the barriers to widening participation. This sets the framework for the project worker's account of ALIC's specific aims and objectives and the aims and achievements of ALIC participants so far.

Although this is still a relatively new initiative lessons are already beginning to emerge, as the evaluator concludes in the final section. There are implications for policies and for mainstream educational provision. There are also issues emerging about the nature of the changes which need to be made and who is to make these changes if there is to be some serious 'joined-up thinking' about tackling the institutional barriers to wider access. The chapter closes with the project worker's reflections on some of the opportunities and challenges to be addressed in ALIC's second and third years.

The Project evaluator
Agendas for widening participation?

'Widening participation' raises underlying questions – questions about participation in learning for what, as well as for whom (see Table 11.1). Is the purpose to transmit and reinforce existing norms and values or to promote critical reflection, leading to challenges and social change – or both? Is the prime objective the attainment of 'useful knowledge' – instrumental skills and training – or 'really useful knowledge', the knowledge which enables people to make sense of the hardships and oppression they experience in their daily lives, and to develop strategies for greater equality and social justice (Johnson 1979; Hughes 1995)? Is the focus primarily economic or is the focus wide enough to include social, cultural and political aims and objectives? Is there the space for education for active citizenship, and is there room for the learning needs of those who may not be actively seeking paid employment, at least in the immediate future, if indeed at all – people with major caring responsibilities or people recovering from mental illness, for example? And is the emphasis upon individual advancement alone or is there also room for group support and collective benefits for the local community?[1]

Do programmes reinforce learners' self-perceptions as deficient individuals (perceptions which may have been reinforced by previous negative experiences of education), empty vessels waiting to be filled with relevant knowledge? Or do programmes strengthen participants' self-confidence and self-esteem, building upon their experiential learning as individuals and as members of groups and communities? These are questions which have been central to educational debates over the years (Bowles and Gintis 1979; Crowther *et al* 1999; Edwards 1997; Freire 1972, Alexander and Martin 1995). How will ALIC be located within these debates?

In addition, in the case of 'widening participation' projects, there are specific questions to be addressed about the relationships between one-off projects, voluntary and community-sector initiatives and statutory mainstream provision. To what extent are 'widening participation' initiatives mutually reinforcing, strengthening creativity and building capacity within and between communities? And to what extent are they pointing the way towards the necessary changes in the structure and delivery of mainstream education and training services more generally, to make them more accessible to under-represented groups?

Or conversely, to what extent are such initiatives effectively substituting for such wider changes, while being seen to be 'doing something' about the presenting problems? Is 'projectitis' even exacerbating conflicts within and between communities as they find themselves competing for their share of scarce and scarcer resources? These are, of course, questions which apply more generally, across a range of current policy interventions, special programmes to address inequalities in health, housing and economic development as well as in education at every level. How might any of these questions apply to ALIC?

Table 10.1 Differing Agendas

Domesticating agendas	Transformatory agendas
'Useful knowledge'/ knowledge and skills for survival	'Really useful knowledge' /critical reflection geared towards progressive social change
Lifelong learning which focuses on economic competitiveness to the *exclusion* of learning for citizenship/ learning for those outside the paid workforce	Lifelong learning which includes learning for active citizenship and democracy and learning for 'life' and leisure as well as learning for paid employment
Learning for individual advancement	Learning for collective/group development as well as for individual advancement
Projects based upon 'deficit' models	Projects which build upon participants' experiential learning, strengthening self-confidence and self-esteem
Projects which lead to competition for scarce resources	Projects which build solidarity and mutual support within and between communities and between communities and educational providers
One-off projects for widening access	Projects which also identify structural barriers to widening access, demonstrating ways of tackling these

Finding the space for innovation and creativity?

To argue that there are differing and competing agendas is by no means to imply that these are mutually exclusive, however. Projects like ALIC will not necessarily be confined neatly within the space of either agenda. On the contrary, in fact, there is no inherent reason why people should not have economic as well as social, cultural and political goals, just as they may combine individual with collective aspirations. Individuals may and do aim to improve their employability through learning while sharing group aspirations for collective community benefits. Can projects like ALIC be sufficiently flexible to meet funders' requirements while providing the space for innovation and creativity, for people to pursue their varying agendas, as these agendas develop and change over time?

On the basis of her experiences of teaching a Scotvec module on a WEA project for unemployed adults, Beveridge (1999) reflected that students may be delighted by their success in obtaining a recognised qualification, whether or not this represented a step towards paid employment. The key problem, as Beveridge saw this, was rather that particular individuals, such as older women without vocational goals, might be denied learning opportunities simply because they did not meet funders' specifications in relation to future employability. Beveridge concluded, nevertheless, that despite the inherent dilemmas it had proved possible to provide a course which combined 'liberal' educational values with instrumental objectives. The course in question offered communications skills – key skills in terms of employability – through democratic educational processes, including the development of critical textual readings and reflections on issues of class, race and gender in Scotland, past and present – issues which were also central to active citizenship and social inclusion. Spaces had been identified and utilised creatively.

These questions, dilemmas and innovative possibilities are all potentially relevant to action learning in the community (ALIC). ALIC sets out to enhance unemployed people's employability through building upon their experiential learning in the community as active citizens, valuing and accrediting this learning, as well as supporting the participants, both as individuals and as a group, while they undertake academic programmes of study at Goldsmiths, University of London, Lewisham College and Community Education Lewisham, the local educational resources committed to 'widening participation'. As the project worker explains, in the following section, ALIC was set up to identify and to address the barriers, both institutional and individual barriers which hold unemployed people back, building upon existing knowledge about the barriers to widening participation. In the words of one of the originators of the project, ALIC was to be a gadfly, a stimulus to institutional change, promoting more 'joined up thinking' on policies and practices for widening access to higher education.

Identifying and overcoming the barriers to participation

Adults face a series of well-known barriers, both situational and motivational. As a number of studies have already identified, there are structural and educational obstacles such as patchy provision, difficulties of access, lack of information, guidance and support in the community as well as in colleges, inflexible pre-educational requirements and colleges which are insufficiently open, welcoming and user friendly (McGivney 1991; 1997). Adults face material barriers, such as lack of money – 'finance', *The Learning Divide* demonstrated, was 'the most important barrier for younger adults, particularly for 20–24 year olds' inhibiting them from taking up learning opportunities (Sargant *et al* 1997:x). Social class, *The Learning Divide Revisited* demonstrates, 'continues to be the key determinant in understanding participation in learning' (Sargant 2000) with the lowest participation rates among unskilled working-class people on limited incomes, particularly those not working. In addition to structural and material barriers, these are the people who are also most likely to face barriers arising from previous negative experiences (Maguire *et al* 1993). The people who are least likely to participate are those with poor previous educational experiences, who lack confidence in their ability to learn, with low expectations of the possible benefits of education (McGivney 1997). Such low expectations may, of course, relate only too clearly to the actual realities in their communities. As Sargeant's research into the learning divide has illustrated, lack of employment opportunities in places such as Northern Ireland and Liverpool very understandably reduces people's motivation for learning as a strategy to improve their employability (Sargant *et al* 1997; 2000). In addition to tackling all the other barriers there need to be genuine opportunities for gaining employment which will provide a fair living wage.

While the evidence about the barriers which need to be addressed is potentially daunting, there is more encouraging evidence about the positive features which can be built upon and strengthened too. In particular, people – especially women – in the very areas which have been most disadvantaged have been developing self-confidence and acquiring knowledge and skills through their involvement in the community as active citizens. People can and do learn in a variety of ways from their experiences in the voluntary and community sectors (Elsdon *et al* 1995).

The connections between adult learning and community and social action have been clearly demonstrated, both in Britain and internationally (Crowther *et al* 1999; Foley 1999). Engagement in social and community action can help people to unlearn dominant oppressive discourses, learning that can transform power relations, through building people's confidence and capacity to handle change (Tuckett 1999). Informal learning in the community plays a crucial role, enabling people, both as individuals and as groups, to develop improved self-confidence and self-esteem and improved quality of life, raising aspirations as well as increasing knowledge and skills (McGivney 1999). For some, this is the trigger for further progression. It is also important to recognise and accept, however, that for others the benefits will be in terms of people's personal lives and in their community involvement (Scottish Office 1996). As the next section explains, ALIC started from the importance of building upon precisely these potential strengths, recognising and validating people's learning from experiences of active citizenship, as well as tackling the structural, educational and material barriers to their participation in more formal learning opportunities.

The Project worker

ALIC in context

South-east London, where ALIC is based, has experienced major processes of industrial restructuring with massive job losses in manufacturing, dock and dock-related industries over recent decades. Local working-class communities have experienced dislocation and fragmentation, tensions which have been compounded for black and ethnic minority communities by experiences of racism, both institutional and direct.

Lewisham is a mixed-class, poly-cultural borough which has been the focal point of a series of urban regeneration funding initiatives. Despite the history of social dislocation related to economic restructuring, the borough is currently characterised by active voluntary and community sectors. Both individuals and groups have learnt from their experiences of participating in regeneration initiatives in recent years. This, in summary, provides the historical and social environment in which ALIC operates. There are major structural and motivational barriers to widening participation to be overcome, but there are also important strengths to build upon in local organisations and local communities.

There have already been initiatives which have sought to widen participation through offering to lighten the financial burden on those returning to education. DfEE initiatives like Access funds, and waivers of tuition fees have improved the situation for further education and now higher education benefit claimants. Not only do these initiatives offer practical support to students already struggling on low incomes; they can also give students the sense that educational institutions and governing bodies are working in their favour and providing useful and practical support. But from our experiences of working with students on low incomes, especially those who have been out of paid work for some time, it is clear that these initiatives have been insufficient. There is evidence of greater need and continuing barriers to be overcome (both situational and motivational). The following description of ALIC, and the environment within which it is working, illustrates some of the needs which have been expressed through peoples' interactions with ALIC, as participants.

ALIC's aims

In March 1999 ALIC was set up to work with people who were unemployed and wanting to make positive changes in their lives. Headed by The Learning from Experience Trust, a proposal was put forward in response to the Government's concerns regarding the limitations in accessibility to higher education for socially excluded groups. We wanted to influence institutional changes and to develop coherent policies and practices for widening access and social inclusion. The Learning from Experience Trust (LET) has a long track record of developing programmes and projects which seek to rebalance the inequity between people with qualifications and those with experience alone. The Trust's mission is summarised in the following statement:

> The Trust's work for the last 15 years has been built on the central idea that people learn throughout their daily lives, and not solely when they are engaged in formal education. We have two main purposes: to develop tools and approaches that help individuals and groups learn more from their life experience and make good use of what they know and to ensure that learning from experience is recognised and valued by society – including by government, educational institutions, employers, community and voluntary organisations, as well as by the public.

Funded by the DfEE and working in partnership with Goldsmiths College, University of London, Lewisham College and the Community Education Department of Lewisham Borough Council, ALIC has taken on the challenging task of recruiting people who will commit themselves to a learning programme using a combination of action learning through community activity and learning from experience-based teaching.

The target is to recruit and work with 45 people by February 2002. The learning programme is participant-focused and has been developed to enable them to build on their skills in communication, learning how to learn and learning in work-based settings. The overall aim of the project is to demonstrate new ways to widen access to higher education for the 45 participants as a means of opening up more fulfilling and better-rewarded career opportunities. This is being achieved through the learning programme, through voluntary activity as community activists, through individual and group support and through personal guidance (offered in relation to educational and career pathways). Participants' employability levels are to be effectively increased by supporting their educational pathways into higher education. This support is provided in three main areas:

- group solidarity – via monthly group activities which focus upon group work, promoting understanding of group processes and building trust amongst participants and facilitators/tutors

- experiential learning – covered in learning through and learning from experience, through voluntary activity in the community, critical reflection and future action planning
- individual support/guidance – one-to-one activities, including action planning, advice sessions (benefits/career etc), mapping exercises and personal life coaching.

In this way we aim to promote learning for economic survival *and* learning for active citizenship and democracy. On the basis of the evidence which is being generated we expect to be in a more powerful position to make the case for the institutional changes which are required if the goals of wider access and social inclusion are to be effectively realised in practice.

The participants

Given further acceleration, we can conclude that knowledge will grow increasingly perishable. Today's fact becomes tomorrow's misinformation. A society, in which the individual constantly changes his job, his place of residence, his social ties and so forth places an enormous premium on learning efficiency. Tomorrow's schools must therefore teach not merely data, but ways to manipulate it. Students must learn how to discard old ideas, how and when to replace them. They must, in short, learn how to learn ... by instructing students how to learn, unlearn and re-learn, a powerful new dimension can be added to education. (Toffler 1971)

Whatever one's perspective on the desirability – or undesirability – of so much uncertainty, the fact of the matter is that globalisation *has* been associated with rapid and continuing processes of economic restructuring and social change. ALIC participants are only too well aware of the potentially negative impact on them and their prospects for future employment. Group members identify future uncertainty as one of their main concerns – the catalyst which has encouraged them to return to education. Their ideas of the future have been coloured by their fears about changes in the employment structure and their anxieties about the uncontrolled rapidity with which technology changes. They have been exploring what skills and status they want for themselves in the future as role models for their children and forthcoming generations. This is in the context of their real sense of concern about their skills becoming outmoded. They want to build upon past experiences and the learning they have already gained both through formal and informal means. And they recognise the need to retrain if they are to be a part of what will be required as relevant and necessary to participate in future societies.

What Toffler (1971) predicted as the key issues are exactly those that the participants also identify as the main reasons for them returning to education.

They mention the need for fundamental changes in educational institutions, arguing the case for developing an educational system that makes sense to them as individuals as well as having equal concern for each and every student. They support the idea of moving away from an education system which has been built on notions of the skills and knowledge required for the workforce of the present day – but not the workforce of the future. Toffler's views on the three objectives which a developing and forward-looking education system must embrace – if it is to create a viable and employable workforce – echo many of the issues which are raised by the ALIC participants themselves, including the need to:

- transform the organisational structure of the education system – make institutions more amenable, user-friendly places in which students who have been out of education for five years or more can feel comfortable
- revolutionise the curricula in further and higher education – to include subjects with which students can identify
- encourage a more future-focused approach to learning – enabling students to have a clearer understanding of what change means for prospective workers and citizens, including the skills to shape and effect change rather than simply endure it.

ALIC participants, then, share ALIC's overall commitment to both types of agenda. They aim to gain the knowledge and skills necessary for survival in an uncertain future. And they are already engaged in sharing critical reflections on the need for wider changes, including fundamental changes in the educational system and in further and higher education institutions.

Barriers

Participants in the project have experienced most of the barriers which have already been identified – and more. In the process of considerable discussion a variety of reasons have emerged as to why their participation in education has been blocked in the past. These range from previous drug offences to past work in the sex industry. For some, mental health issues have been critical. The mental health of adults living in poverty has received far too little attention in the literature on barriers to access – despite the evidence which already exists to document the detrimental effects on people's mental well-being of long-term unemployment, together with the depressing effects of women's experiences of isolation, especially when they feel trapped in the home as a result of caring responsibilities. Becoming defined as a mental health patient raises further issues in its turn, of course. Once acquired, this can become a disabling label, making it even more difficult to enter/re-enter the labour market and further compounding a person's negative experiences. ALIC has worked with a number of people involved in the project who have undergone just such experiences, as well as with those whose feelings of depression, anxiety and despair has not been formally recognised in mental health terms.

Participants have spoken of the incredible barriers they have had to overcome in their lives and the dents which these experiences have made to their self-confidence and self-esteem. As a result, taking even the first steps to get in touch with us is regarded by many as an enormous achievement.

Financial barriers

Stories of financial hardship abound. By definition, ALIC participants, as unemployed people, face the range of material barriers which have already been identified, barriers related to social class, occupational status and lack of money. Overcoming financial barriers has proved problematic in various ways.

Helping students enrol initially is only one aspect of the financial problems which need to be addressed. Continuing support is also required. The DfEE's waiver of tuition fees for unemployed people does not include college registration fees nor subsequent examination board or awarding body registration fees – all of which represent a major financial burden to people subsisting on welfare benefits and on extremely low incomes. In addition, the costs of childcare remain an enormous handicap. Cited nationally as a barrier by 40 per cent of women with children aged between 0–4 years, this represents a major issue for parents on welfare in South-east London. Similarly, travel to and from college and from volunteering activities in the community represents a significant financial issue. Although as a pilot project, ALIC has been able to assist participants to some extent, stepping into the breach when unanticipated costs emerge, there are still unanswered questions about who will pick up the tab, in future, if widening participation initiatives are to be sustainable in the longer term.

There is also concern about future finance (especially if further and higher education is to be pursued) in the light of low incomes, single parenthood and the extra burden of chasing absent fathers. Clearly there are major policy implications here in relation to wider debates about fees and student grants. Community-based agencies in the area have unequivocal views on these issues. Part-time study is the only realistic option for most people they work with. Full-time study involves debt and debt is a millstone, especially for middle-aged and older students. Studying part time while surviving on benefits takes time – up to seven years between starting an access course and graduating. This is a route for 'exceptional and determined' individuals. It is not the way in which access will be widened more generally or educational exclusion because of poverty will be realistically addressed.

While ALIC has been able to provide some limited support in emergency situations and has been able to give assistance with temporary job applications and with funding applications to grant-making trusts, aiming to ensure that participants can access whatever financial help *is* available to them, none of these limited measures represent adequate institutional responses to the wider structural issues of financial constraints. This also raises questions about how effective projects like ALIC can be in calling for more fundamental institutional changes, both in relation to fees and grants and in relation to the benefits system.

Not surprisingly, the benefits system emerges as one of the key constraints. People living in poverty experience the benefits system as being designed to 'catch them out' with claimants feeling that they are constantly having to 'prove their innocence'. In addition to the usual rules and regulations intended to 'encourage' people off welfare and into work rather than education, there are additional restrictions on studying while in receipt of incapacity benefit. It seems as though those in receipt of incapacity benefit are widely viewed as unsuitable 'cases' for learning because of likely restrictions on their future employability. Similar concerns attach to the lack of priority accorded to meeting older people's learning needs, if they were not expected to go on to use their learning in paid employment. Clearly it is not only educational institutions which need to change. Widening access has even further-reaching implications for social welfare policies and institutional practices.

Overcoming personal and motivational barriers

The 1999 cohort of ALIC participants experience a number of shared issues and concerns as long-term benefit claimants, single parents and people over 25 who have been out of formal education for five years or more and who want to return to learn. For many mental health issues are also a fact of life and are indicative of the devastating effects of experiences such as domestic violence, fear of pimps, and drink and drug addiction – not to mention long-term unemployment. Participants speak of the hopelessness they have felt as a result of being out of paid work for extended lengths of time. Depression, inertia and bouts of suicidal thoughts are expressed as very real experiences. This, coupled with living in inner city housing estates characterised by poverty, violence and high crime rates, as some participants do, can lead to feelings of absolute despair. Clearly not all of those who discussed these feelings had been defined as having a 'mental health' problem, although a number have been treated for mental health related illnesses.

Once involved in the project a frequent response to such experiences is to express interest in the kinds of courses and jobs that might make a contribution to other people like themselves in their local communities. Participants' motivation to contribute to their communities is actively welcomed and supported but their initial focus is not simply taken as given, without exploring the range of options in the light of critical reflection.

Their first year with ALIC is a hectic one for the participants. But it has been a useful starting point for them, learning in further and higher education surroundings as well as being part of the ALIC cohort, mixing with people with similar experiences and offering each other mutual support. The personal impact on participants is resounding.

The absence of confidence is identified again and again as the aspect which the participants feel most in their lives. As an expression of concern it tends to act as euphemism for other kinds of social disadvantage, including discrimination on the grounds of race, gender, class, region and disability, all of which are connected as reasons for past lack of achievement in formal education. Building on some of these experiences – specifically 'race' and gender discrimination – becomes central to the curriculum of the project, especially in the areas of communication, literacy and numeracy.

The growing importance of information technology (IT) is also one which causes some anxiety and technophobia in participants already lacking in confidence in themselves as literate, intelligent human beings. Participants in the project, working in partnership with Community Education Lewisham, have opportunities to experience small-group tuition and in two cases one-to-one tuition from an IT tutor, working on developing the ALIC web site. Through this they are learning new IT skills such as web site design and photoshop, as well as developing communication skills and gaining research skills. Placements like these provide useful experiences of voluntary action that also expand employment horizons and opportunities.

The many similarities of experiences and feelings (like lack of confidence) within the student group undoubtedly contribute to group solidarity. Participants learn a lot from each other. When difficulties arise for particular individuals – as a result of personal or educational issues – others in the group are quick to offer insights from their own particular experiences in similar circumstances and to suggest ways of dealing with situations which they have similarly found difficult in the past. The quality of trust is very evident in the kinds of relationships which the participants develop with each other and with ALIC staff. This experience of mutual group support, together with their very important experiences of learning through volunteering and networking in the community, all contribute to their choices of careers and educational pathways.

To summarise, the participants are learning in a variety of ways, gaining confidence and the ability to reflect upon their own practice in community settings as well as gaining certificated knowledge and skills from their college and course-based learning. Group support is the key to this learning as well as the individual support which has been provided by ALIC staff.

Learning pathways

In 1999 the curriculum for project members has involved study related both to active citizenship and to improving their employment opportunities. This includes learning through community activism, attachments to community placements and learning by reflecting on experience in regular group sessions called 'Make your experience count'. Also included are study skills sessions and opportunities to develop personal learning pathways via relevant part-time study programmes at Lewisham College. As well as encouraging critical reflection on experience, community placements and part-time college study, ALIC is seeking to develop a culture of empowerment whereby participants feel comfortable in being challenged and have the tools to demonstrate critical self-reflection in safe and supportive work and learning environments.

The use of community-based placements have been especially valuable, providing a method of enabling group members to understand learning in varying active and dynamic ways. The placements have demonstrated different learning styles, and will continue to be a critical component of any future programmes.

We have also placed considerable emphasis on student support and educational guidance – in relation to career plans, course guidance, education orientation and practical elements like references, UCAS applications, college applications and benefits advice. Without these aspects some participants would not be continuing their studies. For example, one participant in particular had repeatedly started but not completed an educational programme over the last five years. With high levels of appropriate support from the project she has managed to gain sufficient educational confidence in herself to stay on the course and even to offer additional hours at her community placement. This, coupled with bringing up four children, has not been the easiest of tasks, but she has managed and is now reflecting on her future educational path. Other participants have similarly commented on the sense of purpose they have developed through continuing support and collective solidarity.

Future participants in the programme will receive Open College accreditation for the preliminary preparation they undertake to prepare them for the ALIC programme. In addition, adjustments will be made to the community placements to take account of the experiences and feedback from our first cohort of students. The 10-week placement, for example, has been experienced as very short, both by the participants and by their supervisors. Given their other commitments (taking part-time courses and, for many, combining this with caring responsibilities) it is not going to be realistic to extend the period significantly. But more effective use of the time may be achieved by increasing the number of hours per week over the 10-week period and by building in more preparation and strengthening collaboration in three-way partnership between the participants, the supervisors and the ALIC tutors.

In addition to the full-time participants in the project ALIC has also worked with a wider group of people. Not everyone defines themselves as unemployed or looking for work and yet it has become very clear to us there is a role for projects such as this offering educational choices to people experiencing other kinds of social exclusion. Some of these will perhaps participate in ALIC in the near future – others may not, although they may benefit from the project's advice and support. Positive educational experiences can improve people's lives in crucial ways, whether or not this leads directly into paid work, at least in the short term.

Concluding comments

The Project evaluator

Although ALIC is still at a relatively early stage the project is already providing evidence that this approach can succeed in combining learning for employability with learning for active citizenship and democracy, building upon experiential learning in the community to promote progression both for individual advancement and for group development. Learning through active citizenship is clearly a vital part of the programme, giving participants much valued confidence and wider commitment as well as providing them with useful knowledge and political skills. ALIC has been addressing both situational and motivational barriers to participation in higher education through the project's course provision, building upon experiential learning along with individual and group support. As additional participants join the programme in the second and third years the project should be in a position to generate additional evidence to strengthen these claims (or not, of course, depending upon the outcomes).

To suggest that ALIC combines learning for survival in a rapidly changing economic and employment context with critical reflection, geared towards active citizenship and democratic social change, is by no means to imply, however, that such a combination is inherently unproblematic. A number of issues would seem to be emerging, with potentially significant implications both for policies and for practice in widening participation. Key issues which will need careful monitoring and evaluation in the coming period include the following:

1   The changing pattern of employment opportunities in South-east London and the polarisation of the labour market more generally: unless local people stand to benefit from widening employment opportunities (which provide a living wage, taking account of the rapidly escalating costs of housing and the costs of transport in the capital city) then incentives for educationally disadvantaged groups to invest in returning to learn may be expected to be correspondingly reduced.

2   The extent to which discriminatory practices in employment and other areas are effectively challenged: without significant changes, the incentives for black and ethnic minority returners will be particularly reduced.

3   The extent to which educational and related social policies take account of the lessons of programmes and projects to widen participation, learning the lessons from one-off projects for longer-term institutional changes in mainstream policies and delivery mechanisms: unless barriers such as those

related to fees, the lack of financial resources for maintenance, transport and childcare together with barriers inherent in the welfare benefits system are tackled, initiatives such as ALIC will be difficult if not impossible to sustain, in the longer term. This in turn raises questions about the extent to which policy makers are prepared to listen to the experiences of projects such as this and take on board the implications for genuinely joined up thinking.

4   The extent to which educational institutions learn the lessons from widening participation programmes and projects such as ALIC: encouraging more non-traditional students into educational institutions represents no more than the first step – without changing the educational context to make provision more user friendly and without increasing student support services, widening participation may simply lead to widening student drop-out.

5   And the extent to which widening participation agendas recognise the value of learning for individuals, groups and communities, even where this does not lead to improved employability in the foreseeable future: widening participation can significantly improve the quality of life for individuals and for communities whether or not particular individuals, including people with major caring responsibilities and people struggling to overcome a range of health and welfare problems, are enabled to gain paid employment as an immediate result. Evaluations of widening participation initiatives should include reflections on social as well as economic benefits.

The project worker

By offering more guidance and counselling, supporting progression routes, taking education out into the community, targeting under-represented groups and creating new and innovative partnerships, participation has already effectively been widened for some ALIC participants. But the educational provision that has been developed in the past has not been sufficiently user-friendly for ALIC participants. Although ALIC participants are all more than capable of achieving at higher education level, they have had to struggle with initial gaps in their academic skills (as these skills have been traditionally defined). So although financial support, a broader framework of courses and crèche facilities all point to increasing numbers of students and improved inclusion rates, further institutional changes will be required if these new students are to be retained.

Meanwhile the changes to FEFC and HEFCE funding, bring accompanying dangers, potentially encouraging institutions to compete with each other for students from previously under-represented groups. Although the development of partnerships offers one way to address this increasing competitiveness there is a risk that even further 'projectitis' will emerge.

Lewisham is already characterised by a wide variety of projects geared toward providing learning opportunities for people in the community. The networks developed through these projects represent a major source of strength, with the potential for enhanced co-operation, solidarity and mutual support. Despite the range of projects and the networks in the area, though, Lewisham in general, and North Lewisham in particular, is still characterised by concentrations of social deprivation, including high levels of unemployment.

On a more positive note, it is also relevant to comment that through their experiences of working with – and challenging – government and local authority regeneration initiatives, local people have been developing their own responses, building upon local organisational strengths to negotiate their own agendas for change. The voices of the community, however disparate and diverse, are being expressed through innovative approaches, including the development of community-led regeneration projects and programmes. ALIC's commitment to learning for active citizenship has particular and continuing relevance in this context. However valuable local community-based initiatives might be though, projects are not going to be sufficient on their own. The lessons of projects like ALIC will need to be built into mainstream policies and organisational cultures.

Notes

1 ALIC was specifically targeted towards unemployed people, so this chapter does not address issues around the learning needs of people over retirement age.

References

Alexander D, and Martin I (1995) 'Competence, curriculum, and democracy' in Mayo M and Thompson J (eds), *Adult Learning, Critical Intelligence and Social Change*, Leicester: NIACE pp 82– 96

Back L et al (1999) *Between Home and Belonging: critical ethnographies of race, place and identity*, London: CNER

Beveridge M (1999) 'Instrumental objectives and liberal values: squaring the circle' in J. Crowther et al (eds), *Popular Education and Social Movements in Scotland*, Leicester: NIACE

Bowles S and Gintis H (1979) *Schooling in Capitalist America*, London: Routledge

Crowther J, Martin I and Shaw M (1999) *Popular education and social movements in Scotland today*, Leicester: NIACE

DfEE (1998) *The Learning Age: a renaissance for a new Britain*, London: The Stationary Office

Edwards R (1997) *Changing Places?* London: Routledge

Elsdon K, Reynolds J and Stewart S (1995) *Voluntary Organisations: citizenship, learning and change*, Leicester: NIACE

Foley G (1999) *Learning in Social Action*, Leicester: NIACE

Freire P (1972) *Pedagogy of the Oppressed*, Harmondsworth: Penguin

Fryer R (1997) *Learning for the twenty-first century*, London: National Advisory group for Continuing Education and Lifelong Learning

Hughes K (1995) 'Really useful knowledge: adult education and the Ruskin Learning Project' in Mayo M and Thompson J (eds), *Adult Learning, Critical Intelligence and Social Change*, Leicester: NIACE, pp 97–110

Johnson R (1979) ' "Really useful knowledge": radical education and working class culture' in Clarke J *et al* (ed), *Working Class Culture*, London: Hutchinson

Maguire M *et al* (1993) *Factors influencing individual commitment to lifetime learning*, Employment Department

McGivney V (1991) *Opening colleges to adult learners*, Leicester: NIACE

McGivney V (1997) 'Adult participation in learning: can we change the pattern?' in *A National Strategy for Lifelong Learning*, Newcastle: University of Newcastle, pp 127–41

McGivney V (1999) *Informal Learning in the Community*, Leicester: NIACE

Sargant N, Field J, Francis H, Schuller T and Tuckett A (1997) *The Learning Divide*, Leicester: NIACE

Sargant N (2000) *The Learning Divide Revisited*, Leicester: NIACE

Scottish Office (1996) *Lifelong Learning in the Community*, Education and Industry Department, Scottish Office

Schuller T (1998) 'Three steps towards a learning society' in *Studies in the Education of Adults*, Vol 31 No 1, April

Thompson J (1980), Introduction, in Thompson J (ed) *Adult Education for a Change* London: Hutchinson, p 26

Toffler A (1971) *Future Shock*, London: Pan

Tuckett A (1999) Afterword to G Foley (1999) *Learning in Social Action*, Leicester: NIACE

Uden T (1996) *Widening Participation: routes to a learning society*, Leicester: NIACE

11 Working with contradictions in the struggle for access

John Bamber, Alan Ducklin and Lyn Tett

> The lesson is clear. If all students are to maximise their educational potential, the institutions of higher education have to increase their awareness of, and support for, the growing diversity of students who enter higher education. (Stuart Hall 1996)

Introduction

There are two contrasting visions of the widening participation agenda in universities. One suggests that Higher Education's main purpose is to serve the economy so expanding provision is justified on the grounds of giving better choice to those who are able to benefit. The claim is that knowledge is utilitarian so access is about the most efficient and cost-effective way of organising expansion. Broadening access is justified as a way of drawing on all the pools of talent available through a meritocratic system. This economistic vision is becoming the dominant one throughout the 'developed' world. For example, Reich (1991:3) has suggested that:

> We are living through a transformation that will rearrange the politics and economics of the coming century … Each nation's primary assets will be its citizens' skills and insights. Each nation's primary political task will be to cope with the centrifugal forces of the global economy which tear up the ties binding citizens together – bestowing even greater wealth on the most skilled and insightful, whilst consigning the less skilled to a declining standard of living.

This view is also reflected in the National Committee of Enquiry into Higher Education (1997:4) which stated:

> In the next century, the economically successful nations will be those which will become learning societies: all are committed, through effective education and training, to lifelong learning. So to be a successful nation in a competitive world, and to maintain a cohesive society and a rich culture, we must invest in education to develop our greatest resource – our people.

The other perspective is premised upon the idea that scholars and academics have a moral duty to share their knowledge and expertise with the widest community. From this perspective, access should be widened not primarily for reasons of economic efficiency but also for reasons of social justice. The emphasis is much more on exclusion from education as one aspect of being disadvantaged. In Scotland there is a widespread belief that the education system recognises this latter perspective. In reality, however, the formal education system has only ever offered a meritocratic type of equality which also contributes to 'inequality by acting as a safety valve preserving social stability' (Maclean 1994:46). In our view, widening access will need to challenge the dominance of this approach since it results in 'maximally maintained inequality' (Woodrow 1996:6). In this situation the disadvantaged benefit when their inclusion becomes the only means of achieving further expansion in HE. Patterns of provision in Scotland reveal that it is almost entirely the 'new' universities that have changed their intake to include more students with working-class backgrounds whereas the older institutions have remained unchanged (see Paterson 1997; Johnston *et al* 1999).

Just as there are contrasting perspectives regarding the purpose of expanding university provision, there are different responses to the needs of groups who are currently excluded from higher education throughout Europe (Woodrow 1996). At one end of the spectrum HE is about enabling greater access to unchanging patterns of provision. At the other access is radically re-conceived as assisting excluded groups to make a positive contribution to social cohesion. Our account concerns attempts to be inclusive by 'creating inclusive admissions policies and practices while making provision available … at convenient times and places, with the support [for students] to be engaged successfully in completing the qualifications which they need to move ahead with … careers … and with their lives' (Peinovich 1996:63). As such it is an example of practice which occupies a middle ground between the polarities.

We testify that where strong personal aspirations are allied to a well-focused project, rooted in the community and set within a relatively well-resourced and culturally compatible HE course environment, the exclusion of working-class adults can be challenged and, to some extent, overcome. There is, however, no single set of ready-made solutions to the multi-faceted problems of widening access. Policy makers and providers need to be aware of the deeply ambiguous nature of suggested approaches, most of which will reflect both positive and negative characteristics. It is with ambiguity in mind that we examine a number of powerful situational, dispositional and institutional contradictions that educationalists may encounter in attempts to widen access. In concentrating on the last of these three, we suggest that certain actions and strategies can make a positive difference though we are careful to acknowledge that the changes necessary to widen access are immense. In the end, sufficient and effectively deployed resources of the sort that we represent in Box 12.1 must underpin the process. Though some of the elements depicted are common enough, readers will appreciate the difference between current realities and the idealised scenario.

Box 12.1 A mature student's dream day at university

It was 8.15 as Fiona waved goodbye to her 6-year-old son Michael as the childminder collected him for school. Today he would also be attending the after-school club, to which she attributed the recent improvement in his attitude to school work. She watched his little figure disappear down the street and looked forward to seeing him again at 6.00pm when the childminder brought him back. She thought again about the difference that this free service made to the quality of her life. Without it, university would be almost impossible. She returned to the kitchen to finish her breakfast and opened the day's mail. As well as the usual bills, and circulars encouraging her to spend money that she didn't have, was a letter from her academic mentor. It contained some feedback on her ideas for the next course assignment and some positive words about her part in a group presentation to the next group of students on the Access course. All of her group had gone on to higher education and they were talking to the new students about life at university. She went into her living room and switched on the computer, supplied for a nominal rental through the Trust Scheme for mature students like herself. She found that she had to reply immediately or she would forget. A quick note by e-mail was somehow much easier than putting pen to paper. Just after she had started, the familiar 'ping' alerted her to a message. It was a reminder from her professional tutor, Lyn, that they would be meeting at 3.00pm later that day after the theory module. Lyn wanted to know if she had managed to get a copy of the paper from the web site they had been discussing the other day in class. She also wanted to make a date for her termly appraisal, which was due in two weeks. Fiona grimaced at this latter, for although she had been doing well, she always felt nervous about assessments. She reminded herself that this wasn't a typical assessment and that the previous one had been really helpful in identifying progress and pointing out areas of where she still needed to develop. She logged out and made her way into the university making sure that she had her free student pass with her for the train and bus journey. She arrived at 11.00am in time for the learning and teaching module. Always the same format! A short input from the lecturer, small group exercise, followed by a plenary and then a summary of the main points from a member of the class who had been selected the previous week. She was well prepared having managed to read the relevant section of the course handbook and complete the associated 'homework' the night before. She'd also managed to get through a handout provided for the theory module on the train journey in. After the class came a quick meeting over a coffee in the refectory with her study cluster. They swopped a few ideas and prepared five questions that they wanted to put to the lecturer. They also agreed that the next full weekly meeting would look at each other's drafts for the next assignment. After the class, the meeting with Lyn went well. She just had enough time left to go the library and have a look at Section 8 of the on-line study skills course, which was about structuring essays. Too much to take in at one go but

> *she made a note to go back to it. Before logging off she looked in her mailbox to find a message from the Student Advice Centre. They had information about a trust fund that she could apply to, which would top up her maintenance grant. The £6,000 per year didn't cover everything but it was enough to get by. By now her head was full of university and she was glad to break off on the way home to think about getting tea together for herself and Michael.*

At LAST! An inclusive programme?

The ideas for this chapter come primarily from our research into a programme called the Lothian Apprenticeship Scheme Trust (LAST) which was set up in 1995 to enable academically unqualified activists from working class communities, disabled people and minority ethnic groups to gain the BA in Community Education. We also draw from our lengthy experience of working with mature, non-traditional students undertaking the same degree. By enabling participants to work in their own communities and study part-time the LAST sought 'to achieve equality of outcomes for people whose circumstances, geographic, physical or cultural, would not permit them to consider becoming professionally qualified' (LAST 1995:2). Because the participants were working part-time in the community they were referred to as 'apprentices', which reinforced the link with employment rather than education. The apprentices undertook much of their course in conjunction with the BA students who followed a more traditional full-time route, but they were also taught separately and were supported by two full-time tutors and an administrator appointed to the scheme. The apprentices studied on a 40-week year basis, rather than the usual 30, so they were undertaking an accelerated degree. This meant that they had to deal with all the problems that are associated with intensive courses such as having less time to read and reflect and stressful work loads.

LAST adopted proactive recruitment procedures to encourage applications from members of traditionally underrepresented groups. The course structure allowed for part-time provision and was not tied to conventional term times. It meant that the participants were able to combine their studies with working in their communities. Finance was made available through the Urban Programme; a special government fund aimed at socio-economically disadvantaged communities, for travel, dependents' care and disability support. The scheme had its own premises where the apprentices had access to a range of facilities including a substantial collection of course books and relevant journals. More generally, course policy and content heightened staff awareness of the needs of excluded groups, with much emphasis placed, by LAST staff, on individual tuition and guidance. Assessment procedures were flexible and every encouragement made for the apprentices to provide mutual support and reinforce the positive aspects of a diverse student body. The apprentices were encouraged to identify positive learning experiences of all kinds. Even where their experience of formal education had been negative the learning gained from reflecting upon this during the course was taken as a way of turning once negative experiences into positive ones. In addition, the privileging of experience over qualifications enabled apprentices to recognise their own strengths. The involvement of participants' own communities in recruitment and continuing support also served to reduce the 'otherness' of higher education.

Fifteen out of the original 18 apprentices completed the course and received their degrees. It is tempting to claim unqualified success for the scheme but in reality the programme was problematic. A more critical analysis reveals that the cohort divided into three levels of academic performance: high, average and low. Three of the group consistently fell into the first category, a further six into the second and the remaining six into the third. The three who left the course would have brought the total in this category to nine. Half of the original cohort, therefore, had experienced significant levels of difficulty in passing the course. By this we mean continuously invoking extensions to complete work, routinely failing first and second submissions, requiring extensive and unremitting tutor assistance with writing, and achieving the lowest grades consistent with achieving a pass. The difficulties were brought into sharp relief at the point where staff committed to widening access had to fail students who, understandably, were struggling academically.

Our analysis suggests that powerful dispositional and situational factors can serve to contradict attempts to widen access. It is important for educationalists to understand how these factors interact and influence the student experience so that, insofar as it is possible, institutional arrangements can be designed to counteract these contradictions. In addition there are also positive elements that can be utilised and enhanced with appropriate pedagogical and organisational arrangements. It is important that it is made absolutely clear to policy makers and course providers that such a process does not come cheaply. Working effectively with non-traditional students requires high levels of resources and we are fully aware that the general trend in HE is moving in the opposite direction. It is to an examination of these issues that we now turn.

Working with contradictions

Our research confirms Caffarella and Merriam's (1999:63) view that 'learning cannot be separated from the context in which it takes place'. Supporting students, therefore, means taking into account the context in which their learning occurs. For conventional students, passing through HE can be a relatively smooth, integrative process, involving confirmation of what they already know and hold to be true. This is not to deny that such students have to work hard to gain their degrees. Jennings (1995:17–18) puts the point in the following way:

Adults who have moved in and out of formal learning contexts throughout their lives, and who experience little discontinuity in the assumptions and expectations about learning operating across these various situations, can feel a sense of integration upon entry and in their overall experience of subsequent comparable learning environments. What they achieve in that situation is tied in with other kinds of influence within that context and within themselves.

For non-traditional students, however, the passage is more likely to be disjunctive with the need to critically examine and change some of the underlying assumptions on which their lives have been built (see Mezirow 1991). We agree that an integrative experience of HE can indeed depend upon fundamental dispositional change. A consistent finding, for example, was that the apprentices who chose not to use the support systems were those most likely to be in need of them. By the same token, those who did use the systems were more likely to succeed. This would suggest that student motivation to avail themselves of help is a key factor in overcoming the odds. The extent of the motivation required to engage with a course in HE is vividly shown in the following quote:

> Combining being a single parent and the workplace element of being an apprentice, is extremely difficult. I've got a 16-hour a week work commitment and my employer's demand every hour of it. There's supposed to be a three-way agreement; me, the employer and LAST but work is now much less supportive. It's a constant struggle between looking after the kids, work and study. I sometimes have to do my college work from eleven at night till four thirty in the morning. Then I have a quick sleep, then breakfast, get the kid's to school and then off to work. That's what a day's like for me. It's hard but you've got to do it. (Jackie, female, late 20s)

While the level of commitment is ultimately down to individuals, situational factors may be more significant. It is wholly detrimental; for example, that student loans and other central sources of finance are insufficient to meet the needs of older learners with dependent children and rent or mortgages to pay. The recent Cubie Report (1999) in Scotland has ruled that fees should be deferred for Scottish undergraduate students but has not actually abolished them is a small step in the right direction. The starkness of the situation for mature students is portrayed in the following situation:

> I'm earning less now than when I first started the scheme. In order to make ends meet I have to work outside of the apprenticeship as well. I do residential care on a night-shift basis. This has a big impact on my family commitments. I can't always be there for them. Something has to give though, and it's often them. You don't even get a break in the holidays. That's when I work most

of my hours. So there's no space to expand into, to get the college work done. In other words, there's no time off! (Issy, female, 30s)

The quote conveys just how unenviable is the task of balancing the heavy, and often conflicting, demands of work, family, life in general and study. Given such conditions, the fact that a number of apprentices had received paid educational leave at points during the course was a significant bonus.

In addition, it should also be noted that many come from backgrounds where there have been negative experiences of formal schooling and little, if any, previous experience of HE. This was clearly evidenced in one student's experience (Allan, male, 40s): 'I was expelled from secondary school when I was 14 years old. I never really went back into the system after that. That was me finished with it.' As documented extensively in the literature in relation to non-traditional students (McGivney 1990, 1996; Williams J 1997; Woodrow 1996), such experience can result in the feeling that 'HE is not for us'. As another apprentice (Michelle, female, 30s) said: 'People from my area don't go to university, it's seen as just for the "wee swots". But we're breaking the mould and that's scary.' The situation can be compounded by negative attitudes on the part of friends and partners. Deep-rooted feelings can therefore set up a significant psychological barrier to a student engaging fully and openly with a course in HE. In learning terms, the student's motivation to succeed needs to be turned into a 'yes, this is for me' attitude. On the positive side, however, it should also be recorded that many of the LAST and BA students had a deep-seated political commitment to doing well, to showing that it could be done. This is evidenced in Stella's (female, 30s) statement: 'I wanted to achieve it for people like myself. If the whole lot of us had gone through and failed then we wouldn't have achieved what LAST had set out to do. But our success should open gates for people instead of slamming them shut. It proves it can be done.'

Institutional arrangements can exacerbate or alleviate the negative aspects involved in such situational and dispositional factors. Conventional admissions procedures, for example, favour young traditionally qualified candidates who can demonstrate in advance that they have the capacity to benefit. In stark contrast, the LAST programme was, and the BA course continues to be, radically different in favouring life and work experience over qualifications in terms of recruitment. A particular issue for teachers and learners in such situations, therefore, is how that experience features in an academic context. Whaley's (1999:5) comments about learning in HE are useful in this connection:

> Most students need tutor guidance in understanding that experience itself is not sufficient in an academic course; it has to be embedded in 'theory' and used in assignments with scholarly detachment and rigor. Course tutors face a delicate, dual challenge – to develop students' self confidence by accepting and valuing their experience and to develop students'

understanding by encouraging them to venture beyond the 'safety' of their own experience.

A central implication of this statement is the need for a shared understanding between educators and students which ensures that the difficulties encountered are acknowledged and addressed. Extensive mechanisms are needed to support achievement for non-traditional students but these, it should be stressed, do not come easily or cheaply. What we have found is that the LAST and BA students, and by implication other non-traditional students, need introductory level courses such as learning to think sociologically, politically or critically, for example. They benefit from intensive practice and tutoring in writing, comprehension and basic study skills and from extensive verbal and written feedback on draft work by tutors, and from coaching as to how to improve work prior to submission. They favour interactive rather than didactic teaching styles, especially when coupled with opportunities to work collectively in small groups. Course materials that are not, in the initial stages, set at an appropriate intellectual level, can seriously undermine their confidence, which badly affects future performance. In particular, texts that are inaccessible to all but the most able academically will set back, rather than enhance, intellectual development. At the same time, however, there needs to be an emphasis on critical thinking (see Brookfield 1987) to open up and re-examine experience. In itself this could be an emotionally challenging and threatening process; hence the need for a supportive course environment, especially in terms of the relationship with tutors.

Working supportively with non-traditional students, therefore, is a teacher- and resource-intensive business. The requirement is significantly more in terms of face-to-face contact with individual students, marking, personal tutoring and coaching. Their needs are greater and they need more personal attention to reflect upon the emotional baggage that we have referred to above. Given their lack of free time, course materials need to be plentiful and to hand. They have less time for research in the usual sense, which means that photocopied articles provided free and in timely fashion are of great benefit.

Yet there is an ambiguity about such levels of support which also needs to be acknowledged. Those steeped in entry protocols based on school-leaving qualifications, full-time students and conventional methods of assessment warn that providing such high levels can undermine 'standards'. By this they mean that beyond a certain level of assistance it becomes difficult to claim that the end result actually reflects the student's own work. We acknowledge these concerns and can report from our own experience that the extent of such support can have unintended consequences for non-traditional students. The time taken to fail modules from first through to final submission, for example, turned out to be a disadvantage to those who were allowed to carry their fails from one academic year into the next. In such situations a backlog of unfinished work built up which then became a problem to overtake. On the other hand universities need to accept that access for non-traditional students does not end at the point of entry; account needs to be taken of necessary changes in assessment, curriculum and student support. Failure to appreciate this fundamental fact will mean that the probability of academic failure for non-traditional students will be higher than it should or needs to be.

In the end it is a question of where the burden of responsibility lies for ensuring a successful, integrative experience. The idea that access is only about getting into HE is often accompanied by the notion that not everyone is capable of successfully completing a degree, even with high levels of support. In this perspective dispositional factors may be fore-grounded. Alternatively, failure may also be explained in terms of overriding situational factors to which institutional practices fail to respond to adequately. Our analysis of the factors involved with the LAST apprentices and BA students, however, suggests that success and failure is a complex subject. What we have just described is hardly new to those involved with non-traditional students. It may be strange territory indeed for those with no experience of this area in HE. The situation in general, moreover, can be said to be getting worse. Due to recent developments in our own situation, for example, the level and type of support advocated by Hall (SCRE: 1996) is becoming remoter by the day.

> To succeed in higher education students need confidence in themselves and at least minimum competence; but the very methods by which these are built through SWAP are not available in higher education. There is a miss-match of culture. The lesson is clear. If all students are to maximise their educational potential, the institutions of higher education have to increase their awareness of, and support for, the growing diversity of students who enter higher education.

Compounding institutional contradictions

Since the graduation of the LAST cohort in July 1998 the external funding for the project was withdrawn and with it the redundancy/redeployment of the two tutors and the selling off of the Trust's assets. This situation has caused profound difficulties for the second cohort who were undertaking Year studies at the time and have had to be transferred onto either the full-time or part-time study routes. Since that time the College has become a faculty of the University of Edinburgh as part of the pattern of mergers which now sees all of the former teacher training institutions in Scotland incorporated within the university sector as faculties of education. Prior to this change, undergraduate courses had used 100-hour modules as the essential study unit. Initially, this involved 40 hours of class contact per module, with each module being assessed and appropriate SCOTCAT ratings being accumulated for successful module completion. The new course structure makes part-time delivery difficult by spreading teaching in cognate areas across the week, at odd times, and also requires students to undertake courses from outside the department. While we have a part-time route to the BA which was set up under the previous system there is no longer a LAST programme. The existing part-time route has one more year to run.

The merger has also meant a change in the student support systems to reflect the pattern, which exists throughout the rest of the University. From October 1999 all new undergraduates to the Faculty of Education were allocated to a Director of Studies. This need not be a member of academic staff who will teach the particular student nor even someone who, necessarily, works in the course area for a students study programme. In Community Education, however, it was decided to allocate a member of the teaching team to be Director of Studies for the first-year cohort of 30. As a function of size this is certainly possible in contrast to other programmes with much larger numbers of students. The role of a director of studies cannot be equated with the much more proactive and professionally focused functions previously exercised by the LAST and Moray House Professional Tutors. Table 12.1 shows the extent of the difference between the two. In short the Director of Study role is not intended to engage with the student's programme of study, and has no function in regard to monitoring student performance/competence in the area of professional practice and development.

The absence of a professionally oriented support role is one indication of how the form and nature of student support has changed to the detriment of the students. If this is indeed the case, what are the chances of returning to the former levels of support that, in our experience, would appear to be necessary to ensure an integrative learning experience for non-traditional students in HE?

Possibilities for the future

Certainly the new policy framework would appear to support the inclusion of non-traditional students. The decision to include the 'postcode performance' of universities means that there is now a basis for the selective distribution of money earmarked for increasing access to under-privileged students. The Secretary of State for Industry and Education in Scotland announced on 1 May 1998 that at least £1million would be made available to higher education institutions (HEIs) for widening access. This would be to assist them to identify good practices in widening access and to develop increased opportunities for those groups in society who were identified as being underrepresented in higher education. More money is a clear incentive to universities to increase access. In our own institution's mission statement there is clear reference to the need to be inclusive but no overt policy is as yet in place regarding non-traditional, mature students. At the same time, our university is no stranger to the provision of vocationally oriented courses favoured by mature students. There is now a new emphasis nationwide on the quality of teaching with the establishment of

Table 11. 1 – Comparison between Professional Tutor and Director of Studies

Professional Tutor	Director of Studies
Continuity of tutor-student link throughout period of study on professional training programme	To advocate for student at exam board if needs be
Regular contact (weekly when in college), at least one placement visit	To monitor academic progress
Overview of academic development throughout course	To identify further student support needs ie dyslexia etc
Overview of professional development throughout course	To process information for Registry
Tutor ability to directly monitor student progress academically	To meet with student once a term for enrolment purposes
Tutor ability to directly monitor student professional development	To enable student to choose appropriate course in other faculties
Identifiable first port of call for student encountering difficulties	
Potential for student support (especially in year one) for regular feedback on work	
Overseeing study skills and ICT development etc	
Identifying further student support needs ie dyslexia etc	
Tutor second-marking all synoptic assessment work and monitoring modular assessment outcomes	
Tutor ability to advocate on student's behalf on academically related matters with Course Leader and Examination Board	
As above but also potentially related to domestic/personal matters which student feels able to share	
Tutor-student discussions regarding appropriate fieldwork placement to match student learning needs to fieldwork offers. Contact with agencies and visits to students on placement	
Placement briefing and debriefing, individual and group	

the Institute for Teaching and Learning. Perhaps the kind of good practice that we have referred to above within the LAST programme would be seen as necessary rather than as unaffordable?

There is much that is at odds with this ideal, however. The imperatives of the research assessment exercise continue to dominate academic practice in universities, especially those such as Edinburgh, which is taken to be amongst the elite research institutions in the country. Put simply it means that since income for research is deemed somehow to be valued above that which is gained for numbers of students enrolled, then ways and means must be found to reduce staff teaching commitments so that they can enhance their research profile. There is continuing pressure on budgets, which also means consistent attempts to increase staff–student ratios. Established procedures, such as reliance on examinations and written forms of assessment, and course patterns which assume a typical student body of independent, single, young, academically successful people make part-time provision for mature students with financial and family responsibilities extremely difficult. In the end, there is no obvious incentive for the elite universities to break the mould, as they are happily unable to satisfy the demand for places anyway. Finally, even with the renewed emphasis on teaching, the current faith in technology often masks an underlying intention to favour open and distance learning on the assumption that it is possible to teach more students with fewer staff. On balance, the prospects for widening access in the integrative sense that we use the term here would appear to be poor in traditional universities. In other words, the scenario that we have painted in Box 12.1 is likely to remain utopian.

Concluding remarks

All universities have conceptions of equity that reflect ideological positions. Inclusivity can be interpreted as enabling access for previously excluded groups to existing and unchanging patterns of provision. Here the emphasis would be on dispositional factors in the performance of individual students. In our view this emphasis accords with the dominant meritocratic-economistic vision of higher education. Inclusivity could also mean taking into account and seeking to redress the effects of structural inequality, where situational factors are taken to have a crucial bearing on student performance. In turn, the nature of this construction will influence the institutional practice of the university. The discussion can become unnecessarily polarised, however, when the more fruitful line is to appreciate how the dispositional, institutional and structural dimensions interact in shaping the student experience. Too much emphasis on the structural can underplay the impact of institutional arrangements. Similarly, over-privileging institutional factors can create cultures of dependence and undermine the efforts of individual students in determining success or failure. A counter-balancing position is needed in which, while acknowledging the contribution of the student, staff and institutions, build the structures and procedures to challenge the negative effects of inequality.

In the end, what this research has confirmed for us is that class is not an abstract concept but is real and operative in the daily lives of non-traditional students. For this group higher education has been difficult to gain access to and also exceedingly hard to survive. The pressing need for an income to support themselves and their dependants while undertaking all the requirements of a degree leaves no spare time or energy. These circumstances are a far cry from those of the traditional younger, single, middle-class higher education students whose conditions, though they have undoubtedly worsened in the past decade, are still good by comparison. Our point is that in relation to previously excluded groups these wider structural aspects need to be taken into account in terms of course design.

We end by noting that the trend in HE towards greater efficiency through reducing teaching costs per student militates against the very changes in practices that we have argued for here. In the end, large numbers of working class students, who do not have the 'right' (ie legitimated) cultural capital 'in terms of knowledge, dispositions, linguistic codes, problem-solving skills, attitudes, and tastes' (Luttrell 1997:7) participating in HE will only come about through changes in national policy that meet the demands and needs of such prospective students. However, our case study of one small department indicate some of the issues that need to be considered at this level and the action that is necessary if staff wish to create a more inclusive programme. It is possible to argue for, and make changes in, institutions and these inevitably lead to disagreements but by placing the exploration and resolution of debate at the heart of our work we become aware of the diversity of views that arise from these interactions. Being aware of the differing conceptions of inclusivity and the contradictions that they raise is more likely to result in uncomfortable dilemmas and contradictions for individuals but, nevertheless, the struggle to resolve these will lead to growth and development and a better experience for students.

References

Brookfield S (1987) *Developing Critical Thinkers*, Oxford: Oxford University Press

Caffarella R S and Merriam S B (1999) 'Perspectives on adult learning: framing our research', in Rose A (ed), *Proceedings of 40th Annual Adult Education Research Conference*, DeKalb, IL: LEPS Press

Committee of Enquiry into Student Finance (1999) *The Cubie Report*, Edinburgh: The Stationery Office

Hall S (1996) *It was a Worthwhile Slog! Scottish access students in higher education*, Edinburgh: Scottish Council for Research in Education

Jennings L (1995) 'From student to tutor: learning through literature', in Preston P (ed.), *Literature in Adult Education*, Nottingham: University of Nottingham

Johnston V, Raab G, Abdalla I (1999) 'Participation in higher education in Scotland: a geographic and social analysis', *Higher Education Quarterly*, Vol 53 No 4, 369–94

LAST (1995) *Recruitment and Selection Pack*, Edinburgh: Lothian Apprenticeship Scheme Trust)

Luttrell W (1997) *School-smart and mother-wise*, London: Routledge

Maclean C (1994) 'The theory and practice of equal opportunities in Scotland', *Scottish Affairs*, 6, Winter, pp 36–51

McGivney V (1990) *Education's for other people: access to education for non-participant adults*, Leicester: NIACE

McGivney V (1996) *Staying On or Leaving the Course*, Leicester: NIACE.

Mezirow J (1991) *Transformative Dimensions of adult learning*, San Francisco: Jossey-Bass.

National Committee of Enquiry into Higher Education (1997) *Higher Education in the Learning Society*, (Dearing Report) London

Paterson L (1997) 'Trends in higher education participation in Scotland', *Higher Education Quarterly*, Vol 51 No 1, pp 29–48

Peinovich P E (1996) 'Conditions of openness to mature learners in English Universities, 1995: a view from the United States', *Journal of Access Studies*, 11, pp. 59–67

Reich R (1991) *The Work of Nations*, London: Routledge

Whaley P (1999) *The experience of a lifetime? A case study of theory and practice in adult and community education*, unpublished paper given at the 1999 European Conference 'Lifelong Learning – Inside and Outside Schools', Bremen, Germany

Williams J (1997) (ed), *Negotiating Access to Higher Education*, Buckingham: SRHE and Open University Press

Woodrow M (1996) *Project on access to higher education in Europe: working report. Part 1 – Synthesis and recommendations*, Strasbourg: Council of Europe

12 Turning the discourse

Jim Crowther, Ian Martin and Mae Shaw

Reasserting social purpose

Adult education, particularly the adult education of social purpose, has always existed in an uneasy and ambivalent relationship to the academy. Once suspect for trying to make elite knowledge popular and political, it is now beyond the pale because it stands against both profit and political correctness. Consequently in many universities, once singular agents of social purpose, the tradition of socially and politically committed knowledge has simply ceased to exist. And where it does exist, it struggles to survive on the very margins of the academy. In this respect, its fate reflects a wider crisis in the identity and purpose of the university as a social institution. As Bauman (1999) argues, the very notion of *social* purpose is decidedly out of joint with the times:

> It seems that if the knowledge class of the late-modern or postmodern era does assume the role of organic intellectuals at all, it is only the role of organic intellectuals of themselves. What most conspicuously marks off the present-day thought of the knowledge classes is its self-referentiality, its acute preoccupation with the conditions of its own professional activity and the increasingly uncommittal stance it takes towards other sectors of society, indeed, its almost total abandonment of the traditional 'synthesizing' role – the unwillingness to see in the rest of society anything more than an aggregate of individuals, coupled with a proclivity to theorize them as solitary, rather than collective, agents. The 'privatization' of the notion of agency in present-day social thought is a case in point – one of many.

Life and work in the academy today – at least in the rich world – is dominated by two overweening priorities, both which of are driven by the same underlying imperative: first, to publish in high status, international journals (and so to make money through the competitive assessment of institutional 'output'); second, to acquire lucrative, externally funded research (and so to make money in the competitive contract culture). University knowledge has become a commodity, and the successful academic is now a trader in the educational marketplace – as the proliferation of pint-sized professorships and the sprouting of cloned journals of academic entrepreneurialism bear testimony. No matter that the higher the status of the publication the fewer people are likely to read it, or that supposedly 'academic' research is increasingly tied to the politics of policy and/or profit. Inevitably the tradition of social purpose, along with the values of civic engagement and political solidarity which inform it, is one of the first casualties of the culture of the accountant in higher education.

In stark contrast to this bleak political economy of contemporary academic life, Jackson (1995) characterises the social purpose tradition, or what he calls the 'adult education of engagement', in the following terms:

> the view that adults bring something which derives both from their experience of adult life and from their status as citizens to the educational process; that adult education is based on a dialogue rather than a mere transmission of knowledge and skill; that education is not only for personal development and advancement but also for social advancement; that adult education constructs knowledge and does not merely pass it on; that adult education has a dialectical and organic relationship with social movements.

It is worth making several points about this. Such students come to the educational encounter as what Freire calls 'knowing subjects' who, as citizens, have a particular, equal and indivisible political status. The curriculum is derived, partly at least, from the intellectual and personal resources as well as the social and political interests they bring with them. They are social actors – not empty vessels. Moreover, their educational interests and aspirations are shared and collective, and the starting point for learning (whatever its final destination) is their common social purpose as citizens. Learning is essentially about *making knowledge which makes sense of their world* and helps them them to act upon it, collectively, in order to change it for the better. Consequently, such groups of students may be properly said to constitute 'epistemological communities' (Eyerman and Jamison 1991). Finally, adult learning, in this tradition, grows *in and out of* such communities, or social movements, as they exist in the 'real world', struggling and striving outside the walls of the classroom and the gates of the academy. Adult education's relationship to these movements is a symbiotic one (Welton 1995).

What we are talking about, then, is a socially and politically committed form of adult education which is partisan in the broad sense that it reflects particular interests and takes their side. In this respect, it is important to emphasise that this kind of educational work is, essentially, about adopting a political position as distinct from assuming a professional identity. Universities, of course, have never seen such social and political engagement as their (hateful phrase!) 'core business'. Nevertheless, in the past some have tolerated – even nurtured – it on their margins, as the life-work of such luminaries of the social purpose tradition as R H Tawney, G D H Cole, E P Thompson, Raymond Williams and Richard Hoggart testify. Where are the Tawneys and the Williams of today? What does their absence from the academy tell us of its social, political and civic health? How 'research-active' were they? How many externally funded contracts did they wrest from the opposition? So, in these lean and mean times, the task of reasserting the values of social purpose in university adult education is likely to be an uphill struggle. In a fundamental sense, it goes against the very grain of contemporary institutional life: no money is to be made from it, and precious little status is to be gained from it.

It should be emphasised that the notion of social purpose is about acting in solidarity with particular social interests; it is decidedly not about helping 'disadvantaged' groups or squeezing 'non-traditional entry' students into higher education. In this respect, it suggests a qualitative *turning*, as distinct from a quantitative *stretching*, of the current discourse of access and participation. What does this turning of the discourse involve? In short, it implies three things: a distinctive *theory of knowledge*, or epistemology, derived from a particular political analysis and *theory of power*, leading to an appropriate *theory of teaching and learning*, or pedagogy.

The epistemology of social purpose adult education rests upon the claim that the curriculum, *any* curriculum, represents, in the words of Raymond Williams, 'selections from a culture'. Knowledge is never neutral or value-free, and what counts as worth knowing reflects those particular social and political interests which have the power to make it count. Whose voices are heard – and silenced – in teaching and research? The social purpose tradition is not about rejecting the knowledge of the academy, let alone advocating a mindless relativism. Rather, it is concerned to test knowledge against the template of the lived experience of its students and then to harness the ways of understanding and acting which emerge from this process to a common and collective purpose. This purpose is 'social' in the sense that it is conceived in terms of furthering the interests of exploited, oppressed and marginalised groups, and it is part of their continuing struggle for greater democracy, social justice and equality. It should be noted that such students already know a great deal about those shiny shibboleths of New Labour policy: lifelong learning, active citizenship and social inclusion.

These aims and values demand a political analysis and a theory of power that can guide and resource the project. Historically, the tradition of social purpose adult education has been associated with an essentially marxian political economy – deployed for the most part, however, in the interests of democratic political change and determined social reform. The ambivalence of this intellectual legacy is now widely recognised – as is the fact that its reductionist and exclusionary logic (based largely on the assumption of a white, male working class as the privileged agent of social transformation) did much to weaken and impoverish radical adult education (eg see Westwood 1992; Thompson 1997). On the other hand, the present realities of globalisation suggest that the theoretical task now must be to modernise, rather than abandon, the modernism of class analysis and to trace its multiple mediations through gender and race, in particular, as well as some of the other, more nuanced identities and interests of late modernity. In this sense, what matters today is not so much 'diversity and difference' as a coherent and convincing way of making sense of those 'differences that make a difference' (Barr 1999). This suggests a theoretical analysis which locates the 'social' through a combination of a modernist rigour and a postmodern sensibility.

In the social purpose tradition, what counts as knowledge and understanding, is actively constructed in the creative encounter between the expertise of the teacher and the experience of the students, each role conferring a distinctive kind of authority. This, surely, is what Marx meant when he said, 'The educator must himself be educated'. Pedagogy is a matter of principle and purpose rather than mere technique. Methods of teaching and learning must therefore be developed and deployed in order to catalyse this critical pedagogy, that is, to enable the teacher to learn and the student to teach (as well, of course, as vice versa). The idea of a pedagogy which generates such 'knowledge from below' is liberating in two senses: first, because it claims that knowledge itself can be emancipatory and that what counts as knowledge is contestable – as well as being actively contested; second, because it suggests that alternative and sometimes subversive ways of knowing and acting can be liberated through teaching and other kinds of educational work.

How, then, is the tradition of social purpose to survive, let alone thrive, in institutions which are now expected to behave as if they had never had one? The answer to this question demands a sustained critique of the discourse of access and participation in its current form, followed by an account of how it is possible to construct the creative and subversive space in the work of the academy today in order to turn this discourse around.

Access and participation: contesting the discourse

The argument of this chapter is that the dominant discourse of access and participation in higher education is, intrinsically, a limited and limiting discourse. The power of discourse resides in its exclusions and elisions: a discourse 'defines what can be said, which is based on what cannot be said, on what is marginalised, silenced and repressed' (Edwards and Usher 1994). This systematic blinkering of the terms of the debate therefore begs the question: access to what and participation in what, and on whose terms?

Before addressing this question it is necessary to enter a caveat. It is as well not to labour under any delusion that there is, in some simple sense, an educational road to social justice – let alone equality. In this respect it is worth recalling the salutory warning of A H Halsey (1972) that we should avoid treating 'education as the waste paper basket of social policy – a repository for dealing with social problems where solutions are uncertain or where there is a disinclination to wrestle with them seriously'. The social purpose tradition in adult education has always proceeded on the assumption that it is part – only part, yet a vital part – of a much broader process of social, economic and political change. Purposeful educational intervention and collective adult learning are, therefore, a necessary rather than a sufficient condition of the broader 'strategy of equality' envisaged by Tawney and other democratic socialists.

In stark contrast to this, the current policy agenda is based on a meritocratic and individualistic – as opposed to an egalitarian and collective – ideology. There may be nothing intrinsically wrong with meritocracy, but there certainly is when it masquerades as equality. The notion of individualised, meritocratic access onto the ladder of opportunity through participation in a mass system of higher education reflects and reinforces 'an implicit individual, vertical progression model of education' (Ward and Steele 1999). Again, there is nothing wrong with this, but nor is there anything *social* about its purpose. And, of course, it simply ignores the possibility of reasserting the wider, civic role of the academy – which therefore remains, in this particular sense, self-referential and exclusive.

Typically, the dominant discourse of access and participation harbours within itself a narrowly conceived and intellectually debilitating economism. The reduction of the expansive idea of vocation as *learning for living* to the impoverished vocationalism of *learning for a living* is at the heart of New Labour's education policy: apparently, all educational roads lead to the labour market. We now know that when Tony Blair famously announced his new government's priorities as 'Education, education, education', what he really meant was what he subsequently said: 'Education is the best economic policy we have'. As Coffield (1999), commenting on the findings of the major ESRC 'Learning Society' research programme, states, the hegemony of a partial and distorted version of 'human capital theory' remains unchallenged – and largely unremarked:

> The language of one research area within economics has hijacked the public debate and the discourse of professionals so that education is no longer viewed as a means of individual and social emancipation, but as either 'investment' or 'consumption', as having 'inputs' and 'outputs', 'stocks' which 'depreciate' as well as 'appreciate', and it is measured by 'rates of return', an approach which produces offensive jargon such as 'overeducated graduates' and 'monopoly producers'. The discourse which has been sidelined as a result and which must now be brought centre stage is the discourse of social justice and social cohesion.

When Higher Education (especially in the new, 'mass' universities) is reduced to human resource development, it is easy to see how these institutions fall prey to the crude dictats of the new managerialism and the simplistic logic of the accountant. Only the most privileged and exclusive versions of the academy now escape what Collins (1991), writing about the vocation of adult education, characterises as the 'cult of efficiency' and the common sense of 'technical rationality':

A growing, and seductive, tendency to make more and more areas of human endeavour (the practical, moral, and political projects of everyday life) amenable to measurement and techno-bureaucratic control according to what is invoked as a scientific approach.

The emphasis is on how to do things and get them done rather than on wider moral and political questions about what should be done and why. This is reflected in the pervasive modularisation of the curriculum and competence-based forms of assessment (for examples in our own work, see Alexander and Martin 1995; Shaw and Crowther 1995). It is important to be clear about what is actually going on here because the hegemony of instrumental rationality involves 'the extension of the imperatives of the market economy and the bureaucratic state over more areas of social life, money and power become the key media of social co-ordination' (Sanderson 1999).

What we are talking about, then, is, in effect, two very different conceptions of access and participation. The dominant one at present is based on a meritocratic individualism which secures access to and participation in the internal, institutional life of the academy as well, of course, as the social and economic rewards that may – increasingly, however, only for *some* – ensue. In contrast to this, the social purpose tradition stands for what could be termed an external model of access and participation, that is, one in which social interests outside the academy have access to its intellectual resources and the academy itself participates in the life of communities and social movements around it. The first model trades in a currency of individual accreditation and progression. The second has, historically, deployed the intellectual capital of the academy as a resource in the collective struggle of ordinary people outside it to pursue their interests and aspirations as citizens, in their roles as social actors and political agents as distinct from merely producers or consumers.

Social purposes must be rooted in and routed through social interests. Tawney (1926) understood this well:

If you want flowers, you must have flowers, roots and all, unless you are satisfied, as many people are satisfied, with flowers made of paper and tinsel. And if you want education, you must not cut it off from the social interests in which it has its living and perennial sources.

This is the tradition that must be rekindled and these are the connections between the academy and the vital currents of lived experience that must be remade. The continuing evidence of the 'democratic deficit' suggests that we need, in Zygmunt Bauman's words, to 're-invent politics' (Bauman 1999) – and this process must start in communities. Essentially, what is missing today is the opportunity to meet as citizens and, once again, to make democracy work. The point to emphasise is that, historically, the kind of adult education and community-based learning in which citizens met together to talk and learn and argue helped to fill precisely this space – and to make it a uniquely democratic and creative space. Indeed, it could said that in a very real sense collective adult learning, often autonomous and self-directed, *constituted* this space.

Engaging the academy

In seeking to reassert, and reinterpret, the tradition of social purpose adult education in our work, it is as well to bear in mind Gramsci's injunction to sustain the 'optimism of the will' despite the 'pessimism of the intellect'. In order to do this, it is necessary, first, to recognise that universities are both privileged and contradictory places in which academic staff, whatever the pressures and constraints they encounter, still enjoy a degree of relative autonomy. Perhaps this applies most where it seems to matter least: in the more marginal areas of the academy's activities, such as university departments of adult education, where it may still be possible to make a distinction between the particular job we are paid to do and the wider work we choose to undertake. To exploit this autonomy, however, requires that marginality is regarded simultaneously as an asset and a liability and that we engage with the current policy context in a dialectical way. It is essential, for example, to recognise both the opportunities and constraints policy presents and to exploit the ever-present gap between its intended and unintended outcomes. Where there is choice, therefore, we must exercise a strategic 'self-consciousness of choice' (Marris 1982).

Dialectical thinking must start from the specificities of context. In our own case, we have recently experienced a process of institutional merger as part of the wider restructuring of Higher Education. Consequently we now find ourselves ambivalently positioned in relation to another, much larger institution which has a very different culture and tradition from our own. We are not, of course, alone in this. In many parts of the United Kingdom – and elsewhere, no doubt – there has been a spate of shotgun weddings between very different kinds of institution. In our own case, the newly conjoined partners seem to have either a somewhat overdeveloped or, alternatively, a radically under-developed sense of their role as agents of vocational preparation and professional development. In such hasty and expedient couplings, departments of adult education have gone both ways – but, in the end (where they still exist!) they all face the same kind of problems and, we would argue, possibilities. The question is: what kind of space does this new institutional chemistry open up? How can it be made creative by exploiting the competing demands of different constituencies, each of which confer distinctive kinds of legitimacy? More specifically, to what extent is it possible to rescue the political discourse of social purpose from the professional discourse of 'needs meeting' in which it has atrophied so long? These are some of the questions we seek to address in our work, both internally and collegially within the academy and externally and in solidarity with social interests outside it.

Politicising teaching and research

Historically, in the adult education of social purpose ordinary people came together to make their own claim on citizenship and to demand to be included in democracy. In a very real sense they actively and collectively asserted their citizenship as a social practice within the politics of civil society in order to claim the rights of citizenship within the politics of the State. In other words, they struggled to make democracy work. What is now required is to renegotiate and reoccupy this educational space between the personal and political dimensions of people's lives, between difference and solidarity (see Wildemeersch *et al* 1998; Johnston 1999). In this process we must be prepared to learn, once again, how to do this – for instance, from feminist theory and practice as well as the experience of other progressive social movements and communities of struggle.

Consequently, in 're-theorising community' in our work, we are trying, in effect, to reconnect the private lives of individuals with their public lives as citizens. This is the space where, in Habermasian terms, the 'lifeworld' meets the 'systems world'. This has always been the distinctive curricular and pedagogical terrain of the social purpose education which is surely what education for citizenship should really be about. And yet, this kind of engaged adult education has now all but disappeared – squeezed in the vice of possessive individualism and globalised capital. In our view as teachers and researchers in adult and community education, reconstructing this space is at once an urgent educational task, intellectual challenge and political purpose. This is a project not only for ourselves but also for our students who have systematically to relate theory to purpose and practice in the professional placements they undertake as part of their studies. Theorising practice in this way requires, as Alheit (1999) argues, the development of 'meso level' theory in order to connect our educational work with the increasingly complex and fractured reality of individual and social experience in late modernity. And, of course, it is also a project that has particular resonance for us in Scotland today – where there has been so much interest in democratic renewal (see Crowther *et al* 1999).

Our thinking about community in its relation to education starts from the idea of 'community' as a way of describing the level and locus of a particular kind of educational work:

> By referring to 'communities' ... we meant specified groups of actual people, not society as a whole and certainly not a market. In short, we used the term to indicate the 'place' and moment' of engagement with specific groups of people around their interests. (Jackson 1995)

Community, then, is posed as a relational concept which articulates the shared experience of groups, or collectivities, of people (which may be formed around a variety of common identities, interests or issues) at an intermediate level of social reality. In C Wright Mills' (1970) terms, such communities are formed at the interface between the micro-politics of 'personal troubles' and the macro-politics of 'public issues'. It is in the dialectics of community, understood in this way, that people experience, *collectively*, the possibilities of human agency within the pre-existing constraints of structure. Giddens' 'structuration theory' is useful in this respect because it avoids the pitfalls of a crude structure–agency dichotomy by emphasising not only the mutual embeddedness of context and action but also – and in particular for our purposes as educators – the human capacity to make a difference. It also, incidentally, provides one way of combining a modernist political economy with a postmodern sensitivity to the politics of difference – without getting stuck in too many intellectual *culs de sac*! On this view, then, social purpose is redefined as the educational process of deriving the curriculum from the lived experience of people in communities. This is what is distinctive – and, hopefully, subversive – about it.

What does all this mean in terms of the politics of everyday life in excluded communities? And what does it mean for our work? What we have to do is to pose these questions in these communities – and in our curriculum. This process can be illustrated by referring briefly to two examples from our current work with the disability movement: a 'new social movement' which knows a great deal about the problems of exclusion and the challenges of inclusion.

First, a course in our undergraduate programme, 'Special needs and community education', has been retitled 'Inclusive education: the disabling society'. Inclusive education as an aspiration helps to raise the right questions about whose voices are heard (or silenced) in the construction of the curriculum – however obscured these questions may become in the implementation of inclusive education as policy. This distinction is fundamental to the rationale of the course which has been devised, planned and taught alongside activist members of local disabled people's organisations. The argument of the course drives the curriculum, enabling students to interrogate the policy context in which, as professional workers, they will be centrally implicated. In working with the disability movement, whose members daily live out the dialectical relationship between the micro-politics of identity and the macro-politics of position, our aim is primarily to learn from them and to help resource their struggle for citizenship and social inclusion (see Petrie and Shaw 1999). This commitment turns the 'professional' task from integrating 'deficient' people to assessing how education can resource this community's struggle for democracy. Incidentally, an institutional commitment to inclusion as policy, at least in theory, provides the context in which inclusion as aspiration can claim its place in the curriculum.

Second, a related development is a major national research project, funded by the Lottery. This is called 'Experiencing inclusive education: what does it mean?'. Its basic purpose is to make the voice of disabled people heard in the debate about inclusive education and to give them the opportunity to back this up with rigorous research evidence. The project is managed and controlled by a local disability-led action group, which is primarily concerned with increasing disabled people's access to educational opportunities, and it is supported by the expertise and resources of two university departments, the Department of Community Education and the Department of Nursing Studies. The research aims to provide an account which is qualitatively different from the dominant professional discourse of 'special educational needs'. It is derived from the social model of disability which seeks to challenge the individualised medical model by focusing on the environmental barriers, cultural processes and policy frameworks which actively and systematically disable people. This kind of research is one way of turning the rhetoric of 'empowerment' into a reality.

It should be emphasised that in both these cases we are seeking ways of using our work to enable those who are so often defined and excluded as 'other' to generate their own 'knowledge from below' – and to teach us what it means.

Sustaining critical communities

As part of our work we are expected to engage with the field of professional practice outside the academy, and this gives us licence to promote a wider critical culture in a number of ways. One of the responsibilities of university departments of adult and community education is, of course, for staff development and continuing professional education. It is important that opportunities for reasserting social purpose – as distinct from simply promoting 'good practice' – are carried over into this aspect of our work (see Crowther *et al* 1997). In general terms, we try to do this in five ways: by establishing critical distance from both policy and practice in order to secure the intellectual and ideological space for systematic forms of reflection, critique and analysis; by stimulating debate and argument, particularly about the underlying values and purposes of adult and community education in the current policy context; by rehistoricising contemporary social and political struggles in order to excavate from the past what Raymond Williams called 'resources of hope' for the present and the future; by enriching the inter-disciplinary nature of adult and community-based education as a field of academic study, professional practice and social action; and by recognising within all of this both distinctively Scottish and international dimensions.

In light of this, we have attempted to extend the ways in which the field of practice thinks about its work, three of which are briefly discussed here. First, we have used staff development and in-service training as an opportunity to politicise practice. A good example of this is the Really Useful Knowledge (RUK) programme, which was developed in collaboration with the local education authority. The aim was to give practitioners the time and opportunity to relate epistemological questions about what kind of knowledge counts, and who has the power to say so, to issues of social purpose and political action. In this respect, the programme, which took the form of a regular reading and study group, sought to move deliberately away from the 'practical instrumentalism' of much in-service training towards a broader and deeper understanding of the values, purposes and continuing relevance of what the radical tradition characterised as 'really useful knowledge' (see Johnson 1979). Second, we have tried in some of our published work to bring together the voices of acknowledged academic authorities, professional workers and social movement activists to think about the role of adult learning and community-based education in the contemporary Scottish context. In particular, we have been concerned to reinterpret the idea of 'popular education' as a way of harnessing educational work to the social and political purpose of democratic renewal in Scotland, and to understand how this process connects with the struggles of social movements elsewhere in an increasingly globalised world. This is perhaps best illustrated in our recent book *Popular Education and Social Movements in Scotland Today* (Crowther, et al 1999). Third, we strive to keep the radical tradition alive within the academic community in Scotland and to bring a distinctively Scottish intellectual inflection to bear on the debate. For example, the notion of 'creating space for the "democratic intellect"' expresses the purpose of the now well established Edinburgh Biennial Adult Education Conference (see Martin 1996).

The journal *Concept* (Contemporary Community Education Practice and Theory) is central to a wider strategy for sustaining critical communities, and it therefore warrants fuller discussion. The journal, cheaply priced and published three times a year, is complemented by a seminar programme of inspirational events which are intended to stimulate new ideas and critical thinking. Its rationale is clear and simply stated: it aims to create a critical culture in which conventional wisdom is challenged, values are made explicit, and the field of practice is exposed as a range of competing interests. In view of this, it is important to emphasise that *Concept* is definitely *not* a refereed journal. In this respect, it stands quite deliberately against the logic of 'research assessment' and current forms of performance measurement in the academy. Its policy is to make the voices of academics, practitioners and activists as widely heard as possible. This means encouraging and supporting new and unpractised writers. A key concern is to assert both the importance of the relationship between theory and practice in educational work and, at the same time, to demystify and democratise it. Much of this has been brought together and consolidated in a more focused way in a recent collection of papers on working with young people and a special issue of the journal on citizenship – filling what many see as gaps in the 'mainstream' literature and, at the same time, adding to the resources available to students and workers.

There is also a concern to transcend the parochialism of much locally based educational work by including in every issue material which raises awareness of the connections between the local and the global. For instance, the current volume includes a regular series of 'Letters from Latin America', and attempts are now being made to establish links with similar publications in other countries. In this respect, a particularly important development was the special millennium joint issue of *Concept* with the UK journal *Adults Learning* and the Irish journal *The Adult Learner* called, significantly, *Reclaiming Common Purpose*. It is worth quoting from the editorial at some length because it expresses the general commitment which informs much of our work:

> This collaborative issue ... is an attempt, first of all, to take stock – to assess both the damage and the potential for progressive educational practice. But, perhaps more importantly, it is a call for solidarity – which is very different from stakeholding. In educational terms, solidarity means a commitment to relating learning to collective engagement with common struggles and concerns; to developing curriculum from concrete experience by stimulating communal thinking; to repairing damaged alliances and building new ones; and, critically, to working with people as subjects in politics rather than simply as objects of policy interventions of one kind or another. The space this distinction creates will be essential if the cutting edge of common purpose is to be reclaimed ... As history has consistently shown us, reclaiming common purpose means not only serious educational engagement but also serious political commitment to working in solidarity with those who are silenced, marginalised or excluded.

Challenging institutional limits

Finally, we would argue that it is necessary to reassert the values of social purpose both internally, within the walls of the academy, and externally, with like-minded colleagues in other universities (both nationally and internationally). In this, we seek to work against the pervasive politics of possessive individualism and institutional competition in publication and research. Two examples of the attempt to challenge institutional limits follow: one applies to the internal politics of our own university; the other reflects a growing momentum towards international collaboration.

Educational Resources for Renewing Democracy in Scotland is a collection of papers designed as an educational resource pack for use in a wide variety of formal and informal educational settings. It contains 38 papers organised under the following five headings: Making democracy work – key ideas and values; Major Scottish institutions; Contemporary Scottish identities and interests; Issues for democratic renewal in Scotland today; Scotland's place in the international community. The basic premise is that renewing democracy in Scotland should be understood as a long-term educational and cultural process which must start in communities. The strategy is, in short, to harness the resources of the academy to this end. All the papers are short and accessible and have been specially commissioned from members of our own university, ranging across several faculties. The idea is that the combined intellectual capital of the academy should be made available, and not subject to copyright, for a broadly based programme of public education, discussion and debate.

This initiative, of course, runs directly against the grain of the current politics of research and publication but, despite this, it has been welcomed by colleagues we have approached as a novel and worthwhile exercise. In the current policy context of education for active citizenship, this pack is intended to offer a resource for thinking through the intellectual and political issues posed by contemporary democracy and what these imply for active citizenship. It should be noted that this educational process is in striking contrast to the narrowly conceived notions of democracy and citizenship which appear to be inscribed in current policy. Democracy, in our view, demands an informed and politically literate citizenry, and this pack is intended to be a contribution to the process of public education this implies. What we hope will emerge is a kind of locally based education which is, in essence, very close to the historical roots of the social purpose tradition, that is, one of democratic debate and dialogue around common interests, problems and aspirations.

Somewhat in contrast to this, the Popular Education Network is a growing alliance between socialist academics in (to date) 14 different countries who share an essentially materialist analysis of the current globalisation of capital, poverty and inequality. 'Popular education', a term borrowed from Latin America but resonant with many of the features of the radical tradition in British adult education, is understood to be a vital part of the wider struggle for social and political change. Although it is recognised that popular education, in this sense, always proceeds from the specificities and contingencies of particular contexts, our concern is ultimately to establish the international connections between local struggles in the era of globalisation. The analysis which informs the Popular Education Network is, quite deliberately, clear and uncompromising. The aim of the network is to develop a coherent programme of international action and research which brings together politically committed academics, who may be very isolated in their own institutions, to develop forms of collaboration which are based on solidarity rather than contract.

The network originated in discussions between academics in Scotland and Catalonia. One major international conference, Popular Education: Engaging the Academy, has already been held, attended by participants from 12 countries, and similar networks are now being developed in North America and Australasia. It should be noted that this initiative has nothing to do with stretching the academy in order to promote more access and participation; it has everything to do with turning the academy in ways which will enable those who work in it to support, resource and learn from popular struggles for social justice and equality.

Conclusion

In trying to 'turn the discourse' in the ways we have described, we recognise that this task is never easy – it is always and necessarily a struggle. And it is a struggle which has to be fitted in – often squeezed in – among all the other things we are expected to do. To exploit our autonomy in a purposeful way, we have argued that we need to engage dialectically and strategically with the opportunities and constraints we encounter in the academy today. Whatever the problems and pressures of the job, our experience is that there are always new spaces to be opened up and new connections to be made in our work. This process is much more creative, and congenial, in the company of others. In the end, 'One can only think for oneself if one does not think by oneself' (McIntyre 1987). This solidarity needs to be forged both internally within the academy and externally with colleagues, workers and activists elsewhere.

Ultimately, the power of discourse is that, all too easily, it comes to constitute common sense: we work within its blinkers with less and less awareness of how it reduces our sense of the potential and possibilities of our work. The real danger is that we end up policing our own vision, and become the victims of self-surveillance and censorship. To sustain social purpose, this is precisely what we must avoid.

References

Alexander D and Martin I (1995) 'Competence, curriculum and democracy', in Mayo M and Thompson J (eds), *Adult Learning, Critical Intelligence and Social Change*, Leicester: NIACE, pp 82–96

Alheit P (1999) 'On a contradictory way to the "learning society": a critical approach', *Studies in the Education of Adults*, Vol 31 No 1, pp 66–82

Barr J (1999) *Liberating Knowledge: research, feminism and adult education*, Leicester: NIACE

Bauman Z (1999) *In Search of Politics*, Cambridge: Polity Press

Coffield F (1999) 'Breaking the consensus: lifelong learning as social control' *British Educational Research Journal*, Vol 25 No 4, pp 479–99

Collins M (1991) *Adult Education as Vocation: a critical role for the adult educator*, London: Routledge

Crowther J, Martin I and Shaw M (1997) 'Critical culture in Scottish adult and community education', *Adults Learning*, April, pp 203–06

Crowther J, Martin I and Shaw M (eds) (1999) *Popular Education and Social Movements in Scotland Today*, Leicester: NIACE.

Edwards R and Usher R (1994) 'Disciplining the subject: the power of competence', *Studies in the Education of Adults*, Vol 26 No 1, pp 1–14

Eyerman R and Jamison A (1991) *Social Movements: a cognitive approach*, Cambridge: Polity Press

Gramsci A (1971) *Prison Notebooks*, London: Lawrence and Wishart

Halsey A H (1972) *Educational Priority: EPA problems and policies*, Vol 1, London: HMSO

Jackson K (1995) 'Popular education and the state: a new look at the community debate', in Mayo M and Thompson J (eds), *Adult Learning, Critical Intelligence and Social Change*, Leicester: NIACE, pp 182–203

Johnson R (1979) '"Really useful knowledge": radical education and working-class culture', in Clarke J, Crichter C and Johnson R (eds), *Working-class culture: studies in history and theory*, London: Hutchinson, pp 75–102

Johnston R (1999) 'Adult learning for citizenship: towards a reconstruction of the social purpose tradition', *International Journal of Lifelong Education*, Vol 18 No 3, pp 175–90

Marris P (1982) *Meaning and Action: community planning and conceptions of change*, London: Routledge & Kegan Paul

Martin I (1996) 'Creating space for the "democratic intellect": the Edinburgh Biennial Adult Education Conference', *Scottish Journal of Adult and Continuing Education*, Vol 3 No 2, pp 99–113

McIntyre A (1987) 'The idea of an educated public', in Haydon G (ed), *Education and Values*, London: University of London

Petrie M and Shaw M (1999) 'The disability movement and the struggle for inclusion', in Crowther J, Martin I and Shaw M (eds), *Popular Education and Social Movements in Scotland Today*, Leicester: NIACE, pp 159–17

Sanderson I (1999) 'Participation and democratic renewal: from "instrumental" to "communicative rationality"', *Policy & Politics*, Vol 27 No 3, pp 325–41

Shaw M and Crowther J (1995) 'Beyond subversion', in Mayo M and Thompson J (eds), *Adult Learning, Critical Intelligence and Social Change*, Leicester: NIACE, pp 169–81

Tawney R H (1926) 'Adult education in the history of the nation'. paper presented to Fifth Annual Conference of the British Institute of Adult Education.

Thompson J (1997) *Words in Edgeways*, Leicester: NIACE.

Ward K and Steele T (1999) 'From marginality to expansion: an overview of recent trends and developments in widening participation in England and Scotland', *Journal of Access and Credit Studies*, summer, pp 192–203

Welton M (ed), (1995) *In Defense of the Lifeworld*, Albany State: University of New York Press

Westwood S (1992) 'When class became community: radicalism in adult education', in Rattansi A and Reeder D (eds), *Rethinking Radical Education*, London: Lawrence & Wishart, pp 222–48

Wildemeersch D, Finger M and Jansen T (eds), (1998) *Adult Education and Social Responsibility*, Frankfurt am Main: Peter Lang

Williams R (1961) *The Long Revolution*, London: Pelican

Wright Mills C (1970) *The Sociological Imagination*, Harmondsworth: Penguin

Notes on Contributors

John Bamber has been a lecturer in community education at the University of Edinburgh since 1994. Before coming to Edinburgh, he worked in Bristol for three years as a self-employed trainer and consultant for public sector and not-for-profit organisations. His academic interests include voluntary organisations, youth work, developing practice-related learning theory and critical groupwork practice.

Loraine Blaxter began her employment career as a social anthropologist at Queens University of Belfast with a specialism in European rural community studies. She has also lectured in sociology at the University of Papua New Guinea with a research specialism in the informal sector. She has been employed as a lecturer or researcher in Continuing Education at the University of Warwick since 1990.

Anan Collymore has been involved in community development for many years. She has facilitated workshops on maintaining mental health, stress management and life-planning and is about to continue her studies at Goldsmiths College, University of London on the MA in Gender, Culture and Modernity.

Bríd Connolly teaches in the Centre for Adult and Community Education at National University of Ireland in Maynooth. Her research interests include gender, community education and community development. She is particularly concerned with developing new forms of creative teaching and assessment.

Jim Crowther has been involved in adult literacy and teaching and research in adult and community education since 1980. He is currently a lecturer in community education at the University of Edinburgh. He is co-editor of *Popular Education and Social Movements in Scotland Today* and is a founder member of the Popular Education Network.

Alan Ducklin has worked in schools, colleges and teacher education. He is currently a lecturer at the University of Edinburgh and is working with three colleagues on a Scottish Executive-funded research project, looking at differences in gender attainment in Scottish schools and the ways in which schools and local authorities are seeking to address such differences.

Keith Hammond co-ordinates the Outreach Pre-Access project and tutors in philosophy in the Department of Adult and Continuing Education at the University of Glasgow. He did post-graduate work at the European Philosophical Inquiry Centre which pioneered the teaching of philosophy to children aged five and older. His current research is concerned with Aristotle's ethics and community-based adult education.

Christina Hughes has been a lecturer in the Department of Continuing Education at the University of Warwick since 1993. Her research interests are focused on the connections between education, employment and family in women's lives and the development of qualitative methodologies. She is co-editor of *Gender and Education* and Assistant Editor of *Gender, Work and Organisation*. Her forthcoming publications include